The Haider Phenomenon in Austria

The Haider Phenomenon in Austria

Ruth Wodak and Anton Pelinka, editors

Transaction Publishers
New Brunswick (U.S.A.) and London (U.K.)

Library of Congress Catalog Number: 2001034722
ISBN: 0-7658-0117-5 (cloth); 0-7658-0883-8 (paper)
Printed in Canada

Library of Congress Cataloging-in-Publication Data

The Haider phenomenon in Austria / Ruth Wodak and Anton Pelinka, editors.
    p. cm.
  Includes bibliographical references and index.
  ISBN 0-7658-0117-5 (cloth : alk. paper) — ISBN 0-7658-0883-8 (pbk. : alk. paper)
    1. Freiheitliche Partei èsterreichs. 2. Austria—Politics and government—20th century. 3. Haider, Jèrg. 4. Right and left (Political science) I. Wodak, Ruth, 1950- II. Pelinka, Anton, 1941-

JN2031.F73 H355 2001
324.2436'035—dc21

                                   2001034722

Contents

Introduction
From Waldheim to Haider

Ruth Wodak and *Anton Pelinka*

Sometimes—not often—Austria makes political headlines. In past years and decades, this has happened at least twice: in 1986, when the "Waldheim Affair" was debated worldwide; in 1999, when the Austrian Freedom Party, under the leadership of Jörg Haider, received 27 percent of the vote in the national election. The Freedom Party (FPÖ) became part of the Austrian government when it formed a coalition with the Austrian People's Party (ÖVP) on February 4, 2000.

The two events generated discourse, which, both in Austria and beyond its borders, was similar and yet different. The similarities concern the difficulties of confronting Austria's Nazi past (Waldheim was part of the Wehrmacht; Haider, a member of the postwar generation, appealed to "old" sentiments; see Zöchling 1999, Ottomeyer 2000, Scharsach and Kuch 2000). In both cases, Austrians saw themselves as the victim of conspiracies against them, and a nationalistic, chauvinistic discourse emerged, in public as well as in daily life.

The differences lie in the importance of these elections and in their consequences. Waldheim served as a symbol of a generation that had "done its duty" (Manoschek 1986), while Haider stood for a right-wing populist program, and the FPÖ was the first party of its kind to be represented in the government of the European Union (ter Wal 2001).

International reaction to these developments cannot be understood without taking into account Austria's role in the Second World War.

In the following, we will summarize briefly the two phenomena before introducing the chapters in this volume. This short history and both the Austrian and European backgrounds are necessary to understand the strong emotions, international reactions, and scandals of 1986 and 1999/2000.

The Waldheim Affair

Postwar Anti-Semitism in Austria

In his book, *Der ewige Antisemit* (1986), the German-Jewish author Henryk Broder repeated the phrase attributed to Zvi Rix, namely that the Germans will never forgive the Jews for Auschwitz. In surveying past decades in Austria, it would appear that Broder's cynical phrase, an ironic description of the Germans' rationalizing projection, which was aimed at shifting the guilt to the victims, could apply equally well to Austria. Kurt Waldheim's 1986 presidential election campaign effectively put an end to many of the qualms Austrians might have harbored earlier. During the campaign, few Austrians with anti-Semitic convictions felt a need to keep their views to themselves, particularly in the context of private discourse, and anti-Jewish prejudice found various verbal outlets of a more or less explicit nature.

The sociologist Bernd Marin has characterized the postwar situation in Austria as "anti-Semitism without Jews and without anti-Semites" (Marin 1983, 2000). He assumed that anti-Semitism was functionalized and constantly used as a political tool, but that few dared to call themselves anti-Semitic after the Holocaust. This is generally true, although politicians like Oskar Helmer, a socialist and the first Austrian Minister of the Interior of the Second Republic, as well as Leopold Kunschak, the first leader of the Christian Austrian People's Party (ÖVP), made no great secret of their anti-Semitic attitudes even after 1945.

Anti-Semitism existed in Austria immediately before 1938, during the Second World War, and after 1945, and it is still present today. Throughout the past fifty-five years, statistical surveys, opinion polls, and content analysis have developed various standardized quantitative research and survey procedures for identifying and measuring anti-Semitic prejudice. Of course, these procedures are always dependent on the design of the studies, the intentions of the researchers, the questions asked, and the samples themselves (e.g., Weiss 1987, Kienzl and Gehmacher 1987, and Gottschlich 1987). One of the polls (Kienzl 1987) identified an average of 7 percent of Austrians as radical anti-Semites; however, no one has clearly defined what a radical or less radical anti-Semite might be. In Kienzl and Gehmacher's study (1987) which presented this "famous" 7 percent, 40 percent of those asked gave no answer.

The persistence of anti-Semitic attitudes in the above-mentioned opinion polls is ascribed to a small group of right-wing radicals. The number of such (radical) anti-Semites could thus be carefully delimited and their numbers shown to be falling. Anti-Semitism is also frequently identified with a purely racist variety of anti-Jewish prejudice which is equated with Nazism or with the Nazi extermination of the Jews (the "Auschwitz" symbol), thereby effectively excluding or minimizing other anti-Semitic trends in Austria, such as the Christian or the Christian-Social traditions (see Reisigl and Wodak 2001; Mitten 1992).

With the collapse of the Third Reich, many in Austria as well as in Germany were forced to acknowledge the extent of the Nazi crimes. Their doubts, feelings of guilt, and need to justify or rationalize their behavior encouraged the development of strategies for "dealing with the past": playing down the actions and events themselves, denying knowledge of them, or transforming the victims into the cause of present woes. Moreover, since the Moscow Declaration of 1943 was interpreted as an Allied offer of support for Austria's claim to have been the first "collective victim" of Nazi aggression, such reversals were able to draw upon an especially potent form of legitimation.

The putative victim status also made it possible to deny any responsibility that went beyond individual crimes. The newly constructed Austrian identity produced stronger feelings of nationalism, which, in turn, reinforced a specific definition of insiders and outsiders and the separation of "us" from "them."

Compared to the wave of anti-Semitic hostilities unleashed by the events of 1986, prior scandals were minor affairs. In 1986, during the "Waldheim Affair," there was a perceptible shift in public discourse, which developed a distinctive "us" and "them" pattern. The in-groups in this discourse ("Us") were Austria (note the metonymic-synecdochic *totum pro parte*), Waldheim (often taken as a *pars pro toto* for all "respectable" Austrians), the People's Party, the *Wehrmachtgeneration*, all the people who wanted to stop thinking about the past, those who were interested in the future, etc. The out-groups, ("them") were, apart from the Jews, leftists (note the directional metaphor), those Austrians "who foul their own nest" (in German, *Nestbeschmutzer*—note the defamatory nationalist naturalizing metaphor), and *das Ausland*. This macro-toponymic metonymical collective singular describing everything outside the national borders of Austria could mean the international press and, ultimately, "the powerful Jews on the U.S. East Coast" (see Mitten 1992). Between these two poles of referential dichotomization were "Jewish fellow citizens," the beloved "*jüdische Mitbürger*."

In the discourse about Waldheim's Nazi past, the exclusionary boundaries of the "us" group have shifted constantly. Nonetheless, in the context of the disclosures about the president's wartime past, the constant allusion to the "us" group facilitated creation of a *Feindbild Jude*, an image of the Jew as the enemy, which, in turn, reinforced existing prejudices. Certain taboos did exist at the time—for example, the avoidance of making explicit, manifest anti-Semitic remarks on TV or the radio—but even those taboos were broken in 1986 (see Wodak et al. 1990; Gruber 1991; Reisigl and Wodak 2001; Mitten 1992).

Anti-Semitism in postwar Austria must be viewed chiefly in relation to the manner in which alleged or real guilt, with alleged or actual accusations, is dealt with. One can observe that the topic of anti-Semitic prejudice in Austria is not exhausted by merely repeating the clichés of the nineteenth and early twentieth centuries. There are also additional new material roots and motives for anti-Semitism, and several new topoi have been added since 1945. The fear of revenge, although an old motive, has acquired a new urgency in the context of assigning blame for the Holocaust, be it the actual guilt of many or the feelings of guilt of others. Closely related to that is the fear that Jews will reclaim the property which was "aryanized," that is, stolen from them. The Austrians' postwar identity is grounded on the formulation of the 1943 Moscow Declaration, according to which Austria was the first victim of Nazi expansionism/aggression. The incriminating part of the declaration speaks of Austrian responsibility for Nazi crimes. "Digging up the past" is now seen as a threat to this image, all the more so when it recalls events which are not easily denied.[1]

The Waldheim Story

The "Waldheim Affair"[2] is the term conventionally applied to the controversy surrounding the disclosure of the previously unknown past of Kurt Waldheim, former secretary general of the United Nations, during his campaign for the Austrian presidency in 1986. The affair not only focused international attention on Waldheim personally, but also raised broader questions about the history of anti-Semitism in Austria (Mitten 1992a,b). To use a coded idiom more appropriate to post-Auschwitz political debate, "the Waldheim camp"—the Christian democratic Austrian People's Party, which had nominated him—helped construct a *Feindbild*, a hostile image of Jews which served both to deflect criticism of Waldheim's credibility and to explain the international "campaign" against him. The central assumption of this *Feindbild* was that Waldheim (synecdochizingly equated with "Austria") was under attack by an international Jewish conspiracy, the *"Ausland."* Waldheim was thus portrayed as an innocent victim.

The relatively uneventful early phase of the election campaign ended abruptly in March 1986, when the Austrian weekly news magazine *Profil* published documents revealing details of Waldheim's little-known activities during the Second World War. *Profil's* disclosures were followed on March 4 by nearly identical revelations by the World Jewish Congress (WJC) and the *New York Times*. Waldheim had always denied any affiliation of any kind with the Nazis and had claimed in his memoirs that his military service ended in the winter of 1941–42, when he was wounded on the Eastern front. The evidence made public by *Profil*, the World Jewish Congress, and the *New York Times* suggested the contrary: Waldheim had been a member of the Nazi Student Union, and he had also belonged to a mounted unit of the *Sturmabteilung*, or SA, while attending the Consular Academy in Vienna between 1937 and 1939. Other documents revealed that Waldheim had served in the Balkans after March 1942, in the Army Group E, commanded by Alexander Loehr. This unit was known for its involvement in the deportation of Jews from Greece and for the savagery of its military operations against Yugoslav partisans.

Waldheim himself initially denied having belonged to any Nazi organization and claimed to have known nothing about the deportation of Jews from Thessalonica. The general strategy of the Waldheim camp was to brand any disclosures a "defamation campaign," an international conspiracy by "the foreign press" and "the Jews" ("*im Ausland*"). In addition, Waldheim stated that he had simply forgotten to mention such minor events in his life because his injury had been the major *caesura*. In the course of the election campaign, the World Jewish Congress became the main target of criticism, and the torrent of anti-WJC political invective from ÖVP politicians helped promote and legitimize anti-Semitic prejudice in public discourse to an extent that had not been seen since 1945. Waldheim also attempted to link his own fate to that of his generation and country by claiming that he, like thousands of other Austrians, had merely done his duty ("*er habe nur seine Pflicht erfüllt*") under Nazi Germany. This euphemistic, relativizing, positive presentational argumentation topos relies on at least two rules of reasoning: First, if someone does his/her duty, he/she is a conscientious, responsible person; second, a conscientious, responsible person cannot be blamed for his/her deeds (see Benke and Wodak 2001; Heer 1999; Manoschek 2001). Waldheim's self-exculpating argumentation resonated positively not only with many Austrian voters of his generation, but also with members of the younger generations, the children of the *Wehrmacht* soldiers. Waldheim finally won the second round of the election on June 6, 1986, with 53.9 percent of the vote.

Contrary to Waldheim's expectations, however, interest in the unanswered questions about his past did not wane after the election (see Wodak, Menz, Mitten, and Stern 1994). Waldheim did not receive an official state invitation from any country in Western Europe, and some official visitors even avoided traveling to Vienna because they did not want to call on him. In April 1987, the U.S. Department of Justice announced that it was placing Waldheim on a watch list, further reinforcing his pariah status (see Mitten 1986 for more details). More broadly conceived, the "Waldheim Affair" symbolizes the Austrian postwar unwillingness or inability to adequately face the implications of Nazi abominations.

The Haider Phenomenon

The Rise to Power

On October 3, 1999, the FPÖ (currently the second largest party in Austria) won 27 percent of the vote after having run an election campaign based on blatant and explicit ethnicist and racist slogans against foreigners. In this election, the Social Democratic Party lost 6 percent, while the conservative People's Party, the ÖVP, managed to maintain its level of support. The Greens were the only progressive party to succeed in attracting more votes, gaining 2 percent (now about 8 percent). The Liberal Forum with Heide Schmidt failed to win any seats in parliament.

During the campaign, both the Social Democratic Party and the People's Party (the ruling coalition government until October 1999) seemed paralyzed. On October 1, 1999, thousands of people gathered on St. Stephen's Square and applauded FPÖ leader Jörg Haider as he gave his last pre-election speech, welcoming "our Viennese citizens" and promising them protection "against foreigners and against unemployment." The slogans *"Stop der Überfremdung"* ("Stop over-foreignization") ("foreign infiltration" was found in an article about Haider) and *"Stop dem Asylmißbrauch"* ("Stop the abuse of asylum") were accompanied by loud cheers as well as some whistles—a sign of disapproval in Austria – from those who dared. Police were stationed all around the square and the atmosphere was tense, but most bystanders had broad smiles on their faces. Moreover, the headline of the *Neue Kronen Zeitung* was already celebrating Haider's "March into the Chancellery" four days before the election.

What has Haider now become, and what kind of party is the FPÖ in 2000/2001? Does this rise of populism, racism, and hostility towards foreigners/xenophobia correspond to broader social changes in Europe, or is it a uniquely Austrian phenomenon?

After the Second World War, in 1949, "liberals" with a strong German National orientation but no classical liberal tradition (see Bailer-Galanda and Neugebauer 1993:326), who felt they could not support the SPÖ or the ÖVP, founded the VDU (*Verband der Unabhängigen* or League of Independents), which became the political home of many former Austrian Nazis. The FPÖ, founded in 1956, was the successor party to the VDU; it retained an explicit attachment to a "German cultural community." In its more than forty-year history, the FPÖ has, therefore, never been a "liberal" party in the European sense, although there have always been tensions between its more liberal and more conservative members. In 1986, Haider was elected party leader, unseating Norbert Steger, a liberal. Since 1986, the FPÖ has attracted thousands of new voters, and in the fall 1999, accounted for 27 percent of all the votes cast in Austria (1,244,087 voters). By 1993, the

FPÖ's party policy and platform had become anti-foreigner, anti-European Union, and widely populist, very similar to Le Pen's party in France. Since the summer of 1995, the FPÖ has de-emphasized the close ties between the Austrian and the German cultural communities because opinion polls showed that the majority of Austrian citizens no longer accepted such a self-definition. In the fall of 1997, the FPÖ presented a new party program, which, in its calculated ambivalence, emphasized Christian values and succeeded in attracting new voters. The FPÖ is currently the largest right-wing party in Western Europe (Mitten 1994; Bailer-Galanda and Neugebauer 1997; Pelinka 2001) and, more than any other Austrian party, persuasively sets the xenophobic and anti-foreigner tone in Austria. The electoral success the FPÖ achieved with populist slogans is even more surprising in view of the fact that Austria is one of the richest countries in the world today, and its inflation and unemployment rates are among the lowest in Western Europe. Comparisons with the Weimar Republic or with Austria between the two world wars—which the FPÖ often used during the election campaign—are thus completely wrong.

What, then, can account for the success of Haider and his party (a classical *Führerpartei*)? We would like to offer some explanations which illustrate that while there are Austrian peculiarities on many levels, there are also supranational, and indeed global (economic and ideological) implications and phenomena. Since 1945, Austria, a very small, neutral state with a population of eight million, has had difficulty establishing its new identity vis-à-vis Germany and trying to come to terms with its Nazi past (Wodak, de Cillia, Reisigl and Liebhart 1999). Efforts to establish a strong identity and a positive in-group, however, often result in the formation of negative out-groups. After the fall of the Iron Curtain in 1989, Austria lost its function as a "bridge" between the East and the West and still has not found a new compensatory role. Joining the European Union (EU) in 1995 also failed to solve the problem. On the contrary, there has been a noticeable increase in tensions between national state ideology and supranational convictions.

Viewed from a historical perspective, racist, ethnicist and xenophobic prejudices are strongly rooted in the Austrian tradition (as noted above). Ethnic groups have often been blamed for economic and social problems. Before World War II, Jews were discriminated against, and anti-Semitism was a "normal" feature of Austrian political culture. Today, at the beginning of the new millennium, hostility towards foreigners has once again become *quasi* normal. When the first immigrants from the former Eastern Bloc arrived in Austria in 1989–90, all the political parties except the Greens used discriminatory slogans. None, however, were as explicit as those used by the FPÖ in the 1999 election campaign, when the most prominent FPÖ campaign poster read "*Stop der Überfremdung*" ("Stop foreign infiltration "), a term coined by the Nazis and used by Goebbels in 1933. What little opposition there was to the FPÖ discourse came from parts of the Catholic and Protestant churches, Vienna's Jewish Community *(Kultusgemeinde)*, the Green, Liberal, and Communist parties, and some intellectuals. The two major parties, fearing they would lose support if they voiced opposition or used counter-slogans, never publicly condemned the racist and xenophobic propaganda until one week before the election on October 3, 1999.

Moreover, Haider's personality and his suntanned, telegenic appearance are significant factors in the FPÖ's popularity. Haider is certainly a charismatic politician who is adept at using rhetorical persuasion and suggestion in his political self-presentation (for example, in the media). He has proved adept at constructing a new image of himself as a statesman, for example, by participating in summer courses at Harvard University for three successive years.

With respect to the supranational European level, the FPÖ politically functionalizes worries about the EU plans for eastern enlargement, using it to increase the fear of unemployment and of being "colonized by the Islamic culture." The globalization rhetoric of EU policy, with its main focus on flexibility and competitiveness as a safeguard against unemployment, is a further source of misgivings (Weiss and Wodak 1999; Muntigl, Weiss and Wodak 2000). People are afraid of losing the traditional security provided by the Austrian welfare state and implemented over the past twenty-five years of Socialist and grand coalition governments. Change seems inevitable, but the coalition parties have not succeeded in proposing adequate alternative measures. Moreover, they seem to be trapped in the Austrian model of "social partnership," which has made significant change very difficult. The FPÖ, on the other hand, promised to protect jobs, accused the coalition parties of giving in to "international pressure," and proclaimed the need for a *Wende (turning point or change)* in Austrian politics. In response, the trade unions, in a radical departure from their

1993 stance, participated in the anti-foreigner discourse, and increasing numbers of traditional Socialist voters, such as workers, joined the FPÖ. It should be pointed out, however, that foreigners in Austria account for only 10 percent of the population. The populist argumentation, of course, provides no constructive programs, but simply responds to people's fears and gives them simplistic answers (see Taggart 2000; Taguieff 1999) (see ter Wal in this volume).

The search for a new identity and the discursive identification of scapegoats are not only Austrian issues, but supranational ones. The competition of the European economy with the USA and Japan has resulted in a "competitiveness rhetoric" (neo-liberal concepts) which is taking over economic debates (Krugmann 1998) (see Wodak in this volume). The phenomenon of globalization is one of the main factors at the core of anxiety about the future, and it reinforces nationalism, ethnicism, xenophobia, and racism. Thus, although Austria is in many ways unique, it is also a case study for European problems.

The "Measures against the Austrian Government"

The FPÖ is not a uniquely Austrian phenomenon. Some parallels to Haider's party can be found in other European countries. The party's anti-immigration agenda and its xenophobic rhetoric are very similar to those used by the French Front National (FN), the Belgian Vlaams Bloc, or the Italian Lega Nord (see ter Wal 2000). The FPÖ's anti-EU attitude is not so different from the anti-European sentiments of the "anti-Maastricht" wing of the British Conservatives. It can be argued that the anti-NAFTA (North American Free Trade Association) sentiment instrumentalized by some U.S. politicians (like Pat Buchanan [Reform party]) and especially the U.S. Republican party's increasing use of slogans and policies directed against immigrants, do not differ significantly from the approach the FPÖ uses (Riedlsperger 1978).

The specifics that can explain the European reaction to the FPÖ's access to government are to be found not only in the contemporary policies, but in their link to the past. The FPÖ must be seen in the context of Austria's tendency to reject Austrian responsibility for Nazism and to accept the existence of a party like the FPÖ, established by former Nazis for former Nazis, in the mainstream of Austrian politics. The Waldheim affair heightened suspicions that "the Austrians" had not learned their lesson as "the Germans" had (see above).

This is the background for the unusual response of the other fourteen EU governments when the coalition cabinet between the conservative People's Party (ÖVP) and the FPÖ was established in February 2000. Backed by a European Parliament resolution, the EU 14 declared that their bilateral relations with the Austrian government would be downgraded to a purely technical level (see Pelinka and Mitten in this volume).

These measures against the Austrian government, which were soon termed "sanctions" (and which most of the Austrian media called "sanctions against Austria"), turned Haider and his party into a European case. The coalition cabinet, led by Wolfgang Schüssel (ÖVP) and Susanne Riess-Passer (FPÖ), used its isolation in Europe to construct a kind of patriotic agenda: Loyal Austrians should side with their government against the "unjustified, illegal sanctions" (Charim and Rabinovici 2000). Austria's foreign policy focused on a single issue, the sanctions, and nothing else mattered.

Meanwhile, the EU 14 had made their point but were unsure what to do next. They commissioned a panel of three "wise men" to investigate and report their findings. The panel declared that the measures or sanctions might be effective on a short-term basis but would be counterproductive in the long run (Kopeinig and Kotanko 2000).

But even after bilateral official contacts resumed, the Austrian government was not really out of the woods. The report had characterized the FPÖ not only as a right-wing populist party but also as a party with some extremist and radical elements (report, 88, 106; see Kopeinig and Kotanko 2000). The European spotlight is still very much on Austria because of the peculiar nature of the FPÖ.

The report made it clear that Austria's human rights' record was not significantly different from that of other European countries. But that had not been the point of the measures: The EU 14 had sanctioned the Austrian government for giving the FPÖ cabinet status, for legitimizing an extreme rightist party. The EU 14 were motivated by the desire to set an example and to provoke a debate.

Both while the sanctions were in place and after they were lifted, there were interesting developments in the Austrian polity and especially its party system. While there is no scientific proof that these changes were direct results of Austria's international isolation, it is at least probable that the conflict between the Austrian government and its European partners had some impact on the trends.

- Within the governing coalition, the Austrian People's Party benefited. It gained a significant number of votes in the Styrian regional elections in October and is sometimes neck and neck with the Social Democrats in public opinion polls. The loser was the FPÖ, which has posted significant losses in all regional and local elections since February 2000. Recent polls show a general decline in voter approval of the Freedom Party.
- Among the opposition parties, the status of the SPÖ seems to have stabilized, with losses in Styria, wins in the Burgenland and Vienna regional elections, and an approval rating in public opinion polls that is more or less the same as it was in October 1999. The Greens seem to be the big winners: In all regional elections as well as in polls, the party has done and continues to do significantly better than in October 1999. This must be seen in the context of the virtual disappearance of the Liberal Forum (LIF), a centrist but strictly anti-FPÖ party.

This situation could mean the beginning of a two-bloc system: one bloc consisting of a strengthened ÖVP and a weakened FPÖ; the other a "red-green" bloc which is becoming significantly though not dramatically stronger. This would seem to indicate that the ÖVP will continue to be bound to the FPÖ for a long time to come, and that the fundamental consensus of the Second Republic, which is based largely on the formal and informal understanding between the center-right (ÖVP) and the center-left (SPÖ), has come to an end (Pelinka 1998, 15–36).

Some argue that there is also a positive side to this development: Austria has overcome the *Proporz*, its traditional system of clientelism, and is on its way to becoming a more competitive democracy. The rise of the FPÖ is seen as the bitter pill Austria had to swallow for having opened up its two-party cartel. (See e.g., Harvard International Review: Austria's Right. Winter 2001.) But it must be considered that the Austrian version of "consociational democracy" was the method specifically chosen to develop and stabilize a small European democracy in the tradition of the Swiss and Dutch understanding of democracy rather than the Anglo-American (Lehmbruch 1967; Lijphart 1977).

"Normalization?"

One of the reasons the three "wise men" argued that the bilateral measures had been productive was the assumption that the Austrian government felt obliged to respond in a very constructive way (report, 115; see Kopeinig and Kotanko 2000). The two aspects of this positive response were:

- An international agreement to compensate the survivors of the Nazi system of forced labor.
- An international agreement to compensate the victims of the "aryanization" that took place in Austria 1938 and the following years.

Both agreements exemplify Austria's negligence in dealing with Austrian responsibility for Nazi crimes. Negotiations for these agreements had started before the Schüssel-Riess-Passer coalition came to power, but Austria's international isolation had put pressure on the government to reach an agreement as soon as possible. The Austrian government was strongly motivated to demonstrate that it had nothing to do with the Nazi past and that the rationale behind the EU 14's measures had been based on a misconception.

The two agreements demonstrate that it was (and is) not just the FPÖ that gives the Austrian method of dealing with the Nazi past its distinct character. Former governments under the leadership of the Social Democrats had also been unable to reach such agreements: Beginning in 1970, social democratic chancellors, leading either one-party cabinets or coalitions with the (pre-Haider) FPÖ or the ÖVP, had shown little interest in coming up with solutions. What made the agreements possible was the unique isolation in which the newly established Austrian government found itself.

The lesson to be learned for Austrian democracy is that international pressure does pay off; that by itself, the Austrian political system was (and probably is) incapable of finding a decent solution to a problem that originated in Austria decades ago.

Is this an early indication that Austrian politics has lost its specific qualities? In a certain way, the founding of the Schüssel-Riess-Passer government could be seen as a significant step towards normalcy:

- For the first time since 1945, Austrian democracy had produced a "minimal winning coalition"—a form of government typical of most European parliamentary systems. (Müller 1997). The grand coalition which had ruled Austria between 1945 and 1966 and again from 1987 until 2000 was out. The smallest coalition majority in parliament, brought together by the second and third largest parties, started to govern. This, as well as some signs of further decline in the "social partnership" (Karlhofer and Tálos 1999)—the network between business and labor so typical of Austrian political culture—demonstrated that Austria was already less of a "consociational democracy" in Arend Lijphart's sense and more of a "competitive democracy" or a "majoritarian government" (Lijphart 1994).

* Because of his strong desire to be included in such a coalition, Jörg Haider did not go for the chancellorship himself. Instead, he offered the position to the chairman of the ÖVP, despite the fact that the ÖVP had won the same number of seats but received some thousand votes less that the FPÖ. Haider also resigned from his party chairmanship after the sanctions were imposed—a clear indication of the impact those measures had. Haider's retreat could also be seen as one step towards normalcy: Was the FPÖ on its way to becoming a mainstream center-right party?

It is, of course, impossible to predict future developments, but the degree of "normalization" in Austria clearly has a European dimension. As long as Austria's European partners have reason to see the FPÖ as a non-mainstream party, as long as no European party organization admits the FPÖ to its ranks, as long as Haider's official retreat has changed neither his dominant role in the party nor the party's outlook (Scharsach 2000; Scharsach and Kuch 2000), "normalization" remains a concept, not a reality.

Justification and Victim Discourses

Although the two phenomena ("Waldheim" and "Haider") certainly differ in many ways, the discourses surrounding both events are similar and, to a certain extent, predictable. These discourses, as recent qualitative studies (Wodak et al. 1990; Reisigl and Wodak 2001) have shown, follow a certain pattern which gives rise to nationalistic and chauvinistic emotions, symbols, and actions:

First, a conspiracy is constructed to explain why many outside Austria suddenly oppose certain Austrian policies. The conspiracy is often linked to "certain circles" (an allusion to "Jews on the East Coast") or to Social Democratic policies, and it enables politicians and Austrians to deny being guilty of having created or contributed to the problems. Ultimately, it allows them to see themselves in the role of the victims: Austria(ns) as the victim(s) of the EU, of a worldwide Jewish conspiracy, etc.

Secondly, a scapegoat is found to justify the actions of Austrian politicians. Foreigners, Jews, *"Vernaderer"* (a new term used for all those "who speak badly about Austria"), the European Union, etc.— all these different groups are or have been, at some time or another, thought guilty of causing the problems in Austria.

Thirdly, accusations are denied, mitigated or redefined. The media and politicians rarely attempt to use rational arguments to explain how their positions differ from those of their opponents. The "in-group" is presented in a positive light, while the "out-group" is debased and portrayed negatively. Euphemisms serve the same function.

Fourthly, a counterattack is launched: The "others" have done the same thing; or even worse, analogies are used, such as: everyone knows that there is racism everywhere. This line of argumentation seems to imply that "we are all the same."

Fifthly, the roles of the victim and perpetrator are reversed. Waldheim or Haider are not to blame for the problem, nor are certain kinds of policies or discourses. Instead, the guilt is projected onto the victims: the Jews, the foreigners, or the critics are then seen as the cause of the international isolation or the so-called sanctions.

Lastly, the accusations directed at Waldheim or the new Austrian government are redefined as accusations directed at Austria or all Austrians. This justifies a chauvinistic approach (see Wodak 2000a,b; Ötsch 2000; Czernin 2000 for a more differentiated and longer description of these discursive patterns). The "whole of Austria" feels it is under attack and must defend itself.

The "new" discourses since February 2000 manifest some other patterns as well, for example:

"Anything goes": When politicians in Austria deny or distort obvious facts, or even lie, it either only creates a small scandal or nothing at all happens. This is, of course, not a new phenomenon: politicians throughout the centuries and around the world have occasionally been known to have trouble with the truth (see Reichert 1999). What is astounding is that there are no repercussions for obvious distortions, which the media generally exposes within twenty-four hours. One example: Josef Kleindienst, a police officer and former member of the FPÖ, published a book (2000) in which he provided evidence to support his claim that numerous persons from the FPÖ had had illegal access to police personnel files, data and computers. Haider's immediate reaction was to claim that he had never seen Kleindienst before and had never had any contact with him. The next day, several newspapers published pictures of Haider and Kleindienst shaking hands. This so-called *Spitzelaffäre* is still being investigated by the police and courts.

The discourse of silence": Even when public figures make statements that oppose, contradict or violate the preamble of the new coalition agreement, the ÖVP and the chancellor often keep quiet or mitigate the events. Again, an example: In his first speech on June 4, 2000, Ernest Windholz, a high-ranking politician from Lower Austria, repeated the SS oath, *"Unsere Ehre heißt Treue."* A scandal ensued. Windholz denied having known the oath, claiming that his use of the same wording was "pure coincidence" (http://www.derstandard.at, 05.06.2000). The chancellor relativized Windholz's statement and took no action. Education Minister Elisabeth Gehrer (ÖVP), however, recognized a need for more information about the Nazi period and its rhetoric. A booklet intended for use in schools and containing examples of this kind of rhetoric has since been published (February 2001) (but unfortunately, the booklet does not contain these recent examples of politic rhetoric).

"Taking the opposition to court": In May 2000, Haider and his former lawyer and close friend Dieter Böhmdorfer (now Minister of Justice) held a joint press conference in Klagenfurt, Carinthia. Haider voiced the idea that politicians who oppose the "interests of the Austrian state" should be sanctioned and maybe even removed from office. Böhmdorfer replied that the idea was "certainly worth pursuing" (*"sicher verfolgenswert"*). The "three wise men" mention these statements in their report and point out the danger they pose to freedom of expression (report 93–96; see Kopeinig and Kotanko 2000).

Perspectives

Austria has found its way into the European Union. After decades of soul-searching and arguing about being a "bridge" between East and West, Austria developed a clear preference for a Western orientation. The beginnings of this tendency go back into the immediate post–1945 period, when the overwhelming anti-communist attitude of most Austrians—uniting friends and foes of the Nazi regime—had an impact on Austria's international outlook (Stourzh 1998, Bischof 1999, esp. 52–77).

This orientation has come to what appears its logical conclusion: Austria's entry into the European Union. Since joining the EU, however, Austria has had to learn a hard lesson: that membership in the club of European democracies is not without its consequences. It was the Union—more precisely, the governments of the other 14 EU member states—that created the strong point of standards Austria has yet to completely fulfill. It is interesting to note that it was this very union of liberal, Western democracies that pointed out Austria's peculiarities.

What the EU pointed out does not constitute a specific record of Austrian policies. Austria does not treat asylum seekers any worse than most of the other EU member states do. Austria does not violate the rights of ethnic or religious minorities in a way that could be seen as unique and scandalous from a European perspective. But that was not the motivation behind the diplomatic sanctions imposed by the EU 14. The real reason for those measures was the particular character of the Freedom Party. The FPÖ—what it represents, its substance, its very nature—was and still is the main reason why Austria and the Austrian democracy cannot expect it to be "business as usual" with the EU.

There are some indicators that can be used in the future to measure Austria's "normalcy": Will the FPÖ be accepted as a mainstream party in the European Parliament? Will the FPÖ be seen as a party of the same political ilk as the French Gaullists, the Spanish Conservatives, or the Scottish Nationalists? Will the FPÖ be able to win partners beyond the Austrian borders—partners who are not fringe groups of the Italian Lega Nord?

Austria and Austrian society must come to terms with the standards Europe considers self-evident. Austria and Austrian society have to accept the fact that the European Union considers itself the antithesis of the very same message the FPÖ is still sending:

- Historical revisionism through the use of ambivalent rhetoric with clear apologetic subtexts regarding the Nazi past.
- Ethnic egotism and a xenophobic outlook with respect to "the others," defending the borders of and within the EU against immigrants.
- Understanding democracy primarily as an exclusive and not as an inclusive system by constructing obstacles to the political integration of "foreigners."

Austria has to realize that there is sufficient evidence to prove that the process of political "re-socialization," which was so decisive for post–1945 Germany, has not been implemented–at least not deeply enough—in post–1945 Austria (see Harms, Reuter and Dürr 1990). Austria cannot return to square one and restart the process of building an Austrian democracy, but it can agree to pay the price of membership in the club of European democracies. That price is Europeanization, and not only in the sense of customs, agrarian policies, the European Monetary Union, and the European Single Market. Europeanization especially means coming to terms with the fact that Europe has reason to believe that Nazism—not Fascism or Communism—was the most profound experience of the twentieth century.

Until Austrian society changes its cavalier attitude toward its past, Austria will not be fully accepted by the European society which has been shaped by this very experience.

Introducing the Volume

This volume contains eleven papers by internationally prominent scholars from the fields of political science, history, anthropology, and linguistics. The numerous trans—and interdisciplinary approaches make it possible to view the many aspects and dimensions of the "Haider phenomenon": the rhetoric and its impact, daily life in Austria, and the influence of right-wing populism on culture and folklore, as well as the sociopolitical background and developments. Only such a multi-level approach can facilitate an understanding of both the specificities of this Austrian phenomenon and the European dimension of such policies.

Part 1 focuses on the development of the Freedom Party, its politics, and the personality of Jörg Haider. Walter Manoschek discusses Austrian postwar history and how the ÖVP, the FPÖ and the SPÖ dealt with or are dealing with the Nazi past. Reinhold Gärtner continues with a detailed analysis of the FPÖ's anti-foreigner policies, and Ruth Wodak provides an in-depth report on the rhetoric of exclusion, the specific populist rhetoric used by the Freedom Party. John Bunzl then explores the personality of Jörg Haider and his charismatic appeal to many audiences. Finally, Andre Gingrich describes the impact of populist policies on Austrian culture.

Part 2 presents views of the Haider phenomenon from outside Austria. Andrei Markovits provides an American perspective on the Haider phenomenon, while Michal Krzyzanowski chronicles the reactions of the Polish media. Jessika ter Wal compares the FPÖ with the ideologies, policies, and rhetoric of Italy's Lega Nord and the Allianza Nazionale.

Part 3 addresses the latest developments in Austria in the year 2000 in relationship to explanations of Haider's rise to power: the European Union sanctions, their impact on Austria, and the search for a new *Wertegemeinschaft* (value system) in the European Union.

Richard Mitten explains why he believes the sanctions were counterproductive; Anton Pelinka presents arguments for a positive evaluation of the bilateral measures. Finally, Rainer Bauböck contributes a detailed explanation of the Haider phenomenon in the Austrian and European contexts.

Notes

1. The postwar situation in Germany was different (see Stern 1991). The victim discourses are thus not new for Austria; they are a characteristic of Austrian public discourses and sentiments (see Wodak et al. 1994).
2. For a detailed description and interpretation of the chronology of events see Mitten 1992b.

References

Bailer, Brigitte, and Neugebauer, Wolfgang. (1998). "Die FPÖ: Vom Liberalismus zum Rechtsextremismus," in *DöW: Handbuch des österreichischen Rechtsextremismus.* Vienna: Deuticke.

Bailer-Galanda, Brigitte, and Neugebauer, Wolfgang. (1997*).* "Haider und die 'Freiheitlichen'" in *Österreich.* Berlin: Elefanten Press.

Benke, Gertraud, and Wodak, Ruth. (2001). Memories of the War. The Narratives of Wehrmacht Soldiers," in Nelson, D., and Dedaic, M. (eds), *War with Words.* Den Haag: De Gruyter (in print).

Bischof, Günter. (1999). *Austria in the First Cold War, 1945–1955. The Leverage of the Weak.* London and New York: Macmillan and St. Martin's Press.

Broder, Henry K. (1986). *Der ewige Antisemit.* Frankfurt am Main: Fischer Taschenbuch Verlag.

Charim, Isolde, and Rabinovici, Doron (eds.). (2000). *Österreich.* Berichte aus Quarantanien. Frankfurt am Main: Suhrkamp.

Czernin, Hubertus. (2000). *Wofür ich mich meinetwegen entschuldige. Haider, beim Wort genommen.* Vienna: Czernin Verlag.

Gottschlich, Hugo. (1987). "Der Fall 'Waldheim' als Medienereignis." Vienna: Projectreport.

Gruber, Helmut. (1991). *Antisemitismus im Mediendiskurs. Die Affäre „Waldheim" in der Tagespresse*. Wiesbaden and Opladen: Deutscher Universitätsverlag/ Westdeutscher Verlag.

Harms, Kathy, Reuter, Lutz R., and Dürr, Volker (eds.). (1999). *Coping with the Past. Germany and Austria after 1945*. Madison: The University of Wisconsin Press.

Heer, Hannes. (1999). *Tote Zonen*. Hamburg: Edition Hamburg.

Karlhofer, Ferdinand, and Tálos, Emmerich (eds.). (1999). *Zukunft der Sozialpartnerschaft. Veränderungsdynamik und Reformbedarf*. Vienna: Signum.

Kienzl, Heinz, and Gehmacher, Ernst (eds). (1987). *Antisemitismus in Österreich, Eine Studie der österreichischen demoskopischen Institute*. Vienna: Braumüller.

Kleindienst, Josef. (2000). *Ich gestehe. Was ein Polizist über die Exekutive weiß.* St.Andrä/Wördern: Kleindienst Verlag.

Kopeinig, Margaretha, and Kotanko, Christoph. (2000). *Eine europäische Affäre*. Vienna: Czernin Verlag.

Krugman, Paul. (1998). *Pop Internationalism*. Cambridge, MA: MIT Press.

Lehmbruch, Gerhard. (1967). *Proporzdemokratie. Politisches System und Politische Kultur in der Schweiz und in Österreich*. Tübingen: Mohr.

Lijphart, Arend. (1977). *Democracy in Plural Societies. A Comparative Exploration*. New Haven, CT: Yale University Press.

_____. (1984). *Democracies. Patterns of Majoritarian and Consensus Government in Twenty-One Countries*. New Haven, CT: Yale University Press.

Manoschek, Walter. (2001). "Wehrmacht und Holocaust." Vienna (unpublished manuscript).

Marin, Bernd. (2000). *Antisemitismus ohne Antisemiten*. Wien: Campus Verlag.

_____. (1983). "Ein historisch neuartiger 'Antisemitismus ohne Antisemiten,'" in J. Bunzl and B. Marin (eds), *Antisemitismus in Österreich*. Innsbruck: Universitätsverlag.

Mitten, Richard. (1987). "Ohne KURToisie." *Profil* 11 May 1987.

_____. (1992a). *The Politics of Antisemitic Prejudice. The Waldheim Phenomenon in Austria*. Boulder, CO: Westview Press.

_____. (1992b). "New Faces of Antisemitic Prejudice: Reflections on the Waldheim Affair," in R. Wistrich (ed), *Austrians and Jews in the Twentieth Century*. London: St. Martin's Press.

_____. (1994). "Jörg Haider, the Anti-immigration Petition and Immigration Policy in Austria." *Patterns of Prejudice* 28/2, 24–47.

Müller, H.-P. (1997). "Spiel ohne Grenzen?" *Merkur*. Deutsche Zeitschrift für europäisches Denken, Sept./Oct.:805–820.

Müller, Wolfgang C. (1997). "Österreich: Festgefügte Koalitionen und stabile Regierungen," in W.C. Müller, K. Strom (eds.), *Koalitionsregierungen in Europa. Bildung, Arbeitsweise und Beendigung*. Vienna: Signum.

Muntigl, Peter, Weiss, Gilbert and Wodak, Ruth. (2000). *European Union Discourses on Un/employment. An Interdisciplinary Approach to Employment Policy-Making and Organizational Change*. Amsterdam: Benjamins.

Ötsch, Walter. (2000). *Haider light. Handbuch für Demagogie*. Vienna: Czernin Verlag.

Ottomeyer, Klaus. (2000). *Die Haider-Show. Zur Psychopolitik der FPÖ*. Klagenfurt: Drava Verlag.

Pelinka, Anton. (1998). *Austria: Out of the Shadow of the Past*. Boulder, CO: Westview Press.

Reichert, Herman. (1999). *"Lüge" und "Selbstgespräch". Zwei Kommunikationsmodelle*. Vienna: Ed. Praesens.

Reisigl, Martin, and Wodak, Ruth. (2001). "Austria First." A Discourse-Historical

Analysis of the Austrian 'Anti-Foreigner-Petition' in 1992 and 1993," in Reisigl, M., and Wodak, R. (eds.), *The Semiotics of Racism*. Vienna: Passagen Verlag.

Reisigl, Martin, and Wodak, Ruth. (2001). *Discourse and Discrimination*. London: Routledge.

Riedlsperger, Max E. (1978). *The Lingering Shadow of Nazism. The Austrian Independence Movement*. New York: Columbia University.

Reinfeldt, Sebastian. (2000). *Nicht-wir und Die-da. Studien zum rechten Populismus*. Vienna: Braumüller.

Scharsach, Hans-Henning. (1993). *Haiders Kampf*. Vienna: Kremayr & Scheriau.

Scharsach, Hans-Henning (ed.). (2000). *Haider. Österreichs rechte Versuchung*. Reinbek: Rowohlt.

Scharsach, Hans-Henning, and Kuch, Kurt. (2000) *Haider. Schatten über Europa*. Köln: Kiepenheuer & Witsch.

Stern, Frank. (1991). *Im Anfang war Auschwitz. Antisemitismus und Philosemitismus im deutschen Nachkrieg*. Gerlingen: Bleicher.

Taggart, Paul. (2000). "Populism and the Pathology of Representative Politics." Paper presented *in Workshop on Populism*, European University Institute, Florence, January 14–15, 2000.

Taguieff, Pierre A. (1998). "Populismes et antipopulismes: le choc des argumentations," in *Mots*, vol.55 nr. June 1998:5–26.

ter Wal, Jessika. (2000). *Racism and Xenophobia and the Discourse of the Freedom Party in the Year 1999*. Diskussionsforum Technische Universität Wien.

_____. (2001). "Comparing Argumentation and Counter-Argumentation in Italian Parliamentary Debate on Immigration."in Reisigl, M., and Wodak, R. (eds), *The Semiotics of Racism*. Vienna: Passagen Verlag.

Weiss, Gilbert, and Wodak, Ruth. (2000). "Debating Europe. Globalisation Rhetorics in European Union Committees," in Bellier, I. and Wilson, T. (eds). *An Anthropology of Europe*. Berghahn.

Wodak, Ruth. (2000a). "The Rise of Racism—An Austrian or a European Phenomenon?" *Discourse & Society* 11(1):5–6.

_____. (2000b): "Wer echt, anständig und ordentlich ist, bestimme ich!"—Wie Jörg Haider und die FPÖ die österreichische Vergangenheit, Gegenwart und Zukunft beurteilen. In *Multimedia: 5–8*.

Wodak, R, de Cillia, R., Reisigl, M., Liebhart, K. (1999). *The Discursive Construction of National Identity*. Edinburgh: Edinburgh University Press (revised and shortened translation of Wodak, R, de Cillia, R., Reisigl, M., Liebhart, K., Hofstätter, K. and Kargl, M. 1998).

Wodak, R., Pelikan, J., Nowak, P., Gruber, H., de Cillia, R., Mitten, R. (1990). *"Wir sind alle unschuldige Täter!" Diskurshistorische Studien zum Nachkriegsantisemitismus*. Frankfurt/Main: Suhrkamp.

Wodak, R., Menz, F., Mitten, R., and Stern, F. (1994). *Die Sprachen der Vergangenheiten: öffentliches Gedenken in österreichischen und deutschen Medien*. Frankfurt/Main: Suhrkamp .

Zöchling, Christa. (1999). *Haider. Licht und Schatten einer Karriere*. Vienna: Molden.

Part 1

1

FPÖ, ÖVP, and Austria's Nazi Past

Walter Manoschek

When President Klestil swore in the new Austrian government of ÖVP and FPÖ at the beginning of February 2000, the postwar-era in Austria came to an end. Even if this government survives a full term there will be no return to the situation that prevailed before February 2000. The political system in Austria, under strain for over a decade, has finally capsized: the change from a democracy of concord to one of conflict is now final.

After joining the European Union in 1995 and with the increasing differentiation in the Austrian party political system, which allows for more than one type of coalition, consensual democracy in Austria has had its day. Following decades of institutionalized democratic structures, a considerable modernization process has begun. For the first time in the history of the Second Republic, there is a new coalition constellation, that of the Right (ÖVP/FPÖ). Seen from the viewpoint of comparative European politics, what has occurred in Austria resembles those changes in other European countries. From this viewpoint, Austria is more than ever before a part of Western Europe.[1]

But Austria is undergoing its largest crisis since 1945: other European partners are treating the new Austrian government as a pariah, and their representatives have even refused to stay in the same hotel with members of the Austrian government. The prevailing situation is well summed up in a current joke: "Who are the best electricians in Austria?" "Schüssel and Haider—they isolated Austria within a day."

Austria's political isolation at the hands of the rest of the EU partners has two causes: the participation of the FPÖ in the government, and the inadequate review and reappraisal of National Socialism in Austria. Only the combination of the two makes the categorical reaction of the EU partners understandable.

The Nazi dictatorship signified such a massive catastrophe for many peoples that the whole world has to deal with its effects—even if the Austrians do not want to come to terms with their own past, foreign observers will keep reminding them of it. This is especially true since the Waldheim affair in 1986. The reaction of the other fourteen EU partners to the inclusion of the FPÖ in the present government is the best proof of this interest to date. Besides the concern that a similar political situation could arise in another EU country, the Austrian way of dealing with its own Nazi past is an intrinsic component of the EU isolation policy towards Austria. Even if the Austrian population or government rejects such interference from abroad, the international community will continue to judge the internal politics of the country against the heritage of its Nazi past, and at the moment the verdict is a critical one.

For the countries that belonged to the Allies in World War II or were occupied by the Nazis, Germany and Austria are responsible for the crimes of National Socialism—whether Austria likes it or not. Because of the Cold War and Austria's neutral status after 1955, the specific Austrian responsibility in this regard was rarely thematized before the Waldheim scandal.[2] The collapse of Communism and the entry into the EU of Austria changed the situation. The increasing sensibility on the part of other states towards Austria's Nazi involvement was not taken seriously by Austria's political establishment, or its representatives chose to misinterpret the signals from abroad. Once Waldheim's term of office was over in 1992, the situation seemed rectified.

Such was not the case, of course, but self-delusion and ignoring reality are common phenomena in Austria. It is therefore not surprising that Schüssel did not heed the warnings of his EU colleagues about giving the FPÖ ministerial posts.

The formation of the new coalition in February 2000 brought matters to a head, and the reaction was far stronger than during the Waldheim affair. The present government in Vienna will have to learn that membership in the EU is based neither on the Maastricht criteria nor on the gross national product. The resentful defense of the coalition's supporters that Austria pays more into the EU budget than it receives clearly implies that they have not begun to understand what the present crisis is about—that it is simply not compatible with being a member of the European community to invite a political party to partake in a government whose structure is authoritarian and fascistoid and whose leaders use racist and xenophobic arguments, resorting time and again to remnants of National Socialist ideology.[3]

If we review the history of the FPÖ, we see that references made by politicians of that party to ideological elements of National Socialism are, in fact, structural characteristics of the FPÖ world-view and not "verbal slip-ups," as those who wish to play down outrageous statements would have us believe. The FPÖ grew out of the Verband der Unabhängigen VdU (Association of Independents),[4] which was founded in 1949 with the active assistance of the Socialist party (SPÖ). The Socialists hoped that the new movement—688,000 de-franchised former NSDAP members were allowed to vote for the first time at the 1949 parliamentary elections—would split the bourgeois vote, cutting into the support for the ÖVP. The VdU also hoped to profit from this new block of voters, as its own functionaries were old Nazis, neo-Nazis, Pan-Germans and a few liberals. The VdU received a respectable 12 percent of the 1949 vote and began to agitate for its main goal—the abolition of all laws governing de-nazification procedures. The arguments the VdU employed to this end were a typical reversal of the perpetrator-victim dichotomy: the real victims were not those persecuted by the Nazi regime but those who had profited from acquiring Jewish property ("Aryanizers") and former members of the NSDAP, who had been prosecuted on the basis of emergency legislation after 1945 and punished.

The fascism concept of the VdU was a crude version of the totalitarianism theory: Fascism was defined in a very general way as a dictatorship and the suppression of all dissent. As far as the VdU was concerned, Stalinism, Red Vienna of the interwar period, and even the post–1945 Second Republic were fascist because, now and before, Nazis (dissenters) were persecuted on the basis of emergency laws. Accordingly, the "real fascism" problem for the VdU was the de-nazification policies pursued since 1945. Other kinds of fascism belonged to the past, the present fascist danger was represented by the governments of the Second Republic. By portraying anti-fascist laws or anti-fascist politicians as fascists, the VdU turned meaningful political concepts upside-down. The new party used this grotesque fascism concept to attack the de-nazification policies of the government, and in equating Nazism with other political systems, VdU spokesmen were really playing down the crimes of Hitler's regime. When the VdU spoke about fascism, it mentioned neither National Socialism nor the Holocaust, at best indicating the "positive sides" of German fascism, such as full employment and economic growth. When viewed against this political background, notorious remarks made in recent times by Haider and his cohorts cannot be treated as "verbal slip-ups" but rather as being fully in the tradition of the FPÖ and its predecessor VdU. Haider's statement in the Carinthian provincial parliament about "the correct employment policies of the Third Reich," for example, was specified the following day by the FPÖ leader: "Just to make sure that there is no misunderstanding: What I said was just establishing the facts, namely that in the Third Reich an intensive employment policy led to the creation of many new jobs and so abolished the unemployment problem" (*Morgen-Journal* Austria State Radio 1, 14 June 1991).

Haider follows the same tradition when he answers the question as to the difference between Nazism and other dictatorships: "It is not my task to examine whether one form of dictatorship is more humane than another. Question: "Was the Nazi dictatorship the most inhumane?" Haider: "You have passed that value judgement. I don't rate them." (*Profil*, 18 February 1985).

Nazi leitmotifs belong to the vocabulary of the FPÖ. In the spring of 2000, Ernest Windholz, the new chairman of the FPÖ in Lower Austria, thanked those officials who had elected him with the oath of allegiance of the Waffen-SS, "Our honour is loyalty" ("Unsere Ehre heißt Treue"). His sentence was greeted by enthusiastic applause. He later stated that he did not know the real meaning of the quotation. Haider's commentary: "It can't be wrong, if somebody confesses in decency, loyalty, honesty and performance" (Falter 27/2000). Relativizing or playing down key elements of Nazism in different ways is part of the political ideology of the FPÖ. Many leading FPÖ functionaries over the years were previously members of the Nazi party.

The FPÖ was formed as the successor organization of the VdU in 1955, after the proclamation of the Austrian State Treaty. The FPÖ had never been a normal third party like the German Liberals (FDP) or other small liberal parties in West European countries. The FPÖ, indirectly at least, was also the successor of the Austrian NSDAP. The first chairman of the party was Anton Reinthaller, an illegal member of the NSDAP in the pre–1938 era and Minister of Agriculture, member of the Reichstag and SS-Standartenführer following the incorporation of Austria into Germany from March 1938. After his demise, the candidates for the election of FPÖ chairman were Hermann Neubacher, former mayor of Vienna in the Nazi era, Lothar Rendulic, former general of the Wehrmacht, and the SS-Obersturmbannführer Friedrich Peter. All candidates therefore had a strong Nazi pasts. An undefined attitude to the Nazi past and an uninterrupted continuity to German nationalism also characterized the opinions of top FPÖ functionaries and the content of the party program (declaration of adherence to "the German cultural nation").

When Chancellor Kreisky formed a minority government in 1970, with the support of the FPÖ, he appointed four former NSDAP members to ministerial posts, which was a signal to the FPÖ that the SPÖ, in order to gain power, could do business with former Nazis in a pragmatic way. Five years later Simon Wiesenthal disclosed that FPÖ leader Friedrich Peter had been a member of the First SS Brigade, a unit responsible for the murder of thousands of civilians in the Soviet Union. Kreisky and almost all prominent Socialists then unleashed a campaign of defamation against Wiesenthal, which culminated in the charge that Wiesenthal had collaborated with the Gestapo.[5] The case aroused international opinion and severe criticism of Kreisky's behavior. While the controversy did not produce any international consequences in the 1970s, it played an essential part in demonstrating that Austria had a scandalous attitude towards its Nazi past and contributed to the belief held in informed circles abroad that the country was not yet prepared to face up to that portion of its history in an honest way.

With the election of Haider as party leader in 1986, the FPÖ was led by a man who maneuvered skilfully between suggestions and plain speaking in respect to the Nazi past. In regard to Wehrmacht soldiers during the Second World War, Haider said "they made the Europe as we know it today possible. If they had not resisted [Stalin], they would not have been in the East, if they had not fought, we would have today…"(*Profil*, 21 August 1995). In answer to the question of whether the German invasion of the Soviet Union was a war of conquest,

Haider replied that one had to ask oneself nowadays "what it was really like then"(*Profil*, 21 August 1995). He answered that very question later in a public speech before veterans of the Waffen-SS in Krumpendorf in Carinthia. Members of that organization (the Waffen-SS was condemned as a criminal organization at the Nuremberg Trials) were now described by Haider as "decent individuals with character who stick to their beliefs despite strong opposition and remain true to them today as well. That is a good basis, my dear friends, for us younger people to inherit"(*Profil*, 8 January 1996).

The thesis of the German invasion of the USSR as "a preventive war," admiration for the strength of character and ideological loyalty of members of the Waffen-SS, describing concentration camps as labor camps, playing down the crimes of Nazism by equating them with other totalitarian regimes—is the standard repertoire of Haider. His views are shared and supported by the FPÖ as a whole. John Gudenus, a FPÖ member of the Austrian second chamber (Bundesrat), said about the existence of gas chambers: "Gas chambers? I am not going to get involved in that! I believe everything which is dogmatically prescribed." (*Kurier*, 19 October 1995). In 1993, the leading FPÖ man Reinhard Gaugg defined the letters NAZI as "new, attractive, single-minded and ingenious." (*Kurier*, 12 November 1993). Böhmdorfer, Haider's solicitor and Minister for Justice in the present government, has expressed the view that one could not view Nazism "exclusively in the sense of all-out rejection" (*Der Standard*, 11 April 2000). The list of relevant quotations from other FPÖ politicians is legion. Edmund Stoiber, the head of the Bavarian CSU (Christlich Soziale Union) and Prime Minister in that German province, while being one of the most ardent supporters of the present ÖVP-FPÖ government in Vienna, remarked lately that the kind of views as expressed by FPÖ politicians on the Nazi past would force any German politician to resign on the same day. In Austria, however, coming to terms with the National Socialist portion of Austrian history in a meaningful fashion has hardly commenced and a politician's political career is not in jeopardy when he makes scandalous remarks on that subject. The political culture of Austria is such that as long as a politician does not actually break the law when commenting on National Socialism, his views thereon are of no consequence and have no consequences. There are, therefore, no grounds for excluding a party from power whose leaders play down the criminal nature of national socialism.

The Erosion of the "Victim-Thesis" (Opferthese) in the 1990s

Even during the Waldheim affair the long-term government parties SPÖ and ÖVP continued to promote the official line after 1945: presenting Austria as a victim nation and making compromises to the collective memory of Austrian society, which knew that it had been part of the greater German identity between 1938 and 1945 and had not differed from the rest of German society in its attitudes or behavior. Of late, however, President Klestil and the elites in the SPÖ realized that the official Austrian "victim thesis" was no longer acceptable abroad. At the beginning of the 1990s it was replaced by the idea of co-responsibility, which states that Austrian society was not only a victim of the Nazi system but also its junior partner and had therefore to answer for the crimes of Nazism.[6] In July 1991 it was the SPÖ Chancellor Franz Vranitzky who explained in parliament for the first time since 1945, that Austria is "partly responsible for the suffering, that not Austria as a state but citizens of the country had brought over other human beings and other nations."[7]

This new direction, more in tune with historical reality, was not very effective because

1. It was addressed primarily to foreign observers and did not take root in Austrian political discourse;
2. It was not accepted by the ÖVP and the FPÖ.

The FPÖ, while satisfied to see Austria now as part of German history during the Nazi era as set down in the new "co-responsibility thesis," did not free itself from equivocal opinions about the Hitler era and rejects out of hand that Austria was in any way to blame for the crimes of that period.

ÖVP: Ignoring the Nazi Era

The ÖVP chose to ignore the moral dilemma, believing that Waldheim's retirement in 1992 had ended the discussion about the Nazi era in Austria. Two examples may show the insensibility of the ÖVP in such matters:

1. Erhard Busek, at that time Minister for Science in the Coalition government with the SPÖ, stated in 1991 that "we cannot expect

to find acceptance for historical studies about Nazism in the pubs of Austria as the subject matter is half a century old, that is a far back as the battle of Königgrätz for many people,"[8] that is the Austro-Prussian War of 1866!

2. In 1994, a high civil servant responsible for research finance in the Ministry of Science (Günter Burkert)—now director of the Political Academy of the ÖVP—said, "as regards the scientific publications on the fascist and Nazi period, more than enough have been published to date" and further research into aspects of Nazi domination "are private affairs and do not deserve funding."[9] These statements from representatives of the ÖVP were typical of that party's attitude to the Nazi past in the 1990s.

In this context, the previous modest attempts to find an adequate response to the Nazi heritage—Vranitzky's statement on this question or the setting up of a fund to compensate Austrian Jewish victims of the Nazi system—had symbolic significance at best and did not filter down into the political cultural of the country and thus could not influence inter-party negotiation strategies.

The ÖVP-FPÖ-Government and Their Dealing with the Nazi Past

It must be seen as one of history's ironies that the ÖVP and the FPÖ were obliged to sign that part of the preamble to the government statement which states: "Austria admits responsibility for its past and the horrendous crimes of the Nazi regime: Our country takes responsibility for the light and the shade of its own past, and for the deeds, good and bad, of its citizens."

Both the ÖVP and the FPÖ have proven in the past that this is not their actual position. While the FPÖ has a—let's say—unclear relationship to National Socialism, the ÖVP has not progressed beyond Austria's no longer justifiable and lifelong illusion that it was the first victim of National Socialism—a position maintained by the party in the international sphere for the past fifteen years. It is simply inconceivable that the ÖVP, with its conservative-reactionary view of history, will be able to undertake the critical examination of Austria's history of National Socialism.

Other statements by ÖVP politicians do not convince. Ursula Stenzel, an ÖVP deputy in the European parliament, has learned the "co-responsibility" thesis by heart now. Or her colleague in Strassburg,

Marlies Flemming (ÖVP), who on TV turned the truth on its head by stating that the Socialists and the Greens had prevented the reappraisal of the Nazi past and that the new government in Vienna is the first one willing to face this task. It is also doubtful if the appeal by the Austrian Foreign Minister Ferreo-Waldner that "slips of the tongue" on the part of a Carinthian politician—Jörg Haider—should be ignored, especially as the latter has demanded that the compensation paid to work-slaves of the Nazi economy be extended to the displaced Sudeten and Slovenian Germans and Austrian POWs of World War II. Despite the attempts of government spokespersons to explain their position, it is clear that neither of the coalition parties can master the task of confronting Austria's Nazi past.

Just two examples:

In March 2000 it became known that former Austrian soldiers of the Wehrmacht would talk to school classes on their experiences during the Second World War. The initiators of the so-called "Initiative Willingness to Defend" (Initiative Wehrbereitschaft) were recommended to the Minister for Education by the Defence Ministry. It has been revealed that at least four of the twenty perspective speakers are well-known right-wing activists.[10] And the material the group prepared for the meetings with the school children contains phrases like "so-called Holocaust" and denies that there were any Nazi orders to mass murder, unlike the Allies who, the group alleges, conducted such a policy from the air. Or that France and England started the war, and not Germany.[11] When this scandal broke, the Education Ministry was forced to call off the talks in the schools. However, it still remains unclear how both ÖVP-run ministries could attempt to foist the views of well-known extreme right-wingers on school pupils.

Another embarrassing case characterizing Austria's attitude towards the past took place in spring 2000. In Schleswig-Holstein in Northern Germany an anti-aircraft artillery school of the German Bundeswehr was renamed the Anton-Schmid barracks. Schmid was an Austrian sergeant-major who rescued more than 250 Jews from the Wilna ghetto (the camp commander was the Austrian Franz Murer) and thus saved their lives. He was executed for this in 1942. The renaming ceremony was also attended by the speaker of the Austrian Parliament, Social Democrat Heinz Fischer. This invitation on the part of the Germans was a breach in the policy of isolating Austria and can be seen as an occasion when representatives from Vienna were summoned to see how another EU state deals with a problematic past, something which Austrians have hitherto failed to do. This admonitory gesture led Fischer to demand from Austrian Defence Minister Scheibner (FPÖ) that a military barracks be renamed in honor of an Austrian resistance fighter executed by the Nazis. Fischer, by the way, was well aware of the delicacy of the issue, noting that "fortunately" he had not been asked why a German military establishment now carries the name of a Wehrmacht sergeant-major from Vienna and not a barracks in Austria. Fischer admitted that he would not have been able to answer.[12]

He could have said a great deal. For instance, that soldiers of the Wehrmacht in Austria today are seen as victims of the Nazi system in a collective sense, persons "who were forced, similar to the population of other occupied regions, to serve the German war effort,"[13] and whose "attitude to 'Hitler's War' had been a negative one right from the outset."[14] This official victim thesis propagated in postwar Austria is far removed from how citizens who served in the German Army (Wehrmacht) view their own participation in the world conflict. In the course of a representative empirical study being evaluated by the present author it emerged that the tate official standpoint is far removed from that of those Austrians who were soldiers in the Wehrmacht.[15] The poll found that:

- Almost 27 percent had enlisted in the Wehrmacht as volunteers.
- 34 percent stated that the most important soldierly principle was "to achieve final victory"; and an equal percentage held that their war was "a struggle for a Greater Germany."
- Almost 57 percent are of the belief that they fought for "Germany, their Fatherland."
- 48 percent stated that they were soldiers of the Wehrmacht from conviction or devotion.
- 41 percent named the "struggle against World Jewry," and 36 percent "racial purity," as the most important goals of the Wehrmacht."

This high degree of identification with core theses of National Socialism demonstrates that a great percentage of Austrian Wehrmacht veterans felt themselves part of a military community of a Greater Germany, and probably also voted accordingly.

This is a striking example of how the official state attitude toward the Nazi past diverges sharply from collective memory in modern Austria.

Re-education Perforce

The traditional "victim status" of Austria has been in popular decline for some time. A recent poll indicates that 70 percent of the population believes that Austria is co-responsible for the mass-murder of the Jews.[16]

After the Waldheim Affair the present isolation of the Austrian government is the second case within the last fifteen years where a country, because of its attitude to the Nazi past, has been ostracized by the international community. This has led to a kind of non-voluntary re-education, learning one's lesson the hard way. The Austrian Agricultural Commissar in Bruxelles Franz Fischler (ÖVP) sees the core problem in Austrian self-delusion: "We have to come to terms finally with certain chapters of our past, just as has been achieved in Germany and other countries."[17] The Committee for International Relations of the American House of Representatives characterized the FPÖ as "an anti-democratic, racist and xenophobic party."[18] Its inclusion in a coalition government is an affront against the system of principles underpinning the foundation of the European Union because the FPÖ cannot come clear with Austria's Nazi heritage. This failure is no obstacle to political success in Austria, however. All political parties in postwar Austria were assiduous in integrating former Nazis into the mainstream. The SPÖ is the first party to admit during the present crisis that it had made grave errors in this regard.[19] Haider's ascent and the success of the FPÖ were facilitated by the main political currents in Austria. Now the country is confronted with the official EU view that, within the community of European states, Austria's sloppy attitude to the Hitler era is not just an internal matter for the Austrian population but one that affects the basic principles of European unity.

The dilemma of the government in Vienna is that the democratic international community perceives the participation of the FPÖ in the government and the faulty processing of the national socialist past within Austrian political culture as being inseparable. Or expressed differently: the asserted adoption of historical responsibility for National Socialism, as stated in the preamble of the recent government statement, precludes the presence of the FPÖ in the present coalition, and vice versa. The ÖVP leaders prefer to ignore that the mere fact that the FPÖ sits in the government demonstrates the absurdity of all historical and political affirmations in the international sphere or of forced preambles.

Both governmental parties lack (for different reasons) the prerequisites for a profound examination of Austria's National Socialist past. Neither the EU partners nor the widespread opposition to the ÖVP-FPÖ administration within the country wish to continue participating in rhetorical pacification formulas. One does not need to be a prophet to predict that this government coalition will prove itself incapable of solving the crisis without encouragement and strictures from within and without the Alpine republic.

Notes

1. Anton Pelinka, *Austria. Out of the Shadow of the Past*, Boulder, CO, Westview Press, 1998.
2. Günter Bischof, *Austria in the First Cold War, 1945–55. The Leverage of the Weak*, Macmillan Press, London, 1999, 52–77.
3. Brigitte Bailer/Wolfgang Neugebauer, "Haider und die 'Freiheitlichen'" in *Österreich*, Elefanten Press, Berlin, 1997.
4. For a history of the VdU and the FPÖ, see Dokumentationsarchiv des Österreichischen Widerstandes (eds.), *Handbuch des österreichischen Rechtsextremismus*, Vienna, 1994, 357–394.
5. Ingrid Böhler, "Wenn die Juden ein Volk sind, so ist es ein mieses Volk." Die Kreisky-Peter-Wiesenthal-Affäre 1975, in Michael Gehler/Hubert Sickinger (eds.), *Politische Affären und Skandale in Österreich. Von Mayerling bis Waldheim*, Thauer-Wien-München 1996, 502–531.
6. An excellent review essay about new literature on this topic has been written by Günter Bischof, "Founding Myths and Compartmentalized Past: New Literature on the Construction, Hibernation, and Deconstruction of World War II Memory in Postwar Austria," in Günter Bischof/Anton Pelinka (eds.), *Austrian Historical Memory and National Identity* (Contemporary Austrian Studies, Vol. 5, Transaction Publishers, New Brunswick, 1997, 302–341.
7. The statement is quoted in Gerhard Botz/Gerald Sprengnagel (Hg.), *Kontroversen um Österreichs Zeitgeschichte. Verdrängte Vergangenheit, Österreich-Identität*, Waldheim und die Historiker, Frankfurt/Main-New York 1994, 574–576.
8. Letter by Erhard Busek to the Verein zur Förderung von Politischem Bewusstsein im Alltag, 10 May 1991, copy in possession of the author.
9. Letter by Günther Burkert to Emmerich Tálos, 25 March 1994, copy in possession of the author.
10. *Profil*, 6 March 2000.
11. "Initiative Willingness to Defend," Informations 3 and 4.
12. *Der Standard*, 26 May 2000.
13. "Memorandum für die Außenministerverhandlungen in London 1947" (Memorandum for the Negotiations of the Foreign Ministers in London 1947) , in Eva-Maria Csaky, *Der Weg zur Freiheit und Neutralität. Dokumente zur*

österreichischen Aussenpolitik 1945–1955 (The Way to Liberty and Neutrality. Documents of the Austrian Foreign Policy 1945–1955), Vienna, 1980, 121.

14. *Rot-Weiss-Rot-Buch. Gerechtigkeit für Österreich. Darstellungen, Dokumente und Nachweise zur Vorgeschichte und Geschichte der Okkupation* (Red-White-Red-Book, Justice for Austria. Descriptions, Documents and Proofs about the Pre-History and History of the Occupation), Vienna, 1946, 125.

15. The empirical study "Austrians in the Second World War" was carried out in 1982 by Josef Schwarz and first evaluated by the Institut for Contemporary History in Vienna. I thank Gustav Spann from the Institut for Contemporary History in Vienna for putting the dates at my disposal for an evaluation for the Ludwig-Wittgenstein-Award-Project, "Confrontation with a Taboo—History in the Making. Discursive Construction of the Subjective Recollection of the Wehrmacht's War of Annihilation" (Principal Investigators: Ruth Wodak/Walter Manoschek/ Theo van Leeuwen).

16. *Die Presse*, 21 June 2000 and *http://www.integral.co.at/integral/*.

17. *Der Standard*, 1 March 2000.

18. *Der Standard*, 11 March 2000.

19. Statement by the chairman of the SPÖ, Alfred Gusenbauer, 6 April 2000.

2

The FPÖ, Foreigners, and Racism in the Haider Era

Reinhold Gärtner

The Freedom Party's (FPÖ) attitude towards foreigners has not always been a hostile one, at least not where the liberal wing of the FPÖ is concerned and not if foreigners were defined as Germans. But this liberal element has died out over the past fifteen years. German nationalism and German culture have always been planks in its party program, which is not surprising if one bears in mind the history and the ideological roots of the FPÖ. Meanwhile, although this German-nationalistic concept has superficially faded away, it is still present as one characteristic of the FPÖ. In August 1988, Haider pointed out: "You know that the Austrian nation was born with a birth defect (*Missgeburt*), an ideological failure, because membership in a 'volk' is one thing, but membership in a state another" (Tributsch 1994: 217).

The other track is xenophobia, the issue "foreigners" (and its emotion-alization), which became more and more important during the 1980s and 1990s. One possible reason for the decrease in importance of German nationalism is the fact that the FPÖ can no longer gain reasonable new support among the electorate with this issue of foreigners: Those Austrians who still favor German nationalism do not have a real electoral alternative to the FPÖ anyway, so it seems logical not to stress German nationalism too much. This issue is still present, albeit hidden, but xenophobia has replaced it as one of the important concerns of the FPÖ.

In this chapter the FPÖ's attitude towards "foreigners" will be illustrated with a few examples, which are

- the Declaration of St. Lorenzen
- the "Austria First" Referendum
- the new party program and
- concluding remarks on xenophobia and racism.

Up until the liberal Steger era and the participation in the SPÖ-FPÖ coalition (1983–86), "foreigners" were not a very important topic in Austrian politics anyway. Though the migration of foreign workers into Austria began in the early 1960s, neither the grand coalition at the time nor the ÖVP single government (1966–70) or the SPÖ single governments (1970–83) made serious attempts to discuss the fact that hundreds of thousands of foreigners were living (and working) in Austria. Foreigners were accepted as foreign workers—and there were no signals that any government would take any further legal steps to facilitate citizenship laws, living or working conditions. Foreigners in Austria were excluded from political participation, and the political and societal mainstream accepted this exclusion as if it were the most natural thing in the world. Migrant workers should come to Austria, work for some period of time, and then leave the country again. Though this model of rotation didn't work, the Austrian laws governing foreigners assumed this would be the case (Manuschek 1985; Gärtner 1990).

In its policies concerning foreigners, as in other respects such as the attitude towards Austria's Nazi past, Austria has very often been a country with a "not now" attitude, which means that there was obviously never a right moment to do anything. Thus, it was only a question of time until a political party made the "foreigners" issue part of its agenda setting and tried to emotionalize it.

On September 14, 1986, Jörg Haider replaced Norbert Steger as chairman of the FPÖ. While Norbert Steger was liberal and thus represented the weaker part of the FPÖ, Jörg Haider was German national and thus represented the stronger part of the FPÖ. And with Haider's advent, the history of the FPÖ would become very different from the party of his predecessors. During the early Haider years, Austria had to deal with the Waldheim Affair, with the questions about the Nazi past, and the role of Austrians in Nazism. It wasn't long, though, until the FPÖ began proclaiming its new topic, "xenophobia." In the election campaign in Vienna in 1987, it was Jörg Haider who asked if it was necessary to have 140,000 unemployed and 180,000 immigrant workers in Austria (Scharsach 1992: 70). This sounds very much like the Nazi posters which read "500,000 Unemployed—400,000 Jews: The solution is easy" (Marin, *Der Standard* 13 November 1999). Haider has repeated this calculation many times since then.

Thus, we see that immediately after Haider's take over, the FPÖ stressed its anti-foreigner policy as one of its main political issues. And Haider's FPÖ seemed to be ahead of its time. At the time of the collapse of the former communist regimes in Eastern Europe at the end of the 1980s, the Austrian population was asked about its attitudes towards foreigners. In the summer of 1989, immediately after the opening of the borders of Eastern European countries that had until this time been communist, many people in Austria felt sympathy for Hungarians, East Germans, Czechs, and Slovaks, but they also were beginning to fear a possible increase in the crime rate. In spring 1990, the general mood began to change; this was accompanied by a series of articles called "Threats by Foreigners!" published in Austria's most widely read tabloid, the *Neue Kronen Zeitung*. So it was not only the FPÖ which emotionalized xenophobia; some of the media, especially the *Neue Kronen Zeitung* also made aggressive and negative comments. One example was a political cartoon showing a small and obviously helpless Austrian confronted by two big rats with "Crimes committed by Foreigners" tattooed on their skin (Plasser, Ulram 1991: 314). And this bore fruit: In the summer of 1990, 71 percent of Austrians said that people from eastern European countries should stay at home, and 67 percent thought that with foreigners in Austria, the rate of insecurity, disorder and crime would rise (Plasser, Ulram 1991: 320–312).

In a survey in 1991, Austrians were asked whether or not Austria should accept immigrants and asylum seekers from different nations. Forty-nine percent of respondents said "absolutely not" with regard to Hungarians, and 68 percent chose that response for Arabs and Northern Africans (Plasser, Ulram 1991: 322). Twenty-two percent said that foreigners in Austria are "dirty," and 22 percent called them "aggressive."

The "foreigners" issue gained importance at that time especially among FPÖ-clientele. Surprisingly though, FPÖ supporters didn't have significantly more negative experiences with foreigners than the statistical average.

In the 1990 campaign for the National Assembly elections, the topic of "foreigners" became increasingly important. In September 1990, a month before the elections, only 9 percent of all Austrians thought that this would be an important election issue, as compared to 20 percent in Vienna and 14 percent among FPÖ supporters. In a ranking of political issues according to their importance, the "foreigner problem" was not on the list at all in 1989, but it ranked tenth in 1990 and rose to second on the list in 1992 (Ulram, Mueller 1995).

Between November 1989 and March 1990, the Austrian government introduced obligatory visas for Bulgarians, Turks, and Romanians. The then-SPÖ secretary general Josef Cap wanted to require visas for Poles because of their high crime rate, and Haider proudly said that the SPÖ and ÖVP would fulfil already the FPÖ's demands in their foreigner policy.

The Declaration of St. Lorenzen

Earlier, in October 1989, FPÖ officials had presented the declaration of St. Lorenzen ("Lorenzener Erklaerung"). This paper was a first concise summary of what the FPÖ considered to be necessary in an (anti)foreigner policy. It was initiated by Raimund Wimmer, the man Jörg Haider praised as "the father of the political renewal of FPÖ" in 1988 (19th Federal Party Conference, Villach 1988). One of Raimund Wimmer's special remarks was made during the "Inlandsreport" show on ORF (Austrian TV) on November 9, 1989: "We have to make inspections. We cannot let everything [sic!] in (into Austria, R.G.); suddenly even the Negroes will be the majority here—this will take some time, but it will come."

The declaration of St. Lorenzen was a strictly national ("voelkisch") and biological concept, an aggressive attack on the basic elements of equality of Western democracies (Fischer et al 1990: 20–21). In this paper we find FPÖ slogans which were used again in the 1999 election campaign (e.g., "Ueberfremdung—foreign swamping; which is reminiscent of Margaret Thatcher's "swamping" speech of 1978); it is an ideological scheme that sounds very much like the argumentation of Le Pen (National Front/France), Schoenhuber (Republikaner/Germany), and Frey (DVU-Deutsche Volksunion/Germany).

Gero Fischer et al. point out (23): "The program presented by the declaration of St. Lorenzen is definitely German national nationalistic, racist, anti-democratic; with a certain and unmistakable National Socialist thought pattern. It is German nationalistic because it deduces political conclusions on the basis of the alleged affiliation of Austria with the German national tradition and culture ("Volkstum und Kulturraum"); it is racist in its discrimination against foreigners in general and non-European foreigners specifically; and it is anti-democratic because it places different values on people's human dignity and wants to treat them differently." (Fischer et al. 1990: 30). The press commentaries in Austria were corresponding: "FPÖ-group Close to Fascism" (*Kleine Zeitung*, 17 March 1990), "How Closet Nazis ('Kellernazi') are Made Socially Acceptable" (*Der Standard*, 17 March 1990), "The Tip of the Iceberg" (*Kurier*, 17 March 1990) or "Totalitarian Thought Pattern" (*Salzburger Nachrichten*, 17 March 1990).

In October 1989, the FPÖ of Burgenland also presented its "Resolution on the Foreigner Question." This resolution categorized foreigners into three groups: first, members of German minorities; second, European foreigners and, third, non-European foreigners. The second and third groups were associated with drug abuse and other forms of criminal behavior—thus the resolution tried to create a generalizing concept of the foreigner as the enemy: "As regards the content of the term 'extreme right', this resolution is without doubt a document of right wing extremism" (Pelinka 1990: 47).

One of the main actors of the FPÖ's German nationalism was Andreas Moelzer, former editor of the extreme right paper *Aula* (the periodical of the German national students' associations, an important recruiting center for FPÖ politicians) and the FPÖ weekly *Kaerntner Nachrichten*. In 1990, Moelzer published "Joerg! Der Eisbrecher," an enthusiastic portrayal of Haider, and in 1991 he was promoted to the position of Haider's personal advisor ("Grundsatzreferent") and member of Bundesrat (second chamber of the Austrian Parliament). Simultaneously, Moelzer became a member of the FPÖ's party academy (FBW-Freiheitliches Bildungswerk) and handled historic and ideological publications. Also in 1991, Moelzer was appointed as the person politically responsible for the FBW. Due to internal discrepancies, though, Moelzer lost both his seat in Bundesrat and his position in the FBW— he had become head curator of FBW—in 1993. In the late 1990s, Moelzer made a comeback as cultural advisor to governor Jörg Haider in Carinthia, a position he still holds.

Moelzer always has been in favor of staunch, hard-line German nationalism. During his tenure as editor of the *Kaerntner Nachrichten* and of *Aula*, later as the editor of the recently founded right-wing paper *Zur Zeit* and throughout his career, he had many connections to the extreme right. He was also one of the main representatives of the Austrian "New Right" ("Neue Rechte")[1] who tried to introduce more (pseudo)intellectualism into right wing thought. He tried to stress the old FPÖ tenet of German nationalist ideology. In autumn 1993, the FPÖ presented proposals for Austria's political renewal. Moelzer commented on these theses and criticized the absence of terms like "nation," "national conscience," "fatherland," or "volk" but said that despite these omissions, it still contained a declaration of the membership in the German national tradition and culture organization ("Deutsche Volks-und Kulturgemeinschaft"). In 1989, Moelzer dreamt of a pan-German union: Calling Austria the "third German state" would be logical and necessary, "90 million German-speaking people in a closed territory, culturally outstanding and gifted, with economic dynamics, competence and capabilities, organized as a classical 19th century national state would have a vocation for unlimited momentum for European hegemony" (quoted in Gärtner 1996: 113).

Moelzer had parts of Austria in a flurry in 1992, when in a public lecture he talked about the threat of "Umvolkung." Even earlier, Moelzer and others had used this strange term in their articles in *Aula*. Due to public pressure, the FPÖ introduced a party commission which—not surprisingly—stressed that Moelzer had neither deviated from the party-platform nor violated its spirit. At that time, Andreas Moelzer was one of the outstanding examples of the FPÖ's attitude towards foreigners. While he was the editor of *Aula* this publication was clearly racist and extreme right (Gärtner 1996). Moelzer and *Aula* followed a strictly German nationalist direction, with categorizations of foreigners according to alleged values and their willingness to be integrated. There is a strong tendency to disqualify strictly these groups according to their ancestry.

In the late 1980s and early 1990s, the Liberal International also made its first attempts to take a closer look at the FPÖ. Finally, in 1993, the Liberal International decided to expel the FPÖ, which, in turn, decided to withdraw from the Liberal International two days before the summit in Tallinn (June 10, 1993) and immediately before being expelled (Bailer-Galanda, Neugebauer 1997: 191). As early as 1986, the Liberal International took a closer look at the FPÖ and its party publications (especially the *Kaerntner Nachrichten* and *Kaerntner Grenzlandjahrbuch*); in 1987 the party establishment had to distance itself from extreme-right and National Socialist-apologetic discourse in the *Kaerntner Nachrichten* and after the publication of the *Kaerntner Grenzlandjahrbuch 1989*, Haider himself promised to take responsibility for its future content. It was the referendum "Austria First" in early 1993, however, that motivated the Liberal International to take the above-mentioned steps.

"Austria First"

Up to that point, the most striking sign of the FPÖ's anti-foreigner attitude was the "Austria First" referendum ("Volksbegehren"). In January-February 1993, the FPÖ organized a referendum, and the Austrian population was asked to sign twelve points. The referendum was politically not very successful, because only some 417,000 Austrians signed it. But it was a first comprehensive signal that the FPÖ would continue with the emotionalization of anti-foreigner attitudes—and it was meant to mobilize anti-foreigner attitudes. Above all, the topic was in the media for a very long time.

The twelve points of the referendum were as follows:

1. Constitutional amendment: Austria is not a country of immigration
2. A freeze on immigration until an adequate solution for the illegal immigrants has been found, until there is no more problem with housing, and until the unemployment rate is under 5 percent.
3. Obligation for foreign workers to carry an identity card at their place of work. This identity card must show their work permit and health insurance.
4. Increase in law enforcement (aliens branch of the police; detectives); pay raises and better equipment to cope with the problem of illegal foreigners and organized crime.
5. Immediate installation of a permanent border control instead of the army.
6. Easing of the situation in schools by reducing the percentage of pupils with foreign mother tongue in primary and vocational schools to a maximum of 30 percent; instruction of foreigner classes if more than 30 percent of the pupils speak a foreign language.

7. Easing of the situation in schools by making satisfactory knowledge of the German language mandatory.
8. No voting rights for foreigners.
9. No early access to citizenship.
10. Rigorous measures against illegal action (e.g. unions and clubs for foreigners) and against the misuse of social benefits.
11. Immediate deportation of foreign criminals.
12. Establishment of an East European Foundation to eliminate migration.

Until the mid-1980s, at the beginning of Haider's time as chairman of FPÖ, the party's attitude towards foreigners focused less on immigrant workers (although he started to stress anti-immigrant prejudices as early as 1987) and more on the basic question of German vs. non-German. The party platform had always stressed Austria's affiliation with the "Deutsche Volks-und Kulturgemeinschaft"—it was part of the FPÖ's German nationalism. Now, the immigrants were increasingly becoming their primary target.

There were, however, plausible reasons for the FPÖ's tendency to skip the straightforward German nationalism. In their analysis of the 1994 elections, Fritz Plasser and Peter Ulram (1995: 491) point out that voters basically support the Haider FPÖ not because of but despite its ambivalent attitude towards German nationalism and right-wing radical ideas. Putting too much stress on right-wing ideologies has always resulted in a loss of support, but the "foreigners" issue was gaining importance: In 1990 only 11 percent of the Austrian population thought that the FPÖ would solve the "problems with foreigners"; this figure climbed to 28 percent in 1992 and 36 percent in 1994. From 1992 on, FPÖ was ranked first when people were asked which party would effectively solve "problems with foreigners." Thus it was a strategic decision to reduce German nationalism and to put more stress on the topic of foreigners in general.

The FPÖ also shifted to the right in the eyes of the Austrian population. In a 1976 survey, 39 percent of respondents placed the FPÖ in the center of the political spectrum and 23 percent on the right. In 1983, the results were 32 percent center and 33 percent right; in 1989, only 14 percent center and 35 percent right, and in 1993, 11 percent center and 50 percent right.

TABLE 2.1
Thematic Competence of the FPÖ 1990–1994

Issue	Competence ascribed to FPÖ (percent)						Competence: Ranking among political parties						Overall importance					
	90	91	92	93/1	93/2	94	90	91	92	93/1	93/2	94	90	91	92	93/1	93/2	94
Solving problems with foreigners	11	18	28	35	32	36	3	2	1	1	1	1	10	5	2	3	3	5

Source: Plasser, Ulram 1995: 477

The FPÖ Party Platform

In 1997, the FPÖ presented its new party platform. Prior to the final version, there was disagreement within FPÖ as to whether or not the adherence to German culture and values should again be expressly stated.

The title of Chapter III of the platform is "Oesterreich zuerst!" (Austria First!)—subtitled "For us, Austria and its people ('seine Menschen') come first." This chapter is a declaration of loyalty to Austria and its people, their cultural heritage and identity, the quest for solidarity and pride in historic merits. Chapter IV, "Recht auf Heimat" (The Right to a Homeland) deals with the concept of a home in a geographic, ethnic and cultural sense. It ultimately points out that Austria is not a country of immigration: "We reject multicultural experiments because they expressly lead to and result in societal conflicts."

The details, though, are interesting, especially those in Chapter IV, Art. 3, where the FPÖ points out that every Austrian has the right to define his or her identity and affiliation with a certain "Volksgruppe." He/she must not experience any disadvantages from this declaration of identification with a "Volksgruppe." Basically, everybody has the right to define his/her belonging to an ethnic group. Subjective rights, though, can only be granted to those who define themselves as part of one of the autochthonous "Volksgruppen," which are: "Germans, Croats, Roma, Slovaks, Slovenes, Czechs and Hungarians." Chapter IV, Art. 1 continues: "Homeland stands for the democratic republic of Austria and its states, the autochthonous peoples (Germans, Croats, Roma, Slovaks, Slovenes, Czech and Hungarians) and the culture formed by them, the law logically states that the overwhelming majority of Austrians belongs to the German autochthonous group."

Two aspects of the platform's references to "autochthonous groups" seem logical, but only at first sight—basically they are what in previous times was the oath of loyalty to German people ("Volk") and culture:

First, the term *Volksgruppe* is used in Austria for very special minorities, i.e., the autochthonous groups of Slovenes, Slovaks, Czechs, Croats, Roma, and Hungarians. There is no autochthonous group, no minority of "Germans" (Oehlinger 1996). If the program lists the "German Volksgruppe" among minorities, this contradicts the juridical and societal discourse and terminology by demanding minority rights for the German-speaking *majority* population. The Austrian government gave a precise definition of "Volksgruppen" on November 24, 1991 (see also the "European Convention on Human Rights for the Protection of Ethnic Minorities"). "Volksgruppe" here was defined as a group within the population which (a) has traditionally lived in a country, (b) is—in contrast to the majority—a numerical minority, (c) has common ethnic or language characteristics which distinguish it from the majority population, and (d) has its own cultural identity. (Oesterreichisches Volksgruppenzentrum 1995: 71).

Second, the FPÖ platform calls for an individual definition. There is no category "Austrians" and there is no Austrian ethnic group in the program. Thus, German-speaking Austrians are forced to define themselves as Germans. They are, logically, not Czechs, Slovenes, Croats, Slovaks, Roma, or Hungarians; therefore the only category left for them is "German."

An interesting appendix is to be found in Chapter VI, Art. 4, "Schicksalsgemeinschaft Europa": "The fundamental right of every 'Volksgruppe' to continuation and protection against forced assimilation not only places Austria under an obligation to autochthonous minorities but also makes Austria the protector of threatened German minorities in the area of the former Austro-Hungarian monarchy." There are at least two questions:

- Why protection for German minorities and not for others?
- Why not ask for similar rights for Slovenia, Slovakia, the Czech Republic, Croatia or Hungary?

Xenophobia and Racism

According to Robert Miles (1999), racism has two characteristics: first, the process of constituting races by using (alleged) biological differences as criteria for the construction of a collectivity, ascribing to it an unchangeable beginning and status; secondly, the imputation of negative characteristics to groups, which has detrimental effects on that group (p. 105).

Throughout the years, the "anti-foreigner" issue was well prepared. Haider's and other FPÖ representatives' quotations have already become almost legendary. They range from various attempts to turn foreigners against migrant workers to "we're not against foreigners, we're for the indigenous population" and to equating foreigners with criminals (cf. Tributsch 1994, Scharsach 1992, Czernin 2000). That slogan marks a new "quality" not only in the diction of the FPÖ but of the New Right (*Neue Rechte*) in general. The concept is one of ethnocentrism—or ethnonationalism—and it basically says that everybody has the right for his/her home and his/her country, but this right has to be restricted by ethnicity. Thus, "German for Germans" or "Turkey for Turks"—or "Austria for Austrians."

Ethnocentrism—accompanied by a latent German nationalism—became the main argument used to promote the FPÖ's anti-foreigner policy. One characteristic of this policy was to point out that foreigners would exploit the Austrian system of social welfare. There are many examples of this in Haider's book, *Die Freiheit, Die Ich Meine* (*The Freedom I Mean*, quoted in Czernin 2000: 78–84), but very few details. Thus it cannot be proven whether or not the accusations are correct. There are, of course, no examples of Austrians exploiting social welfare illegally. The implication, though, is obvious: If one foreigner gets illegal access to money of the "Austrian tax-payer," they all will. The reader is thus invited to equate foreigners with illegality and milking the system.

Plasser and Ulram call this technique "political dichotomization by constructing concepts of an enemy" (Plasser, Ulram 1995, 480). The FPÖ successfully constructed foreign enemies ("foreigners," "social parasites," "bureaucrats," "those people in Brussels," "corruption," etc.) and, on the other hand, positive auto-stereotypes ("honest, hard-working Austrians/the little man/workers). The old "it's us against them" categorization can—in the case of anti-foreigners policy—be successfully used to create xenophobia.

TABLE 2.2
Percentage of the Working Class Electorate Who Voted SPÖ and FPÖ 1983–1995 (National Assembly elections)

Percentage "workers"	SPÖ-voters	FPÖ-voters
1983	31	10
1986	30	22
1990	28	29
1994	29	28
1995	24	35
Change 1983–1995	–7	+25

Source: Plasser, Ulram, Seeber 1996: 182

TABLE 2.3
Cleavages: Voting by Social Class 1986–1995—in percentage

Election		SPÖ	ÖVP	FPÖ	Greens	Liberals
1986	Blue collar	57	26	10	4	*
	White collar	40	37	14	7	*
	Difference	+17	–9	–4	–3	*
1990	Blue collar	52	21	21	2	*
	White collar	38	27	16	7	*
	Difference	+14	–6	+5	–5	*
1994	Blue collar	47	15	29	4	2
	White collar	29	25	22	12	11
	Difference	+18	–10	+7	–8	–9
1995	Blue collar	41	13	34	3	4
	White collar	32	28	22	7	8
	Difference	+9	–15	+12	–4	–4

Source: Plasser, Ulram, Seeber 1996: 183

TABLE 2.4
Class-Voting: Workers 1979–1999—Percentage

year	SPÖ	ÖVP	FPÖ
1979	65	29	4
1983	61	28	3
1986	57	26	10
1990	53	22	21
1994	47	15	29
1995	41	13	34
1999	35	12	47

Source:Plasser, Seeber, Ulram 2000: 81

It also worked in the National Assembly elections in the 1990s: Thanks to this election strategy, the FPÖ gained support among different socio-demographic groups. Overall, in 1994 the main reason for voting FPÖ was the party's anti-foreigner policy, followed by Jörg Haider, control, policy against scandals and privileges and uncovering abuses. The FPÖ drew 29 percent of the young vote in 1995, and 35 percent in 1999. In 1995, 38 percent of men under thirty voted FPÖ, in 1999, that figure rose to 41 percent. (Plasser, Seeber, Ulram 2000: 94–95). Perhaps the most striking fact was the FPÖ's popularity among blue collar workers.

In Austria, the FPÖ has turned more and more to sometimes hidden, sometimes more open racist argumentation. Thus, it is no longer the question "German" vs. "non-German" that is of importance, but rather the question of our culture vs. other cultures which leads to exclusion. One clear example was given by FPÖ member of parliament, Helene Partik-Pable, in May 1999. On May 1, 1999, Marcus Omofuma, a Nigerian asylum seeker, was deported to Sofia. He died during his flight to Sofia, most likely due to the improper treatment by policemen. When this case was debated in parliament, Partik-Pable said the following:

> Ask the officials about the character of black Africans! They do not only look different, . . . they are different. They are especially aggressive. This is obviously because of their nature." (stenographic protocols of the National Assembly, XX. GP, 168th Meeting, May 10, 1999, p. 85)

There are other quotations that conform to theoretical definitions of "racist"—from Haider's "jungle bunnies" to the election campaign in 1999. It is obvious that the FPÖ's rhetoric has become more and more radical and that xenophobia plays a very important role in FPÖ policy.

The FPÖ has been very successful in emotionalizing xenophobia, but this would not have been possible if other political parties had had a clear and sophisticated policy. It was the Austrian government that did not implement laws against these trends. And it was parts of the media that supported xenophobia, as well. And, finally, it was a widespread prevailing mood among society which made it very easy to act xenophobic.

The FPÖ is alone in the European Parliament—as a non-affiliated party. Unfortunately, though, the ideas favored and presented by the FPÖ are not a uniquely Austrian matter. Parties such as the Belgian

Vlaams Blok have slogans like "Eigen volk eerst"; other parties like the National Front (FN) stress xenophobic issues. Overall, the "foreigners" issue has become one of the common topics across much of Europe; only in methods of discussion does it differ from country to country (Wodak, van Dijk 2000).

Note

1. If the term New Right is used, one has to bear in mind that New Right—as it is understood in English-speaking countries—is different from the term "Neue Rechte" in German-speaking countries. The English term New Right comes from conservative thinking and is—or can be seen as-a turn from the center to the right, thus comparable to a right conservative thinking. The German term Neue Rechte, on the other hand, comes from the extreme right; it is an attempt to hide extreme right thinking and make it sound more tolerable (cf. Gärtner 2000).

References

Bailer-Galanda, Brigitte, Wolfgang Neugebauer. (1997). "Haider und die 'Freiheitlichen'" in *Österreich*. Berlin: Elefanten Press.

Czernin, Hubertus (ed.). (2000). *Wofuer ich mich meinetwegen entschuldige. Haider, beim Wort genommen*. Vienna: Czernin Verlag.

Fischer, Gero, Peter Gstettner, Helmut Konrad, Dietmar Larcher, Anton Pelinka. (1990). "Die 'Lorenzener Erklaerung'—ein Produkt aus der ideologischen Kaderschmiede der FPÖ," in Gero Fischer and Peter Gstettner (eds.), *"Am Kaerntner Wesen koennte diese Republik genesen" An den rechten Rand Europas: Jörg Haiders Erneuerungspolitik*, Klagenfurt/Celovec: Drava.

FPÖ. (1998). Das Programm der Freiheitlichen Partei Österreichs, Die Freiheitlichen—Buendnisbuero, Wien.

Gärtner, Reinhold. (1990). "Arbeitsmigration und immigration policy: Ein Vergleich zwischen Oesterreich und Großbritannien nach 1945," unveroeffentlichte Ph.D. diss., Innsbruck.

Gärtner, Reinhold. (1996). *Die ordentlichen Rechten: Die AULA, die Freiheitlichen und der Rechtsextremismus*. Vienna: Picus.

Gärtner, Reinhold. (2000). "Neue Rechte: Ethnocentrism, Culture and Cultural Identity," in Sociological Research Online, Vol. 1, 2000, *http://www.socresonline.org.uk*.

Manuschek, Helga .(1985). "Auslaenderpolitik in Oesterreich 1962–1985." *Journal fuer Sozialforschung* 25 Jg., 1985, Heft 2.

Miles, Robert. (1999). *Rassismus. Einfuehrung in die Geschichte und Theorie eines Begriffs*. Hamburg: Argument.

Oehlinger, Theo. (1996). "Die Rechtslage ethnischer Gruppen in Oesterreich" in Oesterreichisches Volksgruppenzentrum (ed.), *Volksgruppenreport 1996*, Klagenfurt/Celovec: Hermagoras.

Oesterreichisches Volksgruppenzentrum. (1995). *Internationales und europaeisches Volksgruppenrecht, Oesterreichische Volksgruppenhandbuecher*, Vol. 8, Klagenfurt/Celovec: Hermagoras.

Pelinka, Anton. (1990). "Die Resolution der FPÖ-Burgenland zur 'Auslaenderfrage'," in Gero Fischer, Peter Gstettner (eds.), *"Am Kaerntner Wesen koennte diese Republik genesen" An den rechten Rand Europas: Jörg Haiders Erneuerungspolitik.* Klagenfurt/Celovec: Drava.

Plasser, Fritz, Peter A. Ulram. (1990). "'Die Auslaender kommen!'" Empirische Notizen zur Karriere eines Themas und der Bewusstseinslage im 'Herzen Europas,'" in Andreas Khol, Guenther Ofner, Alfred Strinemann (eds.), *Oesterreichsiches Jahrbuch fuer Politik 1990.* Vienna: Oldenbourg.

_____. (1995). "Wandel der politischen Konfliktdynamik: Radikaler Rechtspopulismus in Oesterreich," in Wolfgang C. Mueller, Fritz Plasser, Peter A. Ulram (eds.), *Waehlerverhalten und Parteienwettbewerb. Analysen zur Nationalratswahl 1994.* Vienna: Signum.

Plasser, Fritz, Peter A. Ulram, Gilg Seeber. (1996). "(Dis)Kontinuitaeten und Spannungslinien im Waehlerverhalten: Trendanalysen 1986–1995," in Fritz Plasser, Peter A. Ulram, Guenther Ogris (eds.), *Wahlkampf und Waehlerentscheidung. Analysen zur Nationalratswahl 1995.* Vienna: Signum.

_____. (2000). "Breaking the Mold: Politische Wettbewerbsraeume und Wahlverhalten," in Fritz Plasser, Peter A. Ulram , Franz Sommer (eds.), *Das oesterreichische Wahlverhalten.* Vienna: Signum.

Scharsach, Hans-Henning. (1992). *Haider's Kampf.* Vienna: Orac.

Tributsch, Gudmund. (1994). *Schlagwort Haider. Ein politisches Lexikon seiner Ausprueche von 1986 bis heute.* Vienna: Falter Verlag.

Ulram, Peter A., Wolfgang C. Mueller. (1995). "Die Ausgangslage fuer die Nationalratswahl 1994: Indikatoren und Trends," in Wolfgang C. Mueller, Fritz Plasser, Peter A. Ulram (eds.), *Waehlerverhalten und Parteienwettbewerb. Analysen zur Nationalratswahl 1994.* Vienna: Signum.

Wodak, Ruth, Teun A. van Dijk (eds.). (2000). *Racism at the Top. Parliamentary Discourses on Ethnic Issues in Six European States.* Klagenfurt/Celovec: Drava.

3

Discourse and Politics:
The Rhetoric of Exclusion

Ruth Wodak

Introduction: Important Functions of Political Discourse

Political discourse and communication are fundamentally based on distinguishing between "us" and "them" as one of the most important functions to allow, on the one hand, positive self-presentation of the speakers/writers and, on the other hand, negative other presentation of opponents. Once such groups have been discursively constructed, various linguistic strategies and tools are used to debase the "other" and to characterize the in-group as positive. This allows for identification with the in-group; it also allows for negative characterization of the out-group, and consequently it becomes possible to blame the out-group for certain social phenomena, which usually have much more complex causes. Such rhetoric has old traditions (see Kossellek 1989; Metzeltin et al. 1996; Wodak 2001a,b,c), going back to Greek and Roman writers and philosophers. The construction of groups and the strategic characterization of these groups must therefore be seen as constitutive for persuasive discourse.

Scapegoating, blaming the victim, victim-perpetrator reversal, trivialization, and denial are among the most common argumentative strategies used to convince voters or listeners/viewers of "necessary" political measures, such as restricting immigration and legitimizing such restrictions which often enough actually contradict the democratic traditions of many nation states (see Van Dijk and Rojo-Martin 1997; Van Dijk 2000; Wilson 1990; Chilton and Schaeffner 1997; Wodak and Van Dijk 2000; Reisigl and Wodak 2001). Of course, depending on the genre and field of political discourse, the linguistic realizations differ: the more anonymous and general the genre, the more explicit exclusionary discourses and discourses of difference tend to be. The more official the setting, the more such prejudices and stereotypes are embedded into positive self presentation. Thus, the context of each utterance has to be taken into account when analyzing its exclusionary force (Wodak et al. 1990; Wodak 2000a,b; Benke 2000; Benhabib 1996).

Right-wing populist discourses in Europe (in France, Switzerland, Italy and Austria) share many common features which ter Wal (1997, 1999), Blommaert and Verschueren (1998), Taguieff (1998) and Taggart (2000) have characterized extensively elsewhere. Nevertheless, it is important to ask how such political movements succeed in addressing so many different voter groups and what main topics or programmatic issues seem so convincing and persuasive to so many. To attempt to answer this question, it is relevant to investigate each movement historically and synchronically by itself, because the countries listed above differ in many respects (see Jones 2000), historically, socially and politically.

In this chapter, I cannot offer a comprehensive analysis of them all. I will therefore restrict myself to Austria and to the success of the FPÖ since 1986 when Jörg Haider became the leader of the FPÖ. Specifically, I will be concerned with the coalition paper of the ÖVP-FPÖ government, which has been in office since February 4, 2000. In analyzing some of the aspects of this coalition paper, it will become clear which topics and argumentative strategies are applied and which theories might explain the specific success of the Austrian right-wing populist movement. While illustrating some theoretical considerations about this phenomenon, it will be necessary to present certain linguistic concepts used in the analysis. However, before embarking upon the more systematic analysis, I would like to provide examples of FPÖ discourses and their exclusionary practices to give readers some impressions about every day discourses in Austria since 1986. This is to be seen as a first ethnographic step in our efforts of explaining and interpreting right-wing populist discourses.

"Us" and "Them": The Simple Division of "the World" into "Good" and "Bad" Guys

In Austria, the tradition of exclusion in the twentieth century goes back as far as Karl Lueger, the famous major of Vienna from 1895 to 1908, who set the standards for who was to be considered a Jew and who was not (*"Wer ein Jud íst, bestimme ich"*). Nowadays, it is Jörg Haider's role to decide who qualifies as a "pure, respectable and upstanding" Austrian (*"echt, anständig, ordentlich"*). To legitimize such a classification, he uses descriptive attributes that usually refer to socially accepted actions, subjects and objects, based on "objective" criteria. Jörg Haider uses the terms "pure, respectable" and "upstanding," especially in contexts that are ideologically useful for him.

Such political rhetoric is supposed to distinguish between the "acceptables" and the "undesirables" (literally between the "good" and the "bad" guys) in our society. Strategies of Manichean depiction and the use of "pure" and "respectable" words are part of its repertoire (see Dieckmann 1964, 1975, 1981). These strategies allow Haider (and other members of the FPÖ) to mediate complex facts in an easily digestible message. Through his talk he thus creates "positive" in-groups and "negative" out-groups, and lets everyone know who "we" are, and who the "others" are. In a time of globalization, great insecurity and uncertainty about the future, this strategy is certainly effective and is a familiar method of classical rhetoric (see above). The complex "reality" is explained in simple terms.

So who are they—those "pure Austrians"? An election poster from the fall 1999 national elections in Austria emblazoned with *Two Pure Austrians*—Jörg Haider and Thomas Prinzhorn—gives an answer. Pure Austrians are "real men" who speak the German mother tongue, not some dark-skinned *foreign* guys. And especially not "bushmen" (literally *bushniggers*) as Haider likes to call them: *"Where will we be when any bushmen will have a chance to provide medical treatment to our fellow Austrians?"* (Haider speaking about a new medical law, *Der Standard*, 13 October 1998*)*. Although Haider has attended summer school at Harvard for the last couple of years, he seems unaware that such formulations violate human rights codes. Helene Partik-Pablé, the FPÖ spokesperson for immigration issues and the main candidate of the FPÖ for the Vienna elections March 2001, a lawyer, agrees with him: *"Black Africans not only look different, . . . they are different, as* *they are especially aggressive" (Tiroler Tageszeitung,* 20 May 1999). This is a classic example of prejudice that is based on generalizations and unfounded allegations.

In these quotes we find a clear definition of the first out-group. In addition, the so-called Black Africans *(Schwarzafrikaner)* are accused of being drug dealers running around in *"designer suits and with mobile phones"* (from one of the FPÖ's election ads, Vienna, September 1999). The discourses about *"Schwarzafrikaner"* have influenced public perceptions widely. Many people (men) with dark skin color are regarded as potential drug dealers and harassed by the police and others on the streets.

It also seems that an Austrian passport is not sufficient for being a "pure" Austrian: *"The expansion of the East and the fact that anyone can be naturalized after 6 years create the threat of a foreign infiltration. I suggest that the federal government wants to create a new voting population, because they can no longer rely on the old one."* (Haider in *Die Presse,* 7 October 1998). The terms "change of national allegiance" *(Umvolkung)* and "foreign infiltration" *(Überfremdung)* for example, which were used by parliamentarian Franz Lafer as early as 1998 *(Neue Vorarlberger Tageszeitung,* 10 July 1998), were already used by Goebbels in 1933 and during the Nazi era. In September 1999, the slogan *"Stop Foreign Infiltration,"* i.e., by "impure" Austrians and "foreigners," was widely circulated by the FPÖ throughout Vienna. Here is an example from the FPÖ's election campaign in 1999: *"We have to defend ourselves against a too rapid Eastern expansion, because the possible number of immigrants would multiply and result in further foreign infiltration."* Since 1989, aggression and fear of further immigration from former Eastern block countries are inflamed by equating this phenomenon with natural disasters (see Mitten and Wodak 1993; Matouschek et al. 1995). The xenophobic fear that foreigners would proliferate faster than "pure" Austrians, was also enforced by the FPÖ's top candidate at the National Assembly's election 1999, Thomas Prinzhorn, now second president of the National Assembly: *"Foreigners and asylum seekers have many advantages. For example, in order to increase their fertility they receive free medicine for hormone treatments from the Social Welfare Office. That is a privilege that is rarely granted to natives."*

Let us now turn to Austria's coming to terms with its Nazi past, and to Jörg Haider's so-called "slips," which portray his attitude and opinions particularly in emotionally loaded situations. Here we find that in addition to "pure" Austrians, there is a second rhetorically created in-group: the "respectable" Austrian. An example of this is the former SS-Obersturmbannführer Walter Reder, who was sentenced to life in prison for the massacre of more than 1,000 people in Marzabotto, Italy during World War II. In 1985, Reder was released early from prison. Haider's comment on this was: *"... Walter was a soldier like any other. He carried out his duty, as he was obliged to by oath"* (*Kärntner Nachrichten*, 14 February 1985). This logic puts Reder on one level with many soldiers of the Wehrmacht that were *not* responsible for such crimes. These are typical strategies of trivialization and denial that have often been used for the justification of national socialists' crimes.

Haider knows other "respectable" men: *"This is why I believe that it is necessary to establish a counter-balance. Otherwise we would end up in a world reigned by chaos. You have fought and risked your lives so that the next generation of our children will have a future within a community, in which order, fairness and respectability are still sound principles ... Because the only valid argument [—while in opposition, to a meeting of Waffen-SS veterans,—author] is that one is upset about the fact that there are still people with character in this world, who stand up to their convictions even in the severest storm, and who have remained true to their beliefs to this day."* (Address in Krumpendorf/ Kärnten 1995, FPÖ's *quick-info*, series 30/96, p.10ff). For Haider, thus, the future belongs to those "respectable" men—a statement that is full of rhetorical catchwords.

Haider's implicit conception of history was scrutinized in *Profil*, 21 August 1995:

Haider: "I have said that the soldiers of the Wehrmacht have made democracy in its existing form in Europe possible. If they had not resisted, if they hadn't been in the East, if they had not conducted military campaigns, we would have ... "
Profil: "What does that mean 'resisted' ... after all, it was a war of conquest of the German Wehrmacht."
Haider: "Well, then we have to ask what really happened."

And what did "really" happen? More argumentative strategies are added to those already mentioned above: recontextualization, re-definition, the offsetting of old myths and the creation of new ones. The result is that an ultimate history is proposed and rewritten as being the authentic one, the one that many veterans agree with. This Haider version of history is also welcomed by some of the so-called "future generations" (as Haider often likes to call himself). This version of history allows the maintenance of the Austrian victim myth (Mitten 2000), which has shaped Austria for a long time. This perception of history includes the practice of equating. When asked, who were the biggest criminals (thus "unrespectable" people) of the twentieth century, Haider equates Hitler and Stalin with Churchill. He did not take into account who represented what ideology in which system of government, what the consequences and results were, nor who the aggressors and the defendants were. The victims, too, were equated:

> *Profil*: "Do you consider the Nazi dictatorship a dictatorship like any other?"
> Haider: "I believe that one should not make gradual distinctions when talking about totalitarian systems. One should reject them altogether . . . .There was an era of military conflicts in which our fathers were involved. At the same time, there were operations occurring within the framework of the Nazi regime that cannot be accepted. But no family members of mine were involved in the latter."
> *Profil*: "Do I understand you correctly? 'Operations'? What exactly do you call 'operations'? "
> Haider: "Oh well, activities and measures against parts of the population that were blatant human rights violations."
> *Profil*: "Do you have any problems calling it genocide or mass murder?"
> Haider: "If you like, then it was mass murder."

This sequence illustrates impressively how vague semantics and euphemisms are used to discuss the Holocaust. It also seems to be difficult for Haider to talk about Jews, Roma, Sinti and other victims of persecution (see also below, analysis of the coalition paper). Haider's equation obviously serves as a base, as was seen in an ORF interview, ZIB 2, September 1998:

> Haider: "Well, it simply is a problem, and I would like to say that we have to find out whether two different measurements are being applied here. If Jewish emigrants are making claims, then there will be endless reparations. If the Sudeten Germans ask the Austrian government to demand reparations in their name from the Czech authorities, it will be said that this part of history needs to be considered finished . . . . One cannot treat equal things unequally."
> ORF: "Do you really consider this to be the same?"
> Haider: " . . . I don't want to be the judge on which matter was worse. . ."
> ORF: "Let's go back to your starting point. You treat the fate of the Sudeten Germans in the same way as the injustice that was done to the Jews?"
> Haider: "Of course, because I refuse to accept that human rights violations are being quantified."

Apart from this equation the question remains why the Austrian government should represent the Sudeten Germans at all? If this were the case, what government would represent the Jews? It is individuals, sometimes represented by their attorneys, who make the claims. In the *Freiheitlicher Gemeindekurier* series 565/1998, the FPÖ expressed the opinion that the commission of established historians had not been assembled correctly:

> After 53 years, there are still applications for reparations. Mr. Simon Wiesenthal reserves the right for himself to nominate a foreigner for a commission, and the president of that commission himself, Clemens Jabloner, said in *Profil* No. 41 that he is from a Jewish family and a member of the Israeli religious community. This is where I question the credibility of this "independent" commission, because, as a matter of fact, Austria's Jewish population is exceptionally well represented in high governmental and private positions, and in banks. But as soon as one talks like that one is considered a "racist" and intimidating.

So according to the FPÖ, fifty-three years is too long after the fact to ask for reparations. However, only in the case of the Jews. The address of Simon Wiesenthal as "Mr." is a purposely chosen linguistic degradation. Foreigners should have nothing to say, even if they are prominent and well-known experts who could guarantee their independence better than anyone else. And finally, Dr. Jabloner, a lawyer, is accused of not being able to judge objectively, which implies the call for "pure" Austrians as they have been described above. In addition, the newspaper employs the myth of the "rich" and "powerful" Jew (which hints at the world—conspiracy topos). Anti-Semitic utterances are made explicitly to devalue the work of the commission of historians.

At this point, it must be added though, that the Austrian government has now negotiated restitution payments with American lawyers January 2001. This is the first time that restitution payments will be given to survivors of the Shoah. The commission mentioned above, of course, was already installed before the new government and the so-called *Wende*. It is difficult to foresee what this decision will mean and if the restitution settlements will be explained to the public in an understandable way.

For Haider, some are allowed to speak their mind, some are not: *"The Holocaust serves as a "cash cow," a method of manipulating interests with high moral standards."* (*Neue Freie Zeitung*, Nr. 36, 2 September 1998). Here, terms derived from discourses about gangsters

and criminals are used rhetorically to describe rightful claims of expelled and persecuted people.

"Respectable" people and objects require a brief comment: pure
and respectable Austrians do respectable things: "In the Third Reich,
they had respectable (*Ordentliche*) employment politics to keep people
occupied, not even the government in Vienna can do that" (Kärntner
Landestag, June 13, 1991). This respectable occupation of people,
which is described here in such positive terms, served, as we all know,
to prepare for a war of extermination. After having said that, Jörg
Haider had to resign as head of the government of Carinthia. But he
has returned. . . . The Austrian memory is short-lived. The FPÖ won
27 percent of the votes on October 3, 1999. All these examples illustrate the specific rhetoric used to construct insiders and outsiders.

These discourses are not the only cause for such a huge electoral
support. But the discourses and evaluations, the distinction between
"good" and "bad" guys, mark perceptions, opinions, and beliefs, which
are widely spread in the population. A systematic analysis of the causes
for the FPÖ´s success could clarify what the impact of such opinions
as demonstrated in this section might be, following the Discourse
Historical approach which has been elaborated elsewhere (Reisigl and
Wodak 2001). Due to space restrictions, I have to refer readers to the
publications cited in this paper for details of our methodology and
theory.[1]

The Coalition Program

The Methodology

After these first examples, I would like to turn to the detailed analysis of the prevailing discourses in Austria and the electoral groups
whom the Haider party addresses and who have voted for the FPÖ, in
the attempt to explain the success of the FPÖ at the 1999 national
elections.

For our analysis, we begin by investigating the following discursive
strategies:

1. How are persons named and referred to linguistically?
2. What traits, characteristics, qualities and features are attributed
   to them?

3. By means of what arguments and argumentation schemes do specific persons or social groups try to justify and legitimize the exclusion, discrimination, suppression and exploitation of others?

4. From what perspective or point of view are these namings, attributions and arguments expressed?

5. Are the respective discriminating utterances articulated overtly, are they even intensified, or are they mitigated?

By "strategy" we generally mean a more or less accurate and more or less intentional plan of practices (including discursive practices) adopted to achieve a particular social, political, psychological or linguistic aim. As far as the discursive strategies are concerned, that is to say, systematic ways of using language, we locate them at different levels of linguistic organization and complexity.

First, there are *referential strategies* or *nomination strategies* by which one constructs and represents social actors, for example, ingroups and out-groups. This is done in a number of ways, such as membership categorization devices, including topical reference by biological, naturalizing and depersonalizing metaphors and metonymies, as well as by synecdoches in the form of a part standing for the whole (*pars pro toto*) or a whole standing for the part (*totum pro parte*).

Second, once constructed or identified, the social actors as individuals, group members or groups are linguistically provided with predications. *Predicational strategies* may, for example, be realized as stereotypical, evaluative attributions of negative and positive traits in the linguistic form of implicit or explicit predicates. These strategies aim either at labeling social actors more or less positively or negatively, deprecatorily or appreciatively. They cannot neatly be separated from the nomination strategies. Moreover, in a certain sense, some of the referential strategies can be considered specific forms of predicational strategies, because the pure referential identification very often already involves a denotatively as well as connotatively more or less deprecatory or appreciative labeling of the social actors.

Third, there are *argumentation strategies* and a fund of *topoi* through which positive and negative attributions are justified, through which, for example, it is suggested that the social and political inclusion or exclusion, the discrimination or preferential treatment of the respective persons or groups of persons is justified.

TABLE 3.1
Strategic Aspects of Self—and Other-Presentation

Positive self-presentation & Negative other-presentation	Reference
	Predication
	Perspectivation and involvement
	Intensification or mitigation
	Argumentation

Fourth, discourse analysts may focus on the *perspectivation, framing* or *discourse representation* by means of which speakers express their involvement in discourse, and position their point of view in the reporting, description, narration or quotation of discriminatory events or utterances.

Fifth, there are *intensifying strategies* on the one hand and *mitigation strategies* on the other. Both of them help to qualify and modify the epistemic status of a proposition by intensifying or mitigating the illocutionary force of racist, anti-Semitic, nationalist or ethnicist utterances. These strategies can be an important aspect of the presentation inasmuch as they operate upon it by sharpening it or toning it down.

Analysis of the Coalition Paper of the FPÖ-ÖVP Government

The discourse topics, *inter alia*, which we find in the short excerpts of the coalition program (see appendix) are the following:

- Dealing with the NS past, the victims mentioned are prisoners of war (Wehrmacht soldiers), the Sudeten Germans, and forced labor.
- In dealing with foreigners, there is a clear distinction between Austrians and "foreigners" who are defined by their mother tongue (not German) and not by citizenship; this means that Austrian citizens whose mother tongue is not German still fall under the label of foreigners.
- In dealing with employment, we find a clear reflection of neoliberal theories (dominance of competitiveness, flexibility, cutting back of social welfare, privatization);
- In dealing with women, they are encouraged to stay home and care for the children; but at the same time, networks for successful women are to be installed.

The linguistic analysis of these texts follows the categories presented above. In our detailed methodology, we rely on *Functional Systemic Linguistics* (M.A.K. Halliday 1994) and on an elaboration of Theo van

Leeuwen's *Actors Analysis* (1996); and, most importantly, on argumentation theory, mainly on Manfred Kienpointner's work (1996) and *Classical Rhetoric*.

Let us now take one example from the many text sequences of the coalition paper "dealing with the Nazi past."

- The Federal Government commits itself to the continuation of the policy of sensitivity and critical confrontation with the Nazi past. The aim is to clarify things without reservation, to dissect the patterns of injustice and to pass on this knowledge to the coming generations as a warning for the future. As regards the matter of Nazi slave labour, the Federal Government, in the light of the interim report of the Austrian Historical Commission and with due regard to the primary responsibility of the companies concerned, will work for appropriate solutions.
- The Federal Government will work for fair solutions to the questions of all persons compelled to perform forced labour during the Second World War, Austrian prisoners of war and the German-speaking populations expelled to Austria as a result of the Benes decrees and the Avnoj regulations . . . (see appendix for more)

The main social actor in this paragraph from the coalition paper is the "Federal government": in a relational process, the aim—probably of the government, but the agent is not specified—is to commit itself, clarify, dissect, pass on, and work. These clauses are all embedded, far removed from any social actors. Material, verbal and mental processes are applied. If we continue our analysis, we find abstract nominalized processes, actually grammatical metaphors, such as the "continuation of the policy of sensitivity," "critical confrontation," "patterns of injustice," and "appropriate solutions," I will comment briefly on some of these. What is a policy of sensitivity? As we do not know what the policy was up to now, this remains very vague. "Sensitivity" can have several meanings in this co-text: it can mean that one should approach this topic carefully, consider the victims and perpetrators, or not go into detail, or it can assume other possibilities. At this point, our theoretical assumptions would have to guide the analysis. Our theories about the official Austrian way of dealing with the Nazi past (see below) suggest that the last meaning will be chosen. This vague definition provides a good example for the necessity of integrating social theory into the microanalysis. But, in any case, we are not informed about any details, nothing in this entire paragraph is spelled out precisely. The material verbs, which do imply activities, have no goal-participants which would serve as more detailed information. "To clarify things without reservation" leads to many questions: which "things"? Implied are—most probably—war crimes, but this is not said. It could also mean Austrian participation in Nazi crimes, or it actually could mean "anything." "Without reservation" serves as moral legitimation. Readers should be given the impression that Austrians would really confront the Nazi past. But, only "things" are supposed to be clarified. The next verb is "dissect." "Dissect patterns of injustice" presupposes that there were "patterns of injustice" and that this embedded clause is the first more precise evaluation of the past. But again, we do not know which patterns, since they are not enumerated in any way. At this point, one could argue that the vagueness is necessary because the genre of a coalition paper implies such a programmatic style. On the other hand, one could also argue that a new government should make its policies as clear as possible. Comparing this particular paragraph with others in the appendix, it is striking that other policies are more detailed in their implementation than this one. Thus, we have to include intertextuality into our analysis; and intertextuality at several levels: comparisons with previous coalition papers, comparisons with other parts of the coalition paper, comparisons with speeches of government politicians, and so on. Finally, one explicit issue is proposed: "Nazi slave labor." A commission of historians who are to investigate all the documents concerned with slave labor was formed one year ago, which means that no precise solutions can be suggested yet, only "appropriate" solutions. The attribute remains vague—appropriate for whom, who decides? When we take into account the opinions of the FPÖ in this matter, which were illustrated above, then we should be quite concerned as to what these measures might be. We need to investigate other genres to be able to interpret this piece of text in more detail. And, looking back at our main question, we need theories about "dealing with the Nazi past" to be able to understand this text as a typical "symptom" of Haider's success.[2]

If we look at the macro structure of this one paragraph, there are several arguments and strategies involved: first, to convince everyone that nothing will change, thus reassuring people who might be frightened. Second, to employ a strategy of camouflage because Haider's utterances about the Nazi past contradict the statements about "injustice." Thirdly, to de-contextualize all the demands on restitution: restitution is restricted to slave labor, prisoners of war (Wehrmacht), and the Sudeten Germans. Jews, Roma and Sinti and other victims are not mentioned. Thus, the government is able to argue that they are, in fact, coping with the important demands of some victims, and through silence, they pass over the other victims. The claims of survivors, which are nowadays being voiced, are then pronounced as not valid: this has led to serious debates and in the last resort to explicit anti-Semitism ("they have survived anyway, what more do they want?").

The Genre of a Coalition Paper

To understand the rhetoric of the coalition paper, it is important to consider the functions of the genre of a coalition paper:

A coalition program is supposed to unite the voters and make a clear political statement in contrast to the previous government and previous coalition programs. Changes, therefore, should be clearly marked, and language used to construct certain ideologies and political positions. A coalition paper has identity-creating and reproducing functions, marking the distinctions between "us" and "them." It should be precise but also vague, permitting different ways of implementation and allowing for unexpected changes in global economies and politics. It has to be innovative and it also has to implement the promises made during the election. It has to legitimize unpopular measures in terms of the party ideologies. And finally, it has to be persuasive and readily comprehensible.

This particular coalition paper is even more complex. It contains a preamble, which the president required before swearing in the new government (see appendix); a statement which emphasizes Human Rights and all explicit European Values from Maastricht and Amsterdam. For this reason, of course, the sections that follow should not contradict this preamble in any way (which might account for the vagueness used).

Changes in the Social Welfare State

While visiting the UK, Haider called himself the "Tony Blair from Austria." Although Tony Blair quickly rejected this comparison, we have to ask ourselves why Haider would use such an analogy. Clearly, he counted on triggering some associations: Blair was very successful in gaining a majority of votes, thus Haider claims to be equally successful although he "only" got 27 percent of the votes. Moreover, Blair is seen and perceived as a reformer. This image also appeals to the FPÖ voters in relation to changes in the Austrian society and economy. To understand the economic changes in Austria and the impact of new neoliberal concepts, one has to consider that up to now the social partnership between employers and employees has dominated Austrian economic policies. The trade unions are very strong, and every change has to be negotiated with them. The relationship between the social partners and the government has made it difficult to permit these necessary economic changes to take place. For this reason, many voters have become frustrated with the status quo. Austria is also the sixth richest country in the world, and the country with one of the lowest inflation and unemployment rates in the EU. The fear of change because of EU enlargement is great (see Krausneker, forthcoming). This made it possible for the FPÖ to launch two discourses.

First, against the privileges and corruption of the leading parties who governed until 1999, and against an almost paralyzed economy that was the result of a form of social partnership in which no changes could be negotiated.

Second, against potential immigrants and low-wage workers from the former eastern Bloc.

The first discourse appeals to many young entrepreneurs and people who are "against those up there," against corruption, and in favor of some kind of change on account of globalization.

The second discourse appeals to workers who are afraid of losing their jobs on account of globalization, and who are afraid of changes. As may be clearly seen, these two discourses necessarily contradict each other. One group endorses changes at a global level, the other group reacts negatively to global issues and looks for scapegoats.

Moreover, the second discourse leads to an interdiscursivity of neoliberal and racist discourses. A scapegoat is needed to legitimize the changes that are being considered and which adhere to neoliberal policies. And those positioned as scapegoats are "foreigners."

Lastly, the FPÖ constructed a topos of fear: fear of unemployment caused by immigrants from the East. According to opinion polls and analyses of the election, the FPÖ has become the workers' party (47 percent of workers voted for the FPÖ).

Conclusions and Discourse Model of Populist Discourse in Austria

If we summarize the different discourses in the FPÖ and in the coalition paper after our short analysis, we find the following:

- Revisionism as motor to deal with the Nazi past
- Exculpation of Wehrmacht from war crimes
- Neoliberal economies which support young entrepreneurs
- Pro-family discourses
- Discourses that support career women
- Anti-EU enlargement discourses
- Anti-privileges discourses

Pro-"Austrian" discourses

Populism is not an ideology (if we follow Karl Mannheim's defini- tion, for example): it is not a clear and causally connected edifice but a mixture of often contradictory measures which appeal to very different voters and also reflect social tensions and changes in the respective society, as mentioned by Taguieff (1998) and Taggart (2000). The FPÖ is a party that has at least ten different motives for potential voters: all those that are against privileges; against those "up there"; for flexibility and privatization; for yuppies; for old soldiers and former Nazis; against trade unions; for young people; for all those afraid of losing jobs; for mothers and employed women; for all "true Austri- ans," to mention just a few. Another important issue is the FPÖ's different notion of democracy; they are not anti-democratic but pro- pose a different kind of democracy, which is similar to Switzerland's. As can be easily seen, abstract theories about populism do not ad- equately grasp this complexity. Neither do they allow for the specifici- ties of Austrian history and culture, and, most importantly, the ques- tion of memory and guilt (see Benke and Wodak 2000).

The specific Austrian past and theories about collective memory and legitimation are necessary for our explanations of the FPÖ's suc- cess. In Austria, the Wehrmacht's past has to be mystified and justi- fied because most men of the older generation and fathers of the younger generation were part of the Wehrmacht. To accuse them means accusing a huge part of the population. Karl Jasper's 1946 essay, *"Die Schuldfrage,"* distinguished four different kinds of guilt: criminal, political, moral, and metaphysical. In our context, his second category "political guilt" has become used as "moral" or "historical" responsibility. "Everybody," he argued, "is co-responsible for the way he is governed" (1979: 21). And he continues, "A *Volk* is responsible for the quality of its policy" (1979, 44). But, as our 1990 study on the Waldheim Affair illustrates, no Austrians (and probably no one else) are happy to be confronted with guilt. As argued by Richard Mitten (2000), there are several ways out of this dilemma, and this can be linked to our analysis of a "justification discourse": if accused or attacked, one denies, plays down, relativizes or turns the tables ("identification with the aggressor"; Anna Freud). And this hypothesis is well illustrated by the rhetoric of the FPÖ.

Moreover, many overtly contracting tendencies can also be grasped by recent research on employment policies in the EU as well as the problems of searching for new "European identities" (Muntigl, Weiss and Wodak 2000). Globalization rhetoric emphasizes—as one central discourse figure—the deconstruction of the nation state. Nationalistic parties apparently tend to react to such economic changes with chauvinistic discourse. In our study it was shown how globalization rhetoric functions and the central role it takes in neoliberal economics in general. Basically, globalization rhetoric constructs one global economic market where everyone has to compete with everyone else. It is, however, not only individuals and enterprises that are constructed as worldwide competitors by this rhetoric but also states, national economies, and supra-national federations such as the EU. The problem here is that the concepts of competition and competitiveness are taken out of their original context, namely a market situation where economic actors compete with each other for profits, and put into a new context where fundamentally non-economic actors, like governments or states, are submitted to the principles of a universal economism. Political actors are then reduced to economic actors and states to big corporations. Politics becomes *ersatz* economics just as, from the contrary perspective, economics becomes *ersatz* politics. As described in our study, and specifically by Gilbert Weiss, the rhetoric of globalization and competitiveness has little to do with either economic or political reality. It neglects the real economic facts and political problems in many respects. Nevertheless, and Paul Krugman does not forget to mention this point, as it serves certain functions:

Finally, many of the world's leaders have found the competitive metaphor extremely useful as a political device. The rhetoric of competitiveness turns out to provide a good way either to justify hard choices or to avoid them. (Krugman 1998: 16)

This is indeed the crucial point when analyzing today's political discourse. The rhetoric of globalization and competitiveness has become an argumentative vehicle for disciplining the aims of social justice and welfare by "economic" arguments. Global competitiveness is the key; and, in order to become competitive, states have to use all available means to keep their currency strong; and they must be flexible—flexible in every respect. At the end of the twentieth century, we have to jump again into the "Darwinian Ocean"—as Lester Thurow (1996: 166) puts it.

Globalization and nationalism imply tensions and contradictions. It is not possible discursively to construct one homogeneous identity, either in the nation state or supranationally. Nowadays, we are dealing with fragmentations, struggles and contradictions; multiple identities seem to be developing, at both individual, national and global levels. Certainty and security are no longer the concepts that accompany our life. Moreover, flexibility has become the basic catchword for all dimensions of our daily interactions. Right-wing populism is one answer to these developments, a step backward on the one hand, a step forward, on the other hand, as illustrated by the conflicting discourses of the FPÖ concerning the diverse responses to globalization.

To summarize these first attempts at systematization, I have constructed the following model:

Certain slogans and arguments that start in the discourse of the elite and spread to other realms are de—and recontextualized in other public spaces and genres. Summarizing, we could conclude that the formula for the specific success of right-wing populist rhetoric in Austria is:

revisionism of history plus ambivalent attitudes to neoliberal economic theories plus racism.

Sheyla Benhabib (1996: 3ff) has summarized the tensions we are

Populist Discourses in Austria

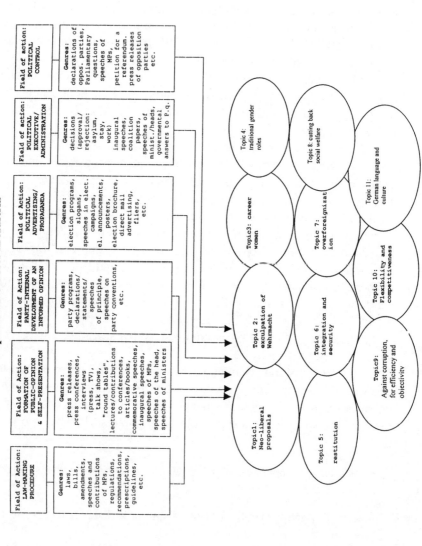

Field of Action:
LAW-MAKING
PROCEDURE

Genres:
laws,
bills,
amendments,
speeches and
contributions
of MPs,
regulations,
recommendations,
prescriptions,
guidelines,
etc.

Field of Action:
FORMATION OF
PUBLIC-OPINION
& SELF-PRESENTATION

Genres:
press releases,
press conferences,
interviews
(press, TV),
"talk shows",
"round tables",
lectures/contributions
to conferences,
articles/books,
commemorative speeches,
inaugural speeches,
speeches of MPs,
speeches of the head,
speeches of ministers

Field of Action:
PARTY-INTERNAL
DEVELOPMENT OF AN
INFORMED OPINION

Genres:
party programs,
declarations/
statements/
speeches
of principle,
speeches on
party conventions,
etc.

Field of Action:
POLITICAL
ADVERTISING/
PROPAGANDA

Genres:
election programs,
slogans,
speeches in elect.
campaigns,
el. announcements,
posters,
election brochure,
direct mail
advertising,
fliers,
etc.

Field of action:
POLITICAL
EXECUTIVE/
ADMINISTRATION

Genres:
decisions
(approval/
rejection:
asylum,
stay,
work)
inaugural
speeches,
coalition
papers,
speeches of
minist./heads,
governmental
answers to P.q.

Field of action:
POLITICAL
CONTROL

Genres:
declarations of
oppos. parties,
Parliamentary
questions,
speeches of
MPs,
petition for a
referendum,
press releases
of opposition
parties
etc.

Topic1:
Neo-liberal
proposals

Topic 2:
exculpation of
Wehrmacht

Topic3: career
women

Topic 4:
traditional gender
roles

Topic 5:
restitution

Topic 6:
integration and
security

Topic 7:
overforeignizat
ion

Topic 8: cutting back
social welfare

Topic9:
Against corruption,
for efficiency and
objectivity

Topic 10:
Flexibility and
competitiveness

Topic11:
German language and
culture

confronted with today in a very precise way:

> Since every search for identity includes differentiating oneself from what one is not, identity politics is always and necessarily a politics of the creation of difference. One is a Bosnian Serb to the degree to which one is not a Bosnian Moslem or a Croat . . . .What is shocking about these developments is not the inevitable dialectic of identity/difference that they display, but rather the atavistic belief that identities can be maintained and secured only by eliminating difference and otherness. The negotiation of identity/difference . . . is the political problem facing democracies on a global scale.

Notes

1. I would like to stress that all the research presented here has been developed together with many colleagues in Vienna and elsewhere , in particular Rudolf de Cillia and Richard Mitten. The most recent elaborations of these studies and the discourse historical approach have been conducted together with Gilbert Weiss and Gertraud Benke (*www.oeaw.ac.at/wittgenstein*), in the Research Center "Discourse, Politics, Identity," located at the Austrian Academy of Science. This chapter, moreover, integrates very valuable creative discussions with Martin Reisigl and also some of his excellent work on linguistic theory and realizations (see Reisigl and Wodak, 2001, Chapter 2).
2. As mentioned above, the new government has negotiated restitution payments for slave labor and for Shoah survivors. It is difficult to understand why the Coalition program does not mention restitution payments; have these been negotiated because of the pressure on Austria after the report of the "three wise men," or out of other motives? We can only speculate at this point. Nevertheless, it is the first government since 1945, which has done so. In which relationship these payments are to be seen to the every day beliefs and antisemitic prejudices is not clear as yet.

APPENDIX

The Coalition Paper (FPÖ and ÖVP), 4 February 2000

Declaration (Präambel)
Responsibility for Austria – A Future in the Heart of Europe

The Federal Government reaffirms its unswerving adherence to the spiritual and moral values which are the common heritage of the peoples of Europe and the true source of individual freedom, political liberty and the rule of law, principles which form the basis of all genuine democracy.

The Federal Government stands for respect, tolerance and understanding for all human beings irrespective of their origin, religion or weltanschauung. It condemns and actively combats any form of discrimination, intolerance and demagoguery in all areas. It strives for a society imbued with the spirit of humanism and tolerance towards the members of all social groups.

The Federal Government works for an Austria in which xenophobia, anti-Semitism and racism have no place. It will take vigorous steps to counter every way of thinking which seeks to denigrate human beings, will actively combat the dissemination of such ideas and is committed to full respect for the rights and fundamental freedoms of people of any nationality – irrespective of the reason for their stay in Austria. It acknowledges its special responsibility as regards the respectful treatment of ethnic and religious minorities.

The Federal Government supports the Charter of European Political Parties for a Non-Racist Society and commits itself to work for the exemplary realisation of its fundamental principles in Austria.

The Federal Government is committed to the protection and promotion of human rights as well as to their unconditional implementation at national and international level. This also makes an important contribution to the prevention of wars and domestic conflicts which result in violations of the rights of people, who may find themselves displaced or even forced to leave their home country.

The Federal Government is committed to the principles of pluralistic democracy and the rule of law common to all members of the European Union, which are also anchored in the Austrian constitution and form the precondition for membership in the Council of Europe. The rights and freedoms enshrined in the European Convention on Human Rights, which are constitutionally guaranteed in Austria, are a clear expression of this commitment.

The Federal Government is committed to the European peace project. Cooperation between the coalition parties is based on a commitment to Austria's membership in the European Union. The Federal Government is bound by those principles of liberty, democracy, respect for human rights and fundamental freedoms, and the rule of law, which under article 6 of the Treaty of the European Union are common to all member states of the European Union. Austria's future, too, lies in the deepening of integration and the enlargement of the Union. Austria's history and geopolitical situation represent a special responsibility to further the process of integration and to anchor the European idea even more firmly in everyday life. The Transatlantic Partnership will have a special significance in order to assure peace and stability during the 21st century.

The European Union as a community of values corresponds to a definite concept for the future development of European integration. This includes, in particular, work on the Charter of Fundamental Rights of the European Union. Austria supports further work towards combating all forms of discrimination according to article 13 of the EU Treaty.

A living culture of democracy and the rule of law demands a relationship between state and citizens that creates new areas of freedom and responsibility for the individual. In a modern efficient state there are functions which can best be carried out by the individual or by non-state actors.

The Federal Government is, however, committed with all emphasis to the maintenance in solidarity of the state welfare services for every citizen who needs state help and support. This applies especially to those people who are unable to take advantage of the opportunities induced by modernisation which are increasingly dominating our lives.

The principle of solidarity also means that consideration must be shown towards the needs and expectations of future generations in order to ensure fair chances for all members of society and their plans for the future.

The Federal Government desires to strengthen Austria's position as a performance and competition oriented economic location. That is the basis for securing existing employment, creating new jobs and ensuring prosperity in our country. Austria's accession to the European Union and an assured participation in the European Monetary Union were and remain important preconditions for the future of the economy and employment in Austria.

Austria's social partnership has proved itself as an important instrument for the location of industry and jobs in Austria, and has contributed to the maintenance of social peace. The Federal Government is committed to comprehensive cooperation with the social partners, but at the same time recommends the necessary readiness to reform the social partnership, for example in respect of the social security structures including the election of representatives of the insured, and strengthening the service character of the social partnership institutions.

The Federal Government is aware that the Austrian people must energetically continue to build on their great achievements of the past and develop Austria's strengths still further.

Austria accepts her responsibility arising out of the tragic history of the 20th century and the horrendous crimes of the National Socialist regime. Our country is facing up to the light and dark sides of its past and to the deeds of all Austrians, good and evil, as its responsibility. Nationalism, dictatorship and intolerance brought war, xenophobia, bondage, racism and mass murder. The singularity of the crimes of the Holocaust which are without precedent in history are an exhortation to permanent alertness against all forms of dictatorship and totalitarianism.

The European Union's project for a broad, democratic and prosperous Europe, to which the Federal Government is unconditionally committed, is the best guarantee against a repetition of this darkest chapter of Austrian history.

The Federal Government is committed to a self-critical scrutiny of the National Socialist past. It will ensure unreserved clarification, exposure of the structures of injustice, and the transmission of this knowledge to coming generations as a warning for the future. As regards the question of forced labour under the National Socialist regime, the Federal Government will endeavour to arrive at objective solutions in the light of the intermediate report by the Austrian commission of historians, while having regard to the primary responsibility of the companies concerned.

The government parties are committed to a new form of government and cooperation. They desire to solve problems, deal with challenges and make consistent use of opportunities, because they are committed to Austria's future in Europe. Austria, as a stable and reliable country, will make her contribution in partnership for a peaceful and secure life together in Europe and the world.

Vienna, 3 February 2000

(Dr. Wolfgang Schüssel)   (Dr. Jörg Haider)

1. Coming to terms with the past

The Federal Government commits itself to the continuation of the policy of sensitivity and critical confrontation with the Nazi past. The aim is to clarify things without reservation, to dissect the patterns of injustice and to pass on this knowledge to the coming generations as a warning for the future. As regards the matter of Nazi slave labour, the Federal Government, in the light of the interim report of the Austrian Historical Commission and with due regard to the primary responsibility of the companies concerned, will work for appropriate solutions.

The Federal Government will work for fair solutions to the questions of all persons compelled to perform forced labour during the Second World War, Austrian prisoners of war and the German-speaking populations expelled to Austria as a result of the Beneš decrees and the Avnoj regulations.

2. Program for the long-term unemployed: "Assistance, Encouragement, Integration"

We want to take a new course in helping the long-term unemployed to enter the job market: The aim of the Federal Government is to provide them with adequate assistance, encourage them to develop their personal skills and to integrate them into a meaningful working process.

Therefore, the long-term unemployed should be obligated to accept suitable jobs in the social services, environmental protection and heritage preservation sectors.

They will then receive a premium in the form of the so-called "citizen money" in addition to their unemployment benefits or emergency relief. Under this scheme, recipients of welfare benefits or emergency relief will be paid an additional amount ("citizen money" premium) of up to 20 per cent of their benefits for doing community work (in the field of health-care or nursing, the preservation of monuments.

3. Effectiveness of the social welfare system and concentration of social benefits

Social justice must be a central element of all policies. Welfare benefits should be based on clear and transparent criteria, they should be financially secured and not distributed indiscriminately.

As a result of rapidly changing labour market conditions and new forms of social life, the welfare state is constantly being faced with new challenges and the requirement to review and adjust the effectiveness, proportionality and accuracy of each individual element of the welfare state, and must ensure that measures are taken to prevent their abuse. We will review the unemployment, accident, health and pension insurance schemes as to whether they are socially just.

4. Women

The new regulation governing the extended duration of child-care/parental leave will enter into force on 1 January 2002 and applies to all parents whose children were born after 30 June 2000 and who on that date will be entitled to parental leave benefits.

An effective family policy and family-related measures should ensure that raising a child and going to work is compatible for both parents. We want to make sure that mothers and fathers have a choice in that they can determine whether both partners are gainfully employed and care for the family at the same time or whether one partner stays at home to care for the family for some time.

Breaking Through the Glass Ceiling

We want to facilitate the rise of women to management positions by means of concrete promotion measures. In this context, it should be examined what the stumbling-blocks are that women have to pass on their way to the top and what the possible counter measures might be.

5. Comprehensive integration

5.1. The central question is the acquisition of good linguistic competence in German.

The intensity of linguistic encouragement and support must be increased. Active integration programmes which start shortly after a person comes to Austria, and which should among other things provide for compulsory German language courses, should guarantee linguistic and socio-cultural integration "from the beginning."

5.2. Already in the *kindergarten,* linguistic encouragement programmes adapted to children should be created. Special incentives should be considered to prompt the use of kindergarten programmes by parents with children who have deficiencies in the acquisition of the German language (linguistic encouragement).

5.3. German language learning should be markedly intensified in the initial stages of primary schools and in other compulsory schools (for example, by increasing the number of weekly German lessons).

5.4. In the *framework of scholastic integration,* these tasks (e.g. increasing the number of German lessons) should have priority in resource management as regards the way in which the about 2,000 current vacancies are shared out.

5.5. In those *sectors where conflicts could arise,* steps should be taken through improved regional distribution to ensure that cultural and linguistic integration in schools can be successful to the best possible degree and that the conditions for people to move in can be made attractive to everybody in individual districts.

5.6. In each class, the *proportion of pupils* in need of special assistance in the area of linguistic and socio-cultural integration should not exceed a limit of roughly one-third.

On the basis of fundamental freedoms and the rights of foreigners, we propose the following measures:

1. Efficient administration of immigration detention; avoid "tourism" by immigration detainees.
2. Improve the quality and number of places in immigration centres (in consultation with regional governments and the justice department) to avoid tourism by immigration detainees.

3. Take steps, in conformity with fundamental rights, against black-
mail used to pressure for release from immigration detention.
4. Consider possibilities for medical action to establish the age of
immigration detainees.)

References

Benhabib, Sheyla (1996). "The Democratic Movement and the Problem of Difference," in S. Benhabib (ed.), *Democracy and Difference: Contesting the Boundaries of the Political*. Princeton, NJ: Princeton University Press.

Benke, Gertraud (2000). "Diskursanalyse als sozialwissenschaftliche Untersuchungsmethode." *SWS Rundschau* (2) p140–162.

Benke, Gertraud, and Wodak, Ruth. (2000). "Neutrality versus Nato: The Analysis of a TV—Discussion on the Contemporary Function of Austria's Neutrality." Contemporary Austrian Studies, *Special Issue on Neutrality* (eds. Anton Pelinka, Günter Bischof, Ruth Wodak) (in print).

Blommaert, Jan, and Verschueren, Jef. (1998). *The Diversity Debate*. London: Routledge.

Chilton, Paul, and Schaeffner, Christine (1997). "Discourse and Politics," in van Dijk, Teun (ed.), *Discourse as Social Interaction. Discourse Studies: A Multidisciplinary Introduction*, Vol. 2. London: Sage.

Dieckmann, Walter (1964). *Information und Überredung. Zum Wortgebrauch der politischen Werbung in Deutschland seit der Französischen Revolution*. Marburg: N.G. Elwert Verlag.

Dieckmann, Walter (1975). *Sprache in der Politik. Einführung in die Pragmatik und Semantik der politischen Sprache*. Heidelberg: Carl Winter Universitätsverlag.

Dieckmann, Walter (1981). *Politische Sprache–Politische Kommunikation. Vorträge–Aufsätze–Entwürfe*. Heidelberg: Carl Winter Universitätsverlag.

Jaspers, Karl (1946/1979). *Die Schuldfrage. Für Völkermord gibt es keine Verjährung*. Munich: R. Piper & Co.

Jones, L. (2000). "Foreigner and Asylum Politics in Western Europe," in Wodak, R. and van Dijk, T. (eds.), *Racism at the Top*. Klagenfurt: Drava.

Kosselleck, Reinhard (1989). *Vergangene Zukunft. Zur Semantik geschichtlicher Zeiten*. Frankfurt am Main: Suhrkamp.

Krausneker, Verena (in print). Einstellungen von ÖsterreicherInnen zur EU-Erweiterung, Project Report, Vienna, Research Center for Discourse, Politics, Identity.

Krugman, Paul (1998). *Pop Internationalism*. Cambridge, MA: MIT Press.

Matouschek, Bernd, Wodak, Ruth, and Januschek, Franz (1995). *Notwendige Maßnahmen gegen Fremde? Genese von Diskursen der Differenz*. Vienna: Passagen Verlag.

Metzeltin, Michael et al. (1996). *Der Andere und der Fremde*. Vienna: Eigenverlag 3 Eidechsen.

Mitten, Richard (2000). "Guilt and Responsibility in Germany and Austria." Paper presented to the conference, „Dilemmas of East Central Europe: Nationalism, Totalitarianism, and the Search for Identity." A Symposium Honouring István Déak, Columbia University, March 24–25, 2000.

Mitten, Richard, and Wodak, Ruth (1993). "On the Discourse of Racism and Prejudice," in *Folia Linguistica. Acta Societatis linguisticae Europaeae. Tomus XXVII/ 3–4/1993*. Berlin and New York: de Gruyter.

Muntigl, Peter, Weiss, Gilbert, and Wodak, Ruth. (2000). *European Union Discourses on Unemployment. An Interdisciplinary Approach to Employment Policy-Making and Organizational Change*. Amsterdam: Benjamins.

Reisigl, Martin, and Wodak, Ruth (eds.). (2001). *The Semiotics of Racism. Approaches in Critical Discourse Analysis*. Vienna: Passagen.

_____. (2001). "Austria First." A Discourse-Historical Analysis of the Austrian "Anti-

Foreigner-Petition" in 1992 and 1993, in Reisigl, M., and Wodak, R. (eds.), *The Semiotics of Racism*. Vienna: Passagen Verlag.
_____. (2001), *Discourse and Discrimination*. Routledge, London.
Taggart, Paul. (2000). "Populism and the Pathology of Representative Politics." Paper presented in Workshop on Populism, European University Institute, Florence, January 14–15, 2000.
Taguieff, Pierre A. (1998). "Populismes et antipopulismes: le choc des argumentations." *Mots*, vol.55 nr.June 1998:5–26.
ter Wal, Jessika (2001). Ideological Implications of Extreme Right-Wing Discourse," in Cornelia Ilie (ed.), *The Study of Parliamentary Debates: Interdisciplinary and Cross-Cultural Approaches*. Amsterdam: Benjamins.
Thurow, L. 1996. *The Future of Capitalism. How Today's Economic Forces Shape Tomorrow's World*. New York: Penguin.
Van Dijk, Teun A. (2000). "Critical Discourse Analysis," in D. Tannen, D. Schiffrin, and H. Hamilton (eds.) *Handbook of Discourse Analysis*. Oxford: Blackwell (forthcoming)
Van Dijk, Teun A., and Rojo, L. (1997). "'There was a problem and it was solved!' Legitimation of the expulsion of 'illegal immigrants' in Spanish parliamentary discourse." *Discourse and Society*, vol. 8/4:523–567.
Wilson, John (1990). *Politically Speaking*. Oxford: Blackwell.
Wodak, Ruth. (2000a). "'Echt, anständig, ordentlich' Wie Jörg Haider und die FPÖ Österreichs Vergangenheit, Gegenwart und Zukunft beurteilen,"in Hans-Henning Scharsach (ed.), *Haider. Österreich und die rechte Versuchung*. Hamburg: Rororo.
_____. (2000b). "La sociolingüística necesita una teoria social? Nuevas perspectivas en el Analisis critico del discurso," in *Discourso y Sociedad* 2(3):123–147.
_____. (2001a). "The Changing of Multinational Organisations: Europe in the Search of New Identities." *Conference Proceedings*, City University of Hong Kong Press (in print).
_____. (2001b). "Multiple Identities: The Role of Female Parliamentarians in the EU Parliament," in J. Holmes and M. Meyerhoff (eds.), *Handbook of Language and Gender*. Oxford: Blackwell (forthcoming).
_____. (2001c). "Diskurs, Politik, Identität," in Panage, Oswald, Goebl, Hans and Brix, Emil (eds.) *Der Mensch und seine Sprache(n)*. Vienna: Böhlau. 133–155.
Wodak, R., Pelikan, J., Nowak, P., Gruber, H., de Cillia, R., Mitten, R. (1990). *"Wir sind alle unschuldige Täter!" Diskurshistorische Studien zum Nachkriegsantisemitismus*, Frankfurt/Main: Suhrkamp.
Wodak, Ruth, and van Dijk, Teun A. (eds.). (2000). *Racism at the Top*. Klagenfurt: Drava.

4

Who the Hell is Jörg Haider?

John Bunzl

Although Jörg Haider has caused massive public irritation and much has been written on him, information and analyses are still schematic and superficial. Often I get the impression that because Austria is not a very important country, it is not worthwhile to deal with this phenomenon seriously; hopefully this will not turn out to have been a costly mistake. As in other cases where there is a lack of understanding and interest, clichés are easily found instead. In the case of Mr. Haider we find two kinds of simplifications: inside Austria he is treated more and more as a successful, "normal," right-wing bourgeois politician who can be dealt with like any other legitimate candidate for participation in government, while outside Austria he is considered beyond the pale because of his remarks that are perceived as neo-Nazi.

This latter perception constitutes an exaggeration and an underestimation, as well. Let me explain: since 1986 when Haider staged a coup within the Freedom Party (Freiheitliche Partei Österreichs, FPÖ) his popularity increased steadily from 5 percent to 30 percent of the general vote. This increase was associated with policies concerning immigration and xenophobia. While the traditional parties dealt with resulting problems according to socioeconomic criteria, the FPÖ added an *ethnic* component. And ethnic politics have very special meanings within the Austrian context.

Historically speaking, "ethnic" or "national" policies in Austria were considered "*German*-national"(deutschnational). Before the "Anschluss" in 1938 a German identity of the republic was assumed by almost everyone. After the disaster of World War II the Austrians were offered the opportunity to "de-Germanize" themselves. This opportunity, of course, was associated with a fatal re-defining of the Anschluss as rape, and consequently of Austria, as victim. While this myth minimized Austrian co-responsibility and led to the foundation of a successful postwar reconstruction, an identity problem still remained. As a superstructure for postwar Austrian development and later prosperity, an "Austrian Nation" had to be invented. Within this concept, however, an "ethnic" component was actually missing, and cultural, political, and religious traditions (often related to the monarchy) were used in its stead. Haider, therefore (in 1988), called it an "ideological miscarriage." This arrangement was always threatened by the *real* history of Austrian involvement with the Third Reich.

With the Waldheim Affair (beginning in 1986), roughly speaking, three options remained:

1. Stick to the myth, blame the outside world, demonstrate xenophobic defiance. That was the line taken by the conservative ÖVP (Österreichische Volkspartei).
2. Criticize the myth in order to confront the real past. That was done with different degrees of success and involvement, by historians and writers, and with a first official declaration by chancellor Franz Vranitzky (Social Democratic Party, SPÖ) in 1991.
3. Criticize the myth in order to rehabilitate the past. The FPÖ, under Jörg Haider, can be understood in this perspective.

The origins of the FPÖ can be found in the German-nationalist "Third Camp" of Austrian politics, which became entirely absorbed by the Nazi party before 1938. After 1945 only three parties were permitted by the Allies: the ÖVP, the SPÖ, and the KPÖ (Communists). Out of electoral and Cold War considerations another party was registered in 1949, the "Independents" (Verband der Unabhängigen), the immediate forerunner of the FPÖ (founded in 1956). The Independents attracted those former Nazis who did not join either of the two main parties. Until 1983 the FPÖ remained a small opposition party containing "national" and "liberal" tendencies.

In that year the FPÖ entered (under the liberal leader Norbert Steger) into a coalition government with the SPÖ. This was precisely the moment when Jörg Haider began his meteoric career.

This young and handsome man, son of a Nazi family in Upper Austria, never challenged his father's traditions, but rather remained faithful to them. This fact had become publicly clear already in 1985 when the then FPÖ minister of defense, Friedhelm Frischenschlager, committed the faux pas of welcoming Walter Reder after his release from an Italian prison. Reder was an SS war criminal of Austrian extraction who had committed atrocities in the village of Marzabotto. While Frischenschlager, having caused a minor local and international scandal, regretted his step, Haider remained defiant. From Carinthia, where he became the provincial party boss, Haider had this to say:

> "Walter Reder was a soldier like hundreds of thousands of others. He performed his duty as demanded by the soldier's oath. . . . All our fathers could have met the same fate."

Carinthia (where Haider is now governor) was not chosen accidentally. This province has a long record of conflict with Slovenes both outside and inside its borders. During World War II this region experienced mass deportations and guerrilla warfare. German nationalist feelings run high there—and Haider, even as a boy of sixteen, had vowed: "The noblest of tasks is resistance against all attempts to separate Austria from Germanness (Deutschtum)"; of Carinthia he proclaimed in 1984: "This land will be free as long as it remains German." Such remarks could be dismissed as the idle talk of a sectarian as long as Haider did not become an important public figure, but international events helped to bring about just that.

Most significant of these international events were the collapse of Communism and the re-unification of Germany. For Haider's FPÖ, these developments were of utmost relevance. First of all, the changes in Eastern Europe triggered a mass *migration* that affected Austria. At the same time the breakdown of an old enemy image (Feindbild) called for a new sense of direction. In this context the FPÖ under Haider managed to re-introduce ethnicity into Austrian politics. In the early 1990s, Andreas Mölzer, the then party theorist, warned of an "Umvolkung"—a Nazi term that, fortunately, has no equivalent in English, but means something like "ethnic transformation." This goes hand in hand with the xenophobic stigmatization of foreigners, expressed in the recent elections (October 1999) by another slogan from the Nazi repertoire: *Stop der Überfremdung* (becoming overwhelmed by foreigners).

Secondly, Haider draws a far-right conclusion from the disintegration of the Soviet Union. He goes as far as re-evaluating Hitler's war against the USSR. In a speech to war veterans and former SS members in October 1990, he had said: "Your sacrifices will only be recognized in the next years for what they were, because European development will make clear that *you* built the foundation for peace and freedom." In other words, the genocidal war in the East saved us from Communism; therefore, it has become obsolete to question "the generation of our fathers."

With regard to the political system in post–1945 Austria, Haider's real concern is not "Proporz" (job allocations in the public sector according to party affiliations), bureaucratization or mis-management as such. He resents the fact that this system was born out of Germany's defeat and under Allied control. Even today he uses the derogatory term "Lizenzparteien," alluding to the fact that the SPÖ and the ÖVP got their "license" from the victors of World War II. The State Treaty and Neutrality are considered cornerstones of a *separate* Austrian political existence. Haider was the first Austrian politician to challenge them openly. And, in this instance, *separate* means: separate from Germany.

But it would be a mistake to say that the FPÖ's success is only, or even mainly, due to these (often camouflaged) positions. It is fair to say that people vote for Haider not *because* he praised the "orderly labor policies of the Third Reich." On the other hand, this fact should not be used to trivialize Haider's success. One million voters knew very well what else he stood for, but chose not to care. The same, by the way, could also be said for the Nazi electorate. People vote for Haider because, as a gifted populist, he manages to bundle together all kinds of grievances and resentments resulting from modernization, globalization, and alienation from political parties and institutions. He promises to "fight the system" (which, paradoxically, worked remarkably well) and gives Austrians a chance to *watch* a self-styled Robin Hood doing the job for them. There has always been a particular fascination with theater in Austria. For Haider, "the system" represents not only a set of alienated institutions as such, but *also* the legacy of Germany's defeat. Therein lies the explosiveness of his cock-tail.

Apparent inconsistencies in Haider's rhetoric should not be overes-timated. In recent years he has downplayed and downgraded what he called the "Deutschtümelei"(Germanism) of his policies; I believe he did so out of tactical and electoral considerations, being that German nationalism was not very popular in Austria. This, apparently, was also why he began an anti-foreigner petition under the slogan, "Aus-tria First"(1993), having, however, an ethnically "cleansed" Austria in mind. A similar calculation appears to guide Haider's policies on the European Union (EU). Blaming EU-membership for many of Austria's (real or alleged) troubles, he can play on widespread feelings, such as fear of competition, immigration, centralization (during the EU-refer-endum, June 1994, Haider claimed that "freemasons rule in Brussels". . .), and pose as a defender of Austrian interests. Behind the opposi-tion to centralization, I assume, "lurks" the old passion for (Germanic) cultural and ethnic identity. It should be remembered that *after* his public repudiation of "Deutschtümelei" (September 1995) he praised Waffen-SS veterans as "honorable people" (October 1995).

In spite of the above Haider should *not* be considered a neo-Nazi. Yes, after having lost the liberal elements, he can run his party as a one-man show and use his populist talents to the utmost. But for what purposes? I believe that his relatively modest goals lie in the realm of personal power and *cultural* hegemony. He wants to take "revenge" on those who (often out of hypocritical motives) have excluded his narrative from the sphere of legitimate public discourse. In this respect he is sending a fatal signal to Austria and the world. And in this respect he should be taken seriously.

Haider once claimed that the FPÖ was not the successor to the Nazi party: "If it were so it would have an absolute majority"(1985). While this may still not be the case, nevertheless, the womb is still fertile-fed by a deep resentment that Austrians, after belonging to the elite of a grand Empire, have been reduced, twice in the twentieth century, to a small and relatively unimportant existence. Monumental changes in the surrounding world have re-awakened slumbering demons.

In a broader sense, these resentments, together with the weakness of a collective ego, predispose Austrians to hostility towards the "other"— the stranger—which is an apparent displacement of their anxiety over losing their own shaky identity. Although opinion polls show quite a strong commitment to Austrian nationhood (in the Central European sense), one should not overlook the relative weakness of this concept in the Austrian context, nor the confusion that exists with regard to its substance.

Austria needs a "renewal"—though not of the kind Haider has in mind. There exist many democratic and supranational traditions that are of value to Austria and the world. On the agenda is a thorough break with an inhuman and catastrophic legacy, not a continuation of it.[1]

Note

1. For a more detailed discussion, see my book, *Between Vienna and Jerusalem. Reflections and Polemics on Austria, Israel, and Palestine*, Peter Lang Publishers, Vienna, 1997.

5

A Man for All Seasons:
An Anthropological Perspective on Public
Representation and Cultural Politics of the
Austrian Freedom Party

Andre Gingrich

"What's wrong with voting for Haider?" says a university student to her friend as they take their seats beside me in a Vienna city bus. "It's as normal as voting for anyone else, and besides, he's sexy!"

"Did you hear what he said last night on TV?" asks the man from the apartment next door, while we take the lift in the morning: "He's the only one who has the guts to speak up to them, and it's even fun to watch!"

Two young workers stroll through Vienna's Stadtpark, on their way to a Friday night party at a local club. "Haider's really one of us. He could even show up at this party—he's so cool!" one of them says to the other, as they pass me on the path to the nightclub.

In personal encounters such as these from autumn 1999, I experience some of the public mood at the eve of the Austrian parliamentary elections: They earned Jörg Haider's "Freedom Party" (FPÖ) 27 percent of the national vote and led to the FPÖ's participation in the country's federal government—amidst strong international and domestic protests. By listening to such conversations, I become better acquainted with the attitudes and qualities that many of his voters attribute to Jörg Haider. For them, Haider represents not only a "normal" voters' option, he is everything that rivaling candidates are not: namely, "sexy," "fun," "cool," "one of us . . . "

Such widely held notions about Haider being fashionable, trendy, and entertaining refer to his image in popular culture and in public representations, and signal the marked success of Haider's strategies throughout the 1990s. By the end of that decade, the FPÖ's ruling group had managed to appear to its voters and many others as the distillation of all the positive cultural values around them, while other party leaders seemed to represent a far less appealing end of the spectrum. The FPÖ leadership appears entertaining and colorful, most others seem boring and dull; the FPÖ leaders are self-assured and active, the others timid and lazy; the FPÖ appears attractive, the rest are unappealing. The FPÖ belongs to "us," not to "them."

In this chapter,[1] I want to explore the various dimensions of popular culture[2] and of public representation in the mass success of Haider's FPÖ at the turn of the century. My methods of inquiry are those of a social anthropologist, and I am particularly interested in two aspects of this topic. First, what are the specific resources of local and popular culture that Haider has employed to achieve his mass success? Second, how do these specific cultural resources interact with elements of wider cultural spheres, in Austria and beyond, to serve Haider's political purposes? These two questions will be pursued in the three sections that follow. The first section deals with Haider's influence in Austria's popular mass culture. Section two analyzes the significance of more traditional forms of "folk culture" in the FPÖ's strategies to mobilize against and attack critical and experimental artists. Section three assesses these key elements of Haider's cultural policies in the context of Austrian society at the turn of the century, within the wider context of the process of European integration and enlargement. I restrict my analysis to the period between autumn 1986, when Haider took over the FPÖ's leadership, and February 2000, when the FPÖ became a partner in the Austrian coalition government—a government that Haider supported and helped shape, although he resigned as party leader and confines himself for the time being to his position as governor of the province of Carinthia.

I begin this investigation with the simple observation that cultural dimensions are indispensable for understanding the FPÖ's mass success; they are part and parcel of the overall political and social phenomenon. In particular, they fulfill three functions: First, a scenario of being embedded in popular mass culture has provided effective and appealing packaging for commercializing the FPÖ's core political agenda. Second, selected elements of popular and folk culture have served the FPÖ well in mobilizing for specific anti-intellectual, neo-nationalist, and neo-liberal goals. Third, "culture" was instrumental in dissociating the FPÖ from its former pan-Germanic inclinations and in newly establishing themselves as culturally well-rooted, good Austrian patriots.

Popular and folk culture registers of attraction and mobilization thus cannot be ignored in any serious attempt to understand the FPÖ's mass success. It might indeed represent a fatal case of intellectual arrogance to disregard the FPÖ's appeal via cultural means. It is simply not enough to repeat that the "packaging" is unimportant. After all, it is the packaging by which the contents are advertised, transported, and sold to consumers. In order to understand what it is that is so attractive to those who consider "buying" the FPÖ line, the cultural dimension deserves analysis.

As a social and cultural anthropologist, I am always interested in the attitudes and priorities of the people I study. From this perspective, it counts right from the beginning if FPÖ voters, and those considering such a vote, think that Haider is entertaining, fun, cool, one of us, and sexy. If these characteristics take precedence for many of these voters, then other factors are secondary for them. It is bad enough for any parliamentary democracy if obvious elements of neo-nationalism and xenophobia, which are conspicuously evident to many, are of secondary importance to almost 30 percent of its voters. But this is exactly the point: *By early 2000, a considerable part of these almost–30 percent of Austrian voters believes that the xenophobic elements in the FPÖ's policies are of secondary significance only.* They consider them partly embarrassing, partly exaggerated by political rivals, partly unimportant or irrelevant, or to some extent, simply nonexistent. Up until early 2000, therefore, a major segment of Haider's voters were not primarily attracted by the xenophobic and neo-nationalist sides of his policies, but by something else. This may well change in the future, but it is important to understand the present. To some extent, the FPÖ's attraction is grounded in a protest against aspects of the established post-World War II political system in Austria. In addition, this protest vote combines with explicit interests and hopes for change. These forces of protest, of special interests and of hopes, are attracted not only by explicit verbal contents of Haider's message, however, but also and perhaps even more importantly, by atmosphere, by appeal, by symbolic forms of identification, by emotional seduction—in short, by public representation.

Glamour Virility:
Mountain Peaks, Lakeshores, and Discotheques

Apart from being a key element in Austria's important tourist economy, skiing is a primary leisure-time activity of the local populace. During a winter weekend, hundreds and even thousands of Austrians may gather at a "ski inn." They will spend their time skiing on the slopes above and below the inn, as well as resting in and around these country restaurants, which overlook any of the many ski resorts in the Austrian Alps. A friend tells me how her sister spent a Saturday's lunch with her family outside such an inn, high in the alps of Carinthia, in the winter of early 1999. Resting from the morning's skiing people are eating, drinking, listening to music, taking a nap or a sunbath, chatting with each other. Gradually, small groups of journalists and bodyguards begin to arrive with the ski lift and gather around the inn's entrance.

Suddenly word passes that "Haider is coming!" A helicopter arrives; several persons get out and walk up to the inn. Amidst the clicking of cameras and the cheering of a few enthusiastic, pre-alerted fans, Haider strolls through the crowd, smiling and waving, until he stops to greet the restaurant owner outdoors. Haider shakes the innkeeper's hand, posing for the cameras, then orders lunch for his crew, after which he quickly moves on to greet as many people as possible in the crowd of surprised weekend skiers. He has taken off his stylish sunglasses; sun-tanned and all smiles, he looks like one of the professional ski instructors of the region. Like them, he casually addresses everyone around him with the informal *Du* (i.e., not with the formal *Sie*). His ski clothes are colorful, elegant, skintight, of the latest fashion. While he chats with local families, my friend's sister's group among them, the meal for his crew is served. It is light, as sportsmen's meals should be; they take it in quickly, without any alcohol. After forty-five minutes, the whole FPÖ crew and their entourage of journalists rise, and Haider's loud and cheerful good-bye is answered by throngs of weekend skiers who are now, by and large, much friendlier and more relaxed towards him than when he arrived. Then the whole FPÖ bunch put on their skis and head downhill; Haider, a good skier, is, of course, in the lead.

"It was like Hollywood, as if Arnold Schwarzenegger or Bruce Willis had dropped in," said my friend's sister, who does not vote for Haider. Scenes like this are typical. Styling himself in the manner of a glamorous and popular screen or sports celebrity is indeed an elementary aspect of Haider's policy of public self-presentation. In a country where winter sports are much more important than they are in the U.S., Haider fully exploits his charismatic presence in this field. To celebrate his fiftieth birthday, to cite another example, a huge evening party was held on a mountain peak not far from his farm in Carinthia. The FPÖ organized the celebration as a major media event—a "snowboard party." Although skiing is still much more popular than snowboarding, in recent years it has come to be seen as a sport of the older generations, as more and more teenagers and twenty-somethings have begun to add snowboarding to their repertoire. During this media event, some young Carinthians gave their provincial governor a snowboard as a birthday gift, which Haider immediately began to use in front of the cameras. The event was clearly and cleverly designed to reinforce Haider's embeddedness in fun events, in winter sports, and in sympathetic association with the younger generation.

Such conscious efforts to construct, enhance, and invigorate the charisma of a star of sports and screen also pervade the FPÖ's presence on the summer scene, where lakeshores and open-air discos provide the typical settings. Especially in Haider's stronghold of Carinthia and in his native Salzkammergut, alpine lakes are focal points of international and domestic tourism. Whenever it seems advantageous, Haider will appear in such contexts, always accompanied by the media, in the persuasive role of a tennis player, a river-rafter, a waterskier, a partygoer, a hiker, or a biker.

These staged appearances emphasize popular sports that require some regular training and skill to look good on camera. Taken together, they construct and re-emphasize Haider's profile as an active, optimistic, ambitious, entertaining, self-assured white man, one who can speak easily to everyone and has a particular way with the young: *This is a star profile of glamour virility.* An important facet of this dazzling profile is added by Haider's other appearances in summer sports, which emphasize, by contrast, alone-ness, a heroic solitude—

be it in the form of breath-taking courage or of tested physical endurance. Haider's televised bungee jumping from a road bridge in the Jaun valley in 1991, at a time when his position in the FPÖ was undergoing a difficult phase, has become a trademark symbol for "fighting it through on his own terms." Similarly, his participation in the New York and other international marathon events were media appearances signaling "the loneliness of the long-distance runner"—the rugged individual determined to reach his goals. Both forms of sportive media performances have been decisive in adding the important, adventurous *lone wolf image*, as an aspect of the main profile of glamour virility.

In a way, these two images of the glamorous celebrity and the lone wolf describe a range of interaction with the common people. They indicate Haider's efforts to be recognized as "part of" the broad masses, not only popular, but also slightly superior, admired by but separate from the masses–even to the point of "solitariness." This last aspect, in particular, exemplifies his strategy of creating an image of the lone individual who sets out to do the difficult and little-rewarded tasks "for" the others.

Strongly embedded in everyday popular culture, Haider's image of glamour virility is contemporary and media-oriented, and targeted at the continental European mainstream. Within this public presentation of self and manipulation of cultural symbols, almost no elements indicate at first glance any rightist political orientation. To many Austrians, this package appears to be innocently imbued with leisure activities, just as an electoral candidate surfing off the California beaches would appear to U.S. voters watching CNN. Haider's mainstream public culture appearances, of course, are those of a white man, but at first this quality looks like "normality par excellence."

But it is in this regard, especially, that Haider 's FPÖ has undergone a striking transformation. From the old-fashioned, elitist male associations that once were central to the party's inner coherence and its public image, the surface has been completely remodeled into the current display of glamour virility. When I was a student at the University of Vienna in the early 1970s, Haider and his associates were known representatives of rightist student and youth groups. Many of the leading members of those groups, including the RFS and RFJ,[3] were also members of (saber) dueling societies: Such fraternities or brotherhoods were widespread in the German-speaking countries and notorious for their pan-Germanic ideology, their ritualized social life, and their exclusively male orientation. Haider himself belonged to the groups "Albia" and "Sylvana" (Zöchling 1999: 41, 75). In the years following the youth and student rebellion of 1968, such dueling societies rapidly lost their influence and public appeal, but behind the scenes, particularly within certain wings of the FPÖ organization and beyond it, these male-bonding associations still provide important networks of alliance and mentoring, and also of rivalry. Because their elitist and traditionalist profile too openly contradicts the party's efforts to appear mainstream and contemporary, however, Haider's FPÖ has pushed most public references and allusions to these dueling associations to the margins. Similarly, these associations' sympathies with pan-Germanism contradict the FPÖ's attempts to situate themselves as "authentic Austrian" patriots.

Since the early nineties, then, the old "brotherhood" image of pan-Germanic dueling networks was pushed radically aside and has been substituted by the more up-to-date image of glamour virility. This image, however, is running into problems of its own as being oriented too exclusively towards men.[4] For a long time, women were quite rare in the FPÖ's leadership, and throughout the 1990s men made up the majority of the FPÖ's growing number of voters. The images of glamour, virility, and of the lone wolf reached out successfully to mainstream family men, among them the "apolitical" and "ambitious" as much as the "angry white" men. But even on the eve of the 1999 elections, which produced a landslide victory for Haider's FPÖ, polls indicated that among women voters, the Freedom Party and the Christian Democrats together had won merely 48 percent, a opposed to 58 percent from male voters. If women alone had to vote in these 1999 elections, therefore, Haider's party might not have made it into government. It is a striking contrast that by the same 1999 elections, however, Haider's FPÖ, for the first time, became the single strongest party (32 percent) among male Austrian voters.[5]

In terms of attracting voters, Haider's glamour, virility, and the lone wolf images may have already peaked. To make a play for support from women, a woman—Susanne Riess-Passer—was installed as the FPÖ leader in the new coalition government formed in early 2000. A devoted follower of Haider, Riess-Passer became not only his successor as official party leader but, as the country's first female vice-chancellor, the highest-ranking woman in the Austrian republics' political history.

It is central to Haider's efforts that his public presentation of self continually reinforces the glamour virility and lone wolf images, but it is important to also note that this takes place almost without words. For Haider's cultural packaging, *no explicit verbal statements had to be inserted into the fashionable and sportive public appearances.* In fact, a large part of Haider's attraction has been his unspoken appeal to the apolitical, including Austrian citizens who don't much care about, or are fed up with, domestic and European Union politics. Almost everyone finds popular entertainment, fun, leisure time, sports, relaxation, and dancing to be normal and sympathetic, and a politician who conspicuously and effectively emphasizes such activities looks more like a normal family man than do those others who constantly talk about complicated political, economic, and social matters. Emphasizing the average, the normal, and the popular thus is Haider's access route through mass culture to mainstream voters.

If we address his explicit words only we miss this point; and labeling his outreach into mass culture as "shallow" or "mindless" disregards the fact that it is cleverly—and deliberately—designed by the FPÖ to seduce voters into identifying with Haider. If at first glance, therefore, Haider engages those who are apolitical, at second glance, his public presentation of self also appeals to those who are fed up with politics. For this segment of potential voters, the lone wolf image intersects persuasively with that of the *outlaw* and the *rebel.* Here, one emotional repertoire, namely, the FPÖ's appeal on the level of the harmless activities of popular culture, is combined with a second emotional repertoire, that of anger. These voters see Haider as the one politician who can articulate their anger, the one who doesn't care about established politics, who breaks the rules, and who "has the guts" to do so. The glamour star looks good on screen, and if he is provocative, he is also entertaining: glamorous celebrity and lone wolf combine in the image of the nonconformist rebel.

This image, too, is conveyed not so much through explicit content as through the implicit codes, symbols, and signs of public appearances. One important code is the contextual usage of Austrian dialect.[6] Most Austrian politicians, including Haider, will use some sort of dialect in their personal encounters with potential voters; the striking difference with Haider is his tendency to switch between standard German and his variant of dialect not only in public speeches, but also in more formal TV or radio interviews—situations in which most other politicians would speak standard German. Speaking dialect on such public occasions carries a distinctly non-standard, local, folkloristic, and even underdog connotation in most parts of Austria. By switching to dialect, therefore, Haider is suggesting that he speaks "the common people's language" when it counts: that he says what they actually think and can come to the point in a clear and unambiguous way.[7]

The nonconformist and rebel image is also enhanced by Haider's dress code. He has developed and cultivated an extremely flexible way of dressing through style shifting, appearing for each public occasion in the appropriate outfit, but always with a subtle difference. Haider might appear in the morning for an Austrian folk music concert wearing folkloristic *Lederhosen*, but will make them distinctive by wearing an unusual, nontraditional shirt; he will show up for political negotiations at noon in the latest Giorgio Armani suit, and later the same afternoon, he might attend a press conference or a youth meeting in jeans. The cosmopolitan European (e.g., Giorgio Armani) and the Austrian rural (e.g., *Lederhosen*) dress codes are standard parts of his register, emphasizing, respectively, the celebrity and the popular images. But it is the casual dress code that Haider has cultivated to the greatest extent. Almost subversively, Haider has incorporated the basic dress code of Green Party politicians of the 1980s, at the same time that the Greens have abandoned the code of "wearing ties as rarely as possible." In short, most other male politicians would wear suits and ties precisely on those occasions when Haider would appear in blue jeans, a designer T-shirt, and a sports jacket. The contrast indicates that Haider is casual and cool, while the others are stiff and formal. Again, without words, Haider's casual dress code enhances his public image as a nonconformist rebel who breaks established rules. This image is particularly appealing to potential protest voters who are disenchanted with their established voting preferences and traditional party loyalties. Haider calls for a change in the post-World War II domestic political order, and indeed change is communicated through every aspect of his self-representation. Whether in the guise of glamour celebrity or lone wolf and nonconformist rebel, his public performances are geared to indicate clear differences from other parties' leaders. In this way, Haider's style of dressing and of public self-presentation manipulates existing expectations of co-occurrence, by emphasizing some through the glamour virility image, while violating others through the rebel image.

Another colleague recounts the following scene: On extremely short notice and through rather remote connections, Haider shows up at the sixty-fifth birthday party of a provincial employee: Maybe 120 people are already at the party, when the doorbell rings and Haider enters with his wife or daughter. He introduces his family, shakes hands with everybody, uses the usual informal *Du* while deferentially indicating that he doesn't want to disturb the proceeding, he is just quickly stopping by to show his appreciation . . . Finally, a few more genial words are exchanged with the host and the birthday person, and Haider is gone. Not one political word has been spoken but the message is clear: Haider cares about the little people, Haider is different, Haider is one of us. In this sort of mainstream celebrity register, very few other politicians are likely to appear. In his nonconformist rebel register, by contrast, Haider might appear on a Friday or Saturday night at any major club or disco anywhere in Austria. On such occasions, his entourage would not be his family, but the aides from his "young boys gang"—the *"Buberlpartie,"* as the media have labeled them. They would all drive up in snazzy sports cars, some of them busily displaying their cell phones, most others addressing the teens and twenty-somethings in the disco, distributing autographed Haider postcards and other FPÖ fan items. If leaders from other parties appear at clubs or discos, which they sometimes do, they look heavy-handed, inexperienced, and even ridiculous. Haider, by contrast, is totally credible in this regard.

Staging all these appearances requires considerable behind-the-scenes logistics, but the public effect appears effortless. Some of Haider's mass appeal through public culture therefore rests on his team's ability to quickly prepare and set up one different stage after another for him, as well as on his own skills of swiftly merging into each subsequent next role. "Acting" certainly is important in this: by early 2000, Haider has established himself as the best actor on the Austrian political stage.

It should now be clear that it takes few words, let alone overtly political statements, for Haider to communicate this mass-media image of glamour virility and non-conformism, rooted in public culture.

For many of his voters, political statements are secondary; what counts first is fun, entertainment, and a stimulating crowd experience. Before and after some of Haider's public meetings, for instance, loudspeakers blast the so-called Haider rap, which combines rap rhythm with a few, taped sentences from Haider's speeches, repeated over and over again. One of these runs: "Better to be a wolf in a sheep's clothing than a sheep in a wolf's clothing." This statement originally was Haider's cynical answer to the accusation by other parties that he was "a wolf in a sheep's clothing": that he was not sincerely committed to parliamentary democracy (the sheep), which he would only exploit for rightist purposes (the wolf). To which Haider replied by metaphorically saying: Well, better that than being pretenders who, in fact, achieve nothing (the sheep in wolves clothing), which was his way of portraying all other party leaders.

Its is ironic that a white, Central European neo-nationalist should use rap rhythms and their Afro-American cultural background as a signature tune for his meetings—but here as in many other cases, ideological considerations are less important than reaching out for the mainstream which, after all, has learnt to appreciate "white" hip hop and rap in German language as a recent element of youth and music culture in Europe. The "Haider rap" is rhythmic, hip, aggressive. Before or after an FPÖ campaign rally, hundreds and thousands of young people may dance to it, moving their bodies in synch with this short rhythmic phrase which, when decoded, suggests: "Better to be a rightist outlaw than a democratic sissy!"

Appropriating Folklore and Targeting Artists

Situated quite apart from Haider's main nonverbal fields of glamour virility and lone wolf rebel are what I would call "special cultural stages." These special stages have a flavor of being folkloristic, or at least more traditional, and they are used by Haider's FPÖ for explicit political mobilization and propaganda. I will briefly examine these special cultural stages before moving on to discuss Haider's frontal attacks against artists.

The special cultural stages I refer to here are the *Bierzelt* and the *Frühschoppen*, popular weekend gatherings that are not ordinarily associated with political events. In fact, they resemble closely the stereotypes that readers in the anglophone world may associate with people from the alpine regions: in this case, the Alpine natives are merrily getting together on weekends and holidays, many of them indeed in *Lederhosen*, to drink, sing, and laugh, almost as if they were playing a role in *The Sound of Music*.

The *Frühschoppen* (which roughly translates as the "morning glass") refers to smaller gatherings on Sunday mornings, when people go to the village pub or small town inn to have a drink on their way home from church. This may take place as an informal custom, or it may be staged as a publicly announced, formal event. In the latter case, an Austrian folk music performance, a lottery, or a political campaign may be on the program. A major *Frühschoppen* event can also take place not inside one of the local pubs or inns, but in a large tent set up outdoors for the purpose during the warmer months. The *Bierzelt* ("beer tent") is similar, but takes place on a weekend afternoon and is always designed for larger crowds. In addition, the *Bierzelt* entails large-scale consumption of beer, and is therefore less popular in the wine-growing areas of eastern Austria. With such regional variations, then, the *Bierzelt* and *Frühschoppen* events take place all over this country of more than seven million inhabitants, in anything from small villages to minor towns, with the one clear exception of Vienna and its almost two million inhabitants.

In this context, Haider's intensive and continual usage of *Bierzelt* and *Frühschoppen* events as a political forum has always conveyed an "anti-Vienna" sentiment, similar to anti-Washington or anti-New York discourses in U.S. domestic politics. Actually, politicians from all political parties have staged *Bierzelt* and *Frühschoppen* appearances during campaign times, but, by and large, others have done so less frequently and for local rather than national political purposes. Jörg Haider, by contrast, has used his *Bierzelt* and *Frühschoppen* performances as key occasions to rally his supporters and deliver programmatic statements.

Haider's staging of such events is clearly distinguished from his mainstream public culture activities. First, the participants are always local core groups of active FPÖ supporters, who often pay entry fees. Second, after brass band music, comic skits, and similar preludes have sufficiently warmed up the crowd, the main program is an explicit, often polemical, political speech by the local candidate and then by Haider himself. Third, by form and content, these events more often than not are designed as explicit provocations, intended to attract the media from the outset.

Haider's performances on such special cultural stages not only mobilize his local supporters, but also usually contain some key message that the media can be counted on to circulate countrywide. Consider these scenes, broadcast throughout the country: Haider stands in front of a tightly packed, agitated crowd of fans and supporters, who eagerly await their idol's next phrase. Haider plays to them, and is capable under such circumstances of moving into a mode of escalating polemics, cruel jokes, and ridicule. His *Bierzelt* speeches are often a blend of simple arguments, angry exclamations, and—most important—jokes of a particularly humiliating kind directed against political opponents—jokes that are not atypical of a wider genre of Austrian humor, and to which the aggressive crowd responds with roaring laughter and frenetic applause. Very often these jokes implicitly oppose body images of political opponents to Haider's self-presentation of body discipline and being sportive.

The crowd in the tent loves it. This, after all, is what they have paid for, this is what they want to hear: remarks with an anti-Polish edge to them, such as Haider's remark about then Polish president Lech Walesa measuring "larger in latitude than in height" (at a time when Polish immigration to Austria was discussed between the two countries); comments with a parallel anti-Viennese tune on the mayor of Vienna, "whose mental maturity lags behind the rapid increase of his body weight" (made in early 2000, when Haider attacked those Austrian politicians who did not criticize the international boycott against the country; Czernin 2000:126); other jokes that also implicate the entire EU such as a reference to Jacques Chirac, resembling a "vest pocket Napoleon" (on the same occasion; Czernin 2000:71), and so forth.

Aggressive German political speeches, roaring laughter in tightly packed beer tents: at this point, at the latest, any association with the more innocent side of *The Sound of Music* is likely to be replaced with images of an entirely different kind. The aesthetic, visual, and rhetorical parallels to Nazi meetings of a similar nature from the late 1920s and 1930s seem to be evident, at least for international observers and sensitive Austrians. Haider himself is educated and intelligent enough to recognize the likelihood that such historical parallels will be made. The very fact that he implicitly plays with such associations is another of his *Bierzelt* provocations.

It is somewhat naïve, however, to point to such superficial parallels as if they revealed the "true character" of Haider's FPÖ. For the average adult in Upper Austria or Carinthia, attending a *Bierzelt* or *Frühschoppen* event is as normal as going to a soccer match or making a weekend family excursion. For everyday people, these folkloristic occasions bear no evident parallel to the Nazi period whatsoever. By and large, the *Bierzelt* and the *Frühschoppen* have continued to be regular forums of Eastern Alpine folk culture, usually serving quite "normal" and apolitical purposes. They existed long before the rise of Nazism; the Nazi's exploited them for their own political purposes; other parties have used them since World War II; and currently it is Haider who uses them. The core of the issue has far less to do with Haider than with Austrian culture and society as a whole. The Nazi appropriation of Alpine folklore, its transformation into eternal icons of "pureness" and "authenticity" in the "Germanic race," is only one story. A second story is that after 1945, many such local cultural leftovers from the Nazi period were never contested, altered, or imbued with new meaning. The Carinthian or Styrian families who went to a Nazi *Frühschoppen* meeting in 1939 were not so different from those going to a brass-band concert *Frühschoppen* in 1947, and the memories and feelings they associated with a *Frühschoppen* were little changed. Certainly there were decisive ruptures on the level of political rule, national symbols, dominant ideology, legal rights, and so forth following 1945. But on the level of local politics, regional culture, and family traditions, changes more often than not were only gradual and minor. Elements of the past[8] lingered on in local folk culture, becoming normalized and self-evident references, part and parcel of local culture in the Austria of the present. Today, they feed into a new wave of nationalism by representing a segment of rural and provincial folk culture that has a diffuse "home country" connotation. Haider thus can easily tap into a broad set of minor and major elements in Austrian folk culture that, despite ongoing changes, still display an element of continuity—a continuity which, and this is the salient point, was not created by Haider. In this regard, Haider simply manipulates, exploits, and enhances what is already there, outside of and underneath official party politics.

In its overall public dimension, however, Alpine folklore is not a sufficient resource, even in the Austria of today, for mobilizing a national voters' majority. The mainstream is found elsewhere, in public mass culture. Alpine folklore helps Haider to rally core groups of militant fans and to attract the radical and extremist right margins through nostalgia. But the "special cultural stage" has no mass attraction per se, no great ability to gain mass support from voters. What *Bierzelt* and *Frühschoppen* do have is a strategic importance for initiating and launching massive attacks against designated political targets.

One target group for such attacks, which no analysis of the cultural element of Haider's policies can ignore, is progressive, experimental, or other avant-garde artists. Although such FPÖ campaigns against artists represent only a sideline of the party's main political strategies, they, nevertheless, are telling and characteristic. There are many examples of such cultural campaigns by Haider's FPÖ against selected painters, writers, and professionals involved in the theater. The FPÖ's cultural campaigns tend to be directed against individually named artists and their work, isolating and publicly attacking provocative aspects of their work in order to mobilize public opinion against the artists and, at the same time, to denounce any public funding for them. The favorite targets of these campaigns are works which allegedly contain blasphemy, sexual perversion, or anti-patriotism. I will mention just a few, in order to clarify the main thrust.

Hermann Nitsch is a widely known representative of the "Vienna actionist" group, which inaugurated the (modest) Austrian variant of the 1968 rebellion by a spectacular public act of defecation at the University of Vienna. Since then, Nitsch has focused on staging performance pieces using pig's blood—his provocative way of addressing the topics of suffering, taboo, and religion. On many of these public, and sometimes publicly funded, occasions, Haider's FPÖ has expressed strong condemnation of any "tax-payers' support" for such art (Zöchling 1999:159). At one point, during a Lower Austrian electoral campaign in the late nineties, the attacks became so heated that Nitsch was forced to retreat into the realm of private performances.

The considerably less controversial Ingeborg Bachmann was by most standards Austria's foremost female poet and writer after 1945; she was also an anti-Nazi democrat. A highly competitive major literary award in all the German-speaking areas is named after her. The competition is carried out annually in Bachmann's native Klagenfurt, the capital of Carinthia, where Haider today is governor. Although sometimes criticized for its commercial and fair-like character, the Bachmann Award for years has attracted many of the most talented artists writing in German. Haider's FPÖ launched a prolonged and aggressive campaign against the award after 1991, when Swiss author Urs Allemann won a prize for a work with the (translated) title *Babyfucker*. The text, the author said, deals with losing orientation and certainties, and with trying out extremes of language. Haider, however, labeled the text "inexcusable" and a "sexual perversion" (Zöchling 1999:159), and as governor used it and other instances as a pretext to withdraw Carinthia's subsidies for the Bachmann award.

In 1995, Haider launched an intensive poster campaign. On huge billboards, passersby were asked: "Do you love Rudolf Scholten, Michael Haeupl, Ursula Pasterk, Elfriede Jelinek, Claus Peymann . . . or do you love culture?" The question suggested that "culture" was something completely different from whatever these five individuals represented. Three of them (Scholten, Haeupl, and Pasterk) were Socialist politicians, involved in one way or another with state or city (Vienna) subsidies for cultural events. Elfriede Jelinek is a renowned author of novels and plays, besides being a leftist feminist, and Claus Peymann, a famous German director with radical political leanings, at that time was heading the Vienna Burgtheater, Austria's premier stage and one of the major theaters of the German language. The FPÖ poster clearly implied that Socialist politicians granted public subsidies to radical artists, whereas "real" culture was something else again (Zöchling 1999:157).

In targeting artists of experimental, critical, or leftist orientations, Haider's cultural campaigns attacked not only the individual aesthetic values of these artists, but also their political opinions. More important, however, is the fact that these campaigns sought to redefine cultural politics in a country with a democratic constitution, mobilizing public opinion in a way that would establish a new legitimacy for the endeavor per se. Imposing restrictive cultural standards has now become a legitimate issue in Austrian cultural politics.

These artists targeted by Haider are, in addition, intellectuals. As anywhere else, serious contemporary art in Austria rarely appeals to the broad masses: intellectuals not only produce such works, they also make up the bulk of its audience. The FPÖ's anti-artist campaigns thus have an underlying anti-liberal and anti–intellectual component. These attacks also combined with targeting "foreigner" artists, such as the Swiss Bachmann prizewinner or the German Burgtheater director (Czernin 2000:104). It was, in fact, within these cultural campaigns that Haider first tried out his own party's reaction to a shift from pan-

Germanism to Austrian nationalism: Pan-Germanism would rarely treat a German national and a German-speaking Swiss as "foreigners," but Austrian nationalism—if need be—might do just that.

These campaigns have worked extremely well for Haider. His party has accepted the dissociation from pan-Germanism and has embraced Austrian nationalism. The fluid differentiation between popular culture and serious art has been artificially enhanced and emphasized. Popular skepticism about and hostility toward intellectuals has been encouraged, strengthened, and brought into the open. In terms of quite specific results, the Bachmann Award now receives strongly decreased subsidies, Claus Peymann has left the country, and Elfriede Jelinek has announced that her plays no longer will be performed in Austria.

Thomas Bernhard, on the other hand, is dead. Perhaps equal in literary standing only to Ingeborg Bachmann, Bernhard was Austria's leading male dramatist and novelist after 1945. In his will, Bernhard ruled out any performance of his plays inside Austria after his death—the writer's unambiguous response to years of vicious criticism of his work by Social Democrats, Christian Democrats, and the FPÖ alike. But Bernhard was Peymann's favorite German-language dramatist, and his Vienna premiere of Bernhard's play *Heldenplatz* created a countrywide scandal. The title itself is controversial, alluding as it does to the square in central Vienna where, in March 1938, tens of thousands of Viennese enthusiastically welcomed Adolf Hitler. Following Peymann's staging of *Heldenplatz*, references to Bernhard were especially explicit in FPÖ campaigns (Czernin 2000:99).

A key FPÖ argument against artists like Jelinek and Bernhard was, and still is, that they are "defamers of Austria" (*Beschmutzer, Beschimpfer von Österreich;* Czernin 2000:99, 113). According to this argument, anyone who constantly criticizes dominant politics in Austria does not love his or her country—an attitude that resonates chillingly with the ultraconservative Vietnam-era slogan, "America—Love it or leave it!" In both the U.S. of that time and in Austria today, one might reasonably assume that those who engage so passionately with their countries' affairs, in fact, care a great deal, but the FPÖ has never ceased to argue that critical or dissident artists are bad patriots. Thus, Haider's shift to "Austrian patriotism" has found a first and very important outlet of articulation and mass mobilization in the field of culture. It is important to recognize that these attacks against specific cultural contents are always implied, but never explicitly spelled out.

Like Haider's public appearances, they implicitly reference a "normality" that has been transgressed, an unspoken normality of patriotism, sexual modesty, and of some reverence for (Catholic) religious values. Attacking artistic "deviance" from a stance of implicit "normality" sought to gain mass support for such normality, by gradually creating a cultural situation in which a shift takes place, from what formerly was unmarked to what now should become marked: cultural normality.

The FPÖ's attacks against specific artists, however, never directly assailed those artists' rights to produce such work. Instead, they have been directed against providing any public funding for them. Why, Haider's cultural campaigns ask, should artists like these (defamers of Austria, sexual deviants, blasphemers) receive public subsidies for their work? (Czernin 2000:104, 115, passim) For a British or U.S. readership, raising the issue of public funding for the arts may sound fair enough, especially considering these countries' experiences in downsizing public art budgets throughout the 1980s and 1990s. In a U.S. congressional debate about Newt Gingrich' s move to downsize NEA and NEH budgets, it was even argued that Austria's State Opera alone received as much annual funding as the NEA then did: According to popular perception, then, huge public subsidies for important cultural activities were regularly spent in Austria, as in many other parts of continental Europe, and as opposed to Britain and the U.S. Debatable as this issue may be, the point is that Haider, from the outset, aggressively combined the issue of cultural budget cuts with a mobilization against individual artists who, according to his standards, deserved no public support or appreciation.

These essentially anti-intellectual campaigns are meant to appeal to citizens who are interested primarily or exclusively in mass entertainment and popular art, as well as to those who are disinterested in art of any kind. The anti-artist campaigns thus come full circle, merging with Haider's appeal to public mass culture. Haider's cultural campaigns, too, address the "common people," those attracted by his star cult of glamour virility, with the implicit overriding question, "You may not care about art, but consider this: Do you want your tax money being spent on defamation of Austria, sexual perversion, and blasphemy?" These cultural campaigns create an artificial rupture between popular culture and "serious" art, aligning the latter with radicals and intellectuals and re-orienting popular culture along neo-conservative and neo-nationalist lines. In this way, the FPÖ has carefully selected easy targets to inflate mass opinion in favor of the party's own agenda—through mobilizing the disinterested against that which does not interest them, recycling their opinion through party campaign propaganda. By isolating single issues from an individual artist's body of work, by presenting these issues in shocking and provocative ways to the broad public, and by denouncing any public funding for such art, the FPÖ has succeeded in intimidating many experimental and critical artists, while enhancing a newly defined "cultural normality." The anti-liberal and anti-intellectual components of the campaigns thus combine aggressively with neo-conservatism and nationalism to have a profound impact on Austrian culture and society as a whole.

Cultural Hegemony and the Rise of Neo-Nationalism

There can be no doubt that Haider's cultural politics are directed at achieving cultural and political hegemony in Austria. This conclusion is not only the result of an outside analysis of his policies and practices; it also derives from the "inside"—from comments made by Haider himself, as one biographer points out (Zöchling 1999:156). Like many rightist politicians in Europe after 1968, Haider is very well acquainted with the more sophisticated theoretical inventory of the left, including some of Antonio Gramsci's work. In and around Europe, writes Haider, ideological struggles of contesting orientations are filtering into people's minds: "He who has a dominant influence on people will gain power" (Haider 1993:73). The cultural politics outlined in this paper represent some of the primary tools he utilizes to gain such dominant influence. Ever since the late 1980s, it has been argued, the FPÖ successfully has set the agenda for those cultural and political topics that local people actually discuss among themselves, even if they are not FPÖ supporters. For over a decade, long before the FPÖ ascended to Austria's 2000 coalition government, the party's agenda has dominated discussions at the *Stammtisch*,[9] that is, at the "regulars'" table in the neighborhood pub.

From an international and comparative perspective, it is evident that nationalism comes to the fore precisely when global factors increasingly undermine local stability (Hannerz 1992:217–267): it is no coincidence that Haider's rise to power set in during the late 1980s, when communism collapsed in neighboring eastern Europe. To an extent, this phenomenon is the local Austrian variant of reactions against changes in the international and domestic post-World War II order that are taking place in many parts of Europe and the EU. On the local level, many of these reactions have taken on nationalist manifestations, with specific anti-immigration and anti-EU policy components. Quite often, these new forms of nationalism inside the EU seek not to enhance strong nation-states in order to protect domestic markets, as was the case in earlier forms of nationalism, but rather to dismantle and downsize welfare states in order to promote global market flows. In light of these differences, I prefer to speak of "neo-nationalism" rather than nationalism. The success of Haider's FPÖ is an important part of an alarming, EU-wide neo-nationalist trend. Like other neo-nationalist leaders, but more successfully than most, Haider has been waging a struggle for cultural hegemony. As these neo-nationalist forces strive to diminish the significance of the state, cultural symbols and representations become an especially important field: in order to successfully attack the existing—and in their view superfluous—state involvement in funding cultural activities, and to embed themselves thoroughly within civil society, they need to profoundly influence all spheres of culture.

Here and elsewhere in this volume, it has been pointed out how a major shift from a pan-Germanism to "Austrian patriotism" was part of Haider's strategy throughout the 1990s. By the end of the 1980s, pan-Germanism no longer was appealing at all to mainstream voters in Austria. A new kind of Austrian self-awareness had gained broad consensus, which politically was largely attributed to the Social Democrats and at that time, to a lesser extent to the Christian Democrats. But, in fact, this new kind of Austrian patriotism was quite a recent phenomenon, coming under new challenges when these parties initiated Austria's entry procedure into the EU. Haider's embrace of Austrian nationalism was not only necessary to become mainstream, it also filled an ideological vacuum left by the other parties. The fact that this new Austrian patriotism was a recent and unguarded phenomenon is a key to Haider's mass success. Precisely because domestic patriotism was more recent, and seemingly more vulnerable than in other small European countries, voters became especially attracted by Haider.

By definition, any neo-nationalist force struggling for domestic cultural and political hegemony has to raise the public profile of national culture, while redefining what it is (Eriksen 1993:109–120). In this sense, the rise of Haider's FPÖ represents a perfect case—a sort of laboratory rat for the rise of neo-nationalism in the EU: The forces of neo-nationalism require meaningful cultural strategies for their political survival and success. In the case of Haider and Austria, these cultural strategies combine an eclectic and professionally mixed blend of global and Western mass culture with elements from the royal court and rural folk cultures of the Austrian past.

We have seen how Haider's bid for cultural hegemony has focused primarily on the main fields of popular and public mass culture. Creating for himself a presence in daring sports, in hip weekend nightlife, and in everyday leisure activities will sound perfectly normal to an English-speaking readership, well used to such devices from their own national and local electoral campaigns. For continental Europeans, however, this is by no means a standard repertoire of political campaigning. Until recently, Austrian political parties relied on a single, and quite simple, conventional repertoire that featured meetings sponsored by established party organizations, formal media interviews, and the broad dissemination of campaign posters. Paradoxically, Haider, the most nationalist of domestic politicians, has imported transnational (Appadurai 1997:48–55) and "foreign" elements into the public and political culture of Austria, and with great success. His introduction of the celebrity cult of glamour virility by means of a densely varying show-business code, has transformed local public culture and politics: its form is now much closer to that of the Anglophone world than before. *Haider, the neo-nationalist, wears transnational and global attire.*

This international show biz effect is slickly packaged with good behind-the-scenes logistics and personal charisma and performing skills. In Austria, this fell on very fertile ground. For centuries of court monarchy, Austrians have been obsessed with performance: music, theater, operetta, and opera. When Haider's "international show biz effect" met the latent domestic enthusiasm for stage entertainment of all kinds, its cultural success was explosive. It is difficult to overestimate the significance of "the stage" in contemporary Austrian cultural life. We have already mentioned the enormous federal subsidy for the Vienna State Opera as compared with that for the NEA; it is also true, and to some astonishing, that little Vienna has as many theaters as gargantuan New York. Hannah Arendt is among those who labeled twentieth-century Austria an "operetta" or a "theatre country," conspicuously differing in that respect from Germany or Switzerland, not to mention Scandinavia or Britain. The *Burgtheater* and the *Staatsoper*, music and operetta, remain widely popular, not only as cherished left-overs from elite-sponsored culture under the Habsburg court, but as representations of the subsequently transformed state culture of the two Austrian republics of the twentieth century. For the audience, appearance and performance count for everything, and the impact on mass perception is profound. Paraphrasing Clifford Geertz's characterization of a Southeast Asian case (Geertz 1980:98–120), one might call Austria the Central European variant of a "theatre society," one in which Haider is the perfect, (almost) postmodern actor on the stage: versatile, eclectic, dramatic, seductive; able to utilize whatever global and local cultural resources are at hand. Much of Haider's polemical and rhetorical aggressiveness also appeals to this latent domestic appreciation for the stage per se: no matter what the contents, the audience appreciates the performance if it is entertaining enough.

If we examine transnational show business styling and local enthusiasm for theatrical performance in the Austrian context, it is clear that both may succeed with little appeal to content. In fact, explicit political arguments are inserted into Haider's cultural politics at a rather late point, often only enhancing the unspoken message that is already out there. The FPÖ's cultural propaganda addresses the average, domestic, German-speaking Austrian citizen, enhancing and re-defining a popular culture normality that is as "banal" as Hannah Arendt's "banality" was. It does not indulge in many words, not to speak of arguments and contents. It does entail an enduring appeal to everyday life, with folklore as a central aspect of it. The *Bierzelt* venue itself is only an additional, publicly visible resource. The most basic element of Austrian folklore, however, is invisible and mental. It is the one that Jörg Haider manipulates carefully and ingeniously, with only a few sentences, as if in by-passing, long after the momentum of identifying with a popular, transnational celebrity on stage has set in.

To most members of these sympathetic audiences, Haider's explicit anti-immigrant and xenophobic slogans therefore become audible only after they have already been hooked by his implicit messages. But when he does become explicit, his sentences ring a resounding bell—the bell of local culture. During an anti-immigration campaign of the 1990s, for instance, one of Haider's stock phrases ran: "We did not fight the Turkish wars" [in the sixteenth and seventeenth centuries] in order to let Turkish immigrants now come into Austria, but in order to keep them out (Czernin 2000:84). With just a few well-chosen references like these, Haider thus can tap into deeply rooted feelings of xenophobia that are already "out there." Everywhere in the monuments, school textbooks, stories, village chronicles, curses, and place names of eastern and southern Austria, notions of an "Oriental danger" and of a "Turkish menace" abound. Haider does not have to use a lot of persuasive propaganda to mobilize and manipulate feelings against foreigners "from the east and southeast"; such attitudes are already there, embedded outside of and underneath official party politics, encoded in local and folk culture as a largely uncontested, historically created social product (Gingrich 1996:106–110, 1999:31–33). Such basic elements of local folklore need only a phrase, a reference, a few sentences to be invoked.

Xenophobic arguments are employed by neo-nationalists all over Europe, of course, but, currently, in Austria they seem to resonate more strongly than elsewhere in the EU. The fact that they are encoded in local folk culture, as demonstrated by Haider's references to the Turkish wars, is one aspect of this. But a similar argument can be made about the pervasiveness of positive identification with elements from the Nazi past among some segments of the local population. This is the part of the ascent to government by Haider's FPÖ that has been most shocking to international opinion. Fully 27 percent of Austrian voters, however, find it acceptable. Other xenophobic aspects of the FPÖ's propaganda inventory are being applied, more or less successfully, by other neo-nationalists in other European parliaments—but sympathetic, and now notorious, statements about the Nazi era are not. To my mind, it is not shocking that Haider has publicly said this or that about the Nazi past, but that 27 percent of the local Austrian population have found this to be either good, or vaguely embarrassing, or perhaps a bit exaggerated, or unclear, unimportant, and irrelevant. My point is that up to the present day in Austria, these xenophobic attitudes, deeply rooted in cherished and unexamined cultural values, have never been subjected to serious cultural upheaval and radical transformation.

One may conclude that Austria deserves Haider. What for a long time has been a well-hidden undercurrent has finally—and belatedly—come to the surface of this society. The good news is that it gives options for significant change in Austria another chance.

Notes

1. For helpful discussions and suggestions concerning this article, I would like to thank Ulf Hannerz, Ulrike Hartmann, Gudrun Kroner, Joan O' Donnell, Alice Pechriggl, Johanna Riegler, Bambi Schieffelin, Gertraud Seiser, Sabine Strasser, and the editors.
2. In this paper, I use the term culture in the way suggested by Scandinavian authors such as Fredrik Barth (1994:352–359), Marit Melhuus (1999: 65–80) or Kirsten Hastrup and Karen F. Olwig (1997: 3–12)
3. RFS stands for "Freedom Students Ring", while RFJ means "Freedom Youth Ring"
4. I will not deal here with press reports or with a recent wave of local gossip about Haider's alleged sexual orientation. The ways in which this issue has been discussed, in the international press as much as locally, would be worth an analysis of its own.
5. Plasser, Ulram, and Sommer 2000: passim. While the Freedom Paraty continuously grew under Haider's leadership (1986–2000), whereby female voters' support also increased in absolute numbers, the relative proportion of female voters support for Haider during the same period steadily decreased nevertheless. The proportion of women among FPÖ voters in national elections went dowm from 52 percent (in 1982, before Haider took over) to 42 percent (1995), to an all-time low 38 percent in 1999. (Hofinger and Ogris 1996; Plasser, Ulram, and Sommer 2000). In short, in 2000 only one out of three among Haider's national voters was a woman.
6. The standard version of Austrian German, as taught in school and spoken in the media, differs only slightly from standard German. In daily interactions, however, the majority of the population uses one of the local dialects prevailing in Austria, which may differ to a considerable extent from standard German.
7. Other aspects of Haider's rhetorical strategies are analyzed in this volume by Ruth Wodak.
8. One might argue that other such cultural elements of the past include the meaning and focus of a certain type of monument. Almost every village square in Austria prominently displays a stone pillar that commemorates "our soldiers" (or "heroes") who "fell for the home country" in the 1914—18 *as well as in the* 1939—45 wars. These are signposts of local identification. I do not criticize the wish of any village family to commemorate its war dead. But these monuments focus on soldiers exclusively, and they refer to Nazi Germany as the "home country." (They make no reference, of course, to any civilian victims, let alone deserters, persecuted minority members, and victims from the resistance.) Austria as a whole has never gone through any cultural upheaval, from above and below, that might have changed the values and meanings of these signposts.
9. The *Stammtisch* is an important site of local cultures in Austria and the eastern Alps in general, where people get together to carry on such topical conversations. The *Stammtisch* is the "regulars'" table in a neighborhood pub, inn, coffee shop, or restaurant, reserved for a steady network of friends, colleagues, or associates who gather there once a week or once a month.

References

Appadurai, Arjun. (1997). *Modernity at Large. Cultural Dimensions of Globalization.* Minneapolis and London: University of Minnesota Press.

Barth, Fredrik. (1994). "A Personal View of Present Tasks and Priorities in Cultural and Social Anthropology," in Robert Borofsky (ed.), *Assessing Cultural Anthropology.* New York and Toronto: McGraw-Hill.

Czernin, Hubertus (ed.). (2000). *Wofür ich mich meinetwegen entschuldige. Haider, beim Wort genommen.* Vienna: Czernin.

Eriksen, Thomas Hylland. (1993). *Ethnicity and Nationalism. Anthropological Perspectives.* London and Boulder, CO: Pluto.

Geertz, Clifford. (1980). *Negara. The Theatre State in Nineteenth-Century Bali.* Princeton, NJ: Princeton University Press.

Gingrich, Andre. (1996). "Frontier Myths of Orientalism: The Muslim World in Public and Popular Culture of Central Europe," in Bojan Baskar and Borut Brumen (eds.), *MESS—Mediterranean Ethnological Summer School*, vol. II, 99–127. Ljubljana: Institut za multikulturne raziskave.

_____. (1999). "Österreichische Identitäten und Orientbilder. Eine ethnologische Kritik," in Walter Dostal, Helmuth A. Niederle, and Karl R. Wernhart (eds.), *Wir und die Anderen. Islam, Literatur und Migration.* Vienna: WUV.

Haider, Jörg. (1993). *Die Freiheit, die ich meine.* Frankfurt am Main.

Hannerz, Ulf. (1992). *Cultural Complexity. Studies in the Social Organization of Meaning.* New York: Columbia University Press.

Hastrup, Kirsten, and Karen Fog Olwig. (1997). "Introduction," in Karen Fog Olwig and Kirsten Hastrup (eds.), *Siting Culture. The Shifting Anthropological Object.* London and New York: Routledge.

Hofinger, Christoph, and Günther Ogris. (1995). "Achtung, Gender Gap! Geschlecht und Wahlverhalten 1979–1995 in Österreich," in F. Plasser, P. Ulram, and G. Ogris (eds.), *Wahlkampf und Wählerentscheidung. Analysen zur Nationalratswahl 1995.* Vienna: ZAP.

Plasser, Fritz, Peter Ulram, and Franz Sommer. (2000). "Analyse der Nationalratswahl 1999. Muster, Trends und Entscheidungsmotive," in F. Plasser, P. Ulram, and F. Sommer (eds.), *Das österreichische Wahlverhalten.* Vienns: ZAP.

Melhuus, Marit. (1999). "Insisting on Culture?" *Social Anthropology*, vol. 7, part 1, 1:65–80.

Tributsch, Gudmund (ed.). (1994). *Schlagwort Haider. Ein politisches Lexikon seiner Aussprüche von 1986 bis heute.* Vienna: Falter.

Zöchling, Christa. (1999). *Haider. Licht und Schatten einer Karriere.* Vienna: Molden.

Part 2

6

Austrian Exceptionalism:
Haider, the European Union,
the Austrian Past and Present

Andrei S. Markovits

Introduction

This chapter focuses on the developments pertaining to the controversy surrounding the coming to power of a "black/blue" coalition
government in Austria in early 2000. It analyzes the antecedents to
this event and places it in the context of Austria's postwar political
arrangements.

The chapter has three parts. The first part offers an argument as to
why I think the European Union's action of boycotting the Austrian
government was not only morally appropriate but also immensely effective, despite virtual unanimity regarding its alleged failure. The
second part delineates in some detail the structural and cultural antecedents to the current situation. In particular, it analyzes the precursors
in Austrian politics that led to the rise of Jörg Haider and his particular
brand of politics. I will briefly describe a situation that will make clear
why Europeans reacted to much more than Jörg Haider and the current
FPÖ: Indeed, they reacted to a particularly inadequate and unwilling
confrontation on the part of key Austrian institutions regarding Austria's
involvement with its Nazi past. It is in this context that I will look at
some of the features of this missed opportunity, in particular the three

95

main actors of Austria's postwar politics: the Social Democratic Party (SPÖ); the People's Party (ÖVP); and Haider's party itself, the Freedom Party (FPÖ). The third, and final, part of the chapter will argue how, paradoxically, it has been the "de-Austrianization" of Austrian politics, to use Anton Pelinka's apt formulation, or the secularization of its particularly parochial culture of the so-called "Lager" or political camps which encompassed every possible aspect of public, even private life, that has led to the "Westernization" or normalization of Austrian politics, at least in form if not necessarily in content. It is then in the wake of this Westernization, this secularization, that the chapter concludes on a rather optimistic note.

The European Union's Response

First of all, the European Union as such—as the entity "European Union (EU)"—did not take a stand against Austria. Rather, it was a coordinated action in which fourteen members of the EU, acting completely as their own individual sovereign, decided to boycott Austria on regular bilateral relations—or, more precisely—to contain bilateral relations with Austria strictly to an administrative level. Thus, no Austrian representative on the cabinet level was welcomed on any bilateral mission in the capitals of these fourteen European countries. No Austrian ambassador was allowed to meet cabinet members of the fourteen governments. Moreover, the European Parliament passed resolutions condemning the formation of a coalition government in Austria which included the FPÖ. Lastly, the European Commission declared unambiguously that Austria would be closely watched—and if the country was found to be in violation of the EU's strict human rights principles, the Commission reserved the right to start procedures to cancel Austria's participation in the European Council. Pursuant to the Amsterdam Treaty this would be the first step towards Austria's expulsion from the EU. The driving forces behind these uniquely drastic steps were the German government, in particular the Social Democratic Chancellor Gerhard Schröder and the Green Foreign Minister Joschka Fischer; the French government, led by the conservative (RPR) President Jacques Chirac and the socialist (PS) Prime Minister Lionel Jospin; the Spanish government, led by the conservative Prime Minister Jose Maria Asnar; and the Belgians. It is important to point out that—contrary to the repeated claims by the Austrian government that

the EU members' action was a spiteful social democratic cabale or-
chestrated by the Austrian Social Democrats who proved to be sore
losers—the European reaction reached across party lines and spanned
the gamut of the acceptable middle that has governed Europe so successfully throughout the postwar period: center-left social democrats
and center-right conservatives.

Second, it is important to point out that the Europeans' reactions in
no way interfered with the Austrians' political articulations, nor did it
intervene in any way with Austria's political sovereignty. It was not a
preemptive strike or a fait accompli; instead it was merely an unambiguously clear reaction. The Europeans never told the Austrians for
whom to vote; what government to have; how to run their internal
affairs. What they did say—and they did so loud and clear—was that
Austrians were free to choose whomever they wanted; but that Europe
was equally free not to like the Austrians' choice. [Or to use Daniel
Cohn-Bendit's inimitable language: "You are free to have bad breath,
but we are free not to like you for it."] Politics is clearly a contact
sport and any action activates a re-action. That is the name of the
game, and the Europeans reacted to something that they clearly found
uniquely objectionable. And what they found so objectionable was the
unique character and history of the FPÖ, coupled with Austria's mea-
ger attempts to come to terms with its Nazi past. These two factors
were far more important than Jörg Haider's personality and particular
form of leadership.

Third, Europe's reaction must also be seen in the context of its
becoming a community of values, a community that—as the Germans
like to point out—adheres with increasing intensity to something called
a "Wertekanon," a canon of values. It has also entered the political
vernacular by the French terminology of "acquis communautaire,"
which, especially in its German version of "europäische Errungen-
schaften," sounds haughty and arrogant but also helps establish an
important baseline of values that any newly forming political entity
needs for its internal as well as external legitimation. By the end of the
1990s, the EU no longer was merely a common market, a large bureaucracy regulating British beef, Swedish cigarettes, used cars, and
French cheese, although it remains that, too. Rather, it has come to
stand for basic values of human decency which, to be sure, are vaguely
defined and rather broad, but which, nevertheless, have some important common denominators and a clear baseline that is accepted by all:

And one essential ingredient of this baseline has been that everything and anything associated with National Socialism and open racism is simply beyond the boundaries of the acceptable. This is a clear remnant of the Yalta world. And it is, in fact, different from the views and values concerning other forms of dictatorships and evil regimes, including Stalinism and all other forms of fascism. Does this make the latter legitimate? No, it certainly does not. Does it make it right that the Europeans took over six months to react in concert to Serbia's appalling behavior in the Kosovo disaster and well over one year to the massacres in Bosnia—and that they could only act in concert under the leadership of the much-despised United States (which, of course, further added to the Europeans' dislike of Americans)? Or that some, like the French, cannot wait for the moment to conduct business as usual with a mass murderer like Saddam Hussein? No, once again, it certainly does not. Are the Europeans flawed? Yes, they most certainly are. Do they have a singularly applicable universal code of moral right? No, they do not. Do they treat all dictatorships equally? No, they do not. To be sure, it is easier to attack a small and weak thug like Serbia's Slobodan Milosevic than a large and powerful one like Russia's Vladimir Putin whom all Europeans—as well as Americans—accommodated in his butchery of the Chechen people with not even the threat of any ambassadorial pull-outs as signs of discomfort and protest, let alone the threats of any kinds of boycotts. But these severe and morally wanting shortcomings do not mean that the Europeans then have to accept anything and everything, particularly developments in a country that had over the years clearly become part of the inside, part of the family, a status which Austria by all measures had clearly attained. But it is noteworthy that unlike Austria, the FPÖ had been ostracized from the European family as early as 1993 when it was excluded from the Liberal International by dint of its racist and anti-Semitic stands and thus became an ostracized party in the European Parliament that did not belong to any overarching and international faction as did all other Austrian parties: the Social Democrats to the large Europe-wide social democratic faction; the Greens to the smaller but still important European Green faction; and the Austrian People's Party, the ÖVP, to the parliamentary association of European conservative parties.

In the wake of the Europeans' unique reaction to the FPÖ's entering the Austrian government, the question was frequently posed as to why the Europeans did not act remotely as emphatically and forcefully when, in 1994, Gianfranco Fini's Allianza Nationale entered the Italian center-right government under the leadership of Silvio Berlusconi's Forza Italia. The answer is twofold: First, the European Union was something entirely different in 1994 than it had become by 2000. There is simply no doubt that in the meantime, spurred by the Amsterdam Treaty, the EU is actively engaged in a gradual state-building process: It has a clear capital; it has clear, though shifting, boundaries; it has a common currency; it has a central bank; in the wake of the Kosovo crisis, it now has a foreign and security (defense) minister rolled into one—Mr. Gasp, as the Germans call him—in Javier Solana, the former secretary general of NATO; it has a flag and it even has an anthem (Ludwig von Beethoven's "Ode to Joy"), albeit only in its melodic form, with no lyrics at all. All it lacks is an airline, which it sort of has in the form of mighty Airbus Industries. Europe is in the process–however slow and cumbersome–of establishing a federation that, in certain key cases among which issues of political ethics and human values such as rejection of racism definitely take pride of place, supersedes the sovereignty of the individual states. These centripetal developments also exact clearer rules and a more specific concept of acceptable behavior and legitimate political discourse. In a sense, then, the federation has become like a club, which means that it has clear insiders and equally clear outsiders. For the insiders, however, certain rules apply that the club intends to enforce. This is also part of the state-building process. Thus, just as the federal government in the United States deemed it appropriate to impose its values on race relations on deeply reluctant southern states that tried to resist any reforms to their racist ways under the banner of state rights and state autonomy, so, too, does the EU as a budding federation reserve itself the right to impose certain sanctions on one of its members whom it has deemed to have violated one of the club's major rules that construe the club's very identity and essence. The status of the EU was not this club-like, its construct as a federation not as far advanced in 1994 as in 2000. Second, and far more important, the Allianza Nationale simply never evoked the same threatening images and fears in Europeans as did the FPÖ which, in turn, has everything to do with the fact that Italian Fascism, though a heinously murderous and dictatorial political regime, was much closer to other fascisms in Europe than to National Socialism in Germany (and Austria), which was truly sui generis. Italian Fascism was not nearly as anti-Semitic as German National Socialism. Indeed, Jews from Vichy France fled to Fascist Italy because they felt safer under the latter. But most important, Italians helped defeat fascism themselves and hanged Mussolini in Milan. Nothing comparable ever happened in Germany or Austria where the local population did not even make any credible attempts to challenge National Socialism (excepting the famous July 20 *putsch* against Adolf Hitler) let alone help defeat it. Adding insult to injury, a leading FPÖ member, then serving as defense minister in the "red/blue" coalition government of the mid–1980s, welcomed with all military honors the infamous SS Major Walter Reder while Reder was wanted and condemned as a war criminal in Italy. And Europeans knew this difference and have continued to feel it. Moreover, not having reacted to Haider would in no way render the Europeans' non-reaction to Fini's Allianza Nationale's presence in the 1994 Italian government justifiable or acceptable. Just because one was negligent and remiss in certain instances does not mean that one therefore has the permission— indeed the obligation—to make being remiss and negligent a matter of policy, habit, and routine. And Nazism is still not part of Europe's routine. This is one of the great legacies of the Yalta world. But with that world now fast becoming history, there is a new contest afoot to create a new order of things, which, indeed, includes a community and hierarchy of values. The battle for a new hegemonic political and moral order has already begun. To see this, all one need do is read, with rigor and care, the editorial pages of certain key European dailies, like the *Frankfurter Allgemeine Zeitung*. And nowhere is it a given that the values that had been associated with National Socialism will remain for good beyond the acceptable. In fact, I am convinced that National Socialism–unlike Stalinism—exerts a certain attraction on people, contains a certain seduction of evil, even eroticism, which makes it very powerful and attractive, whether it be to adult Europeans or teenage killers in an upper middle-class Colorado suburb. Hate sites on the Internet are almost exclusively associated with Nazism and are full of Nazi iconography. They invoke National Socialism, not Stalinism. While I am not an expert in pornography, I am quite certain that the prominence of Nazi imagery far outweighs that of any of its Stalinist counterparts. There are probably very few, if any, hate sites or pornographic web pages invoking the Cheka, the NKVD or the KGB the way they habitually do SS and other Nazi symbols. Alas, of the two major evils of the twentieth century, National Socialism appears to be much more attractive as we begin the twenty-first century.

The European Union clearly put its foot down with its unique action against Austria. As Chancellor Schröder aptly phrased it: "We have to make every effort to contain this to Austria. We may fail, but we have to make the effort." The EU clearly conceived of its action as the construction of a "cordon sanitaire" around Austria, or making it clear to other European countries that parties such as the FPÖ will not be tolerated and will remain beyond the politically acceptable in the European community. As such, it was a clear act of precedence setting. One needs only to read the Hungarian intellectual Miklos Haraszti's prescient analysis on the op ed page of the *New York Times* to see how Haider and his legitimation by the conservatives in Austrian politics has become an attractive and acceptable political model to many East Europeans.

What of the consequences of this EU action? Was it such an ignominious failure as many have claimed? Did the EU have to revoke the sanctions in September 2000 with egg on its face, having caused much ado about nothing? I beg to differ.

From my normative vantage point, this boycott included many positive consequences proving yet again, that the only way to attain even the semblance of success in politics is through pressure. There have never been any free lunches in politics, and there never will be. None of the consequences to follow would have occurred without the EU's action.

First, the EU's policy rendered Austrian President Thomas Klestil a man of stature and importance to a degree that was clearly lacking before this event. The fact that Klestil first objected to some candidates for ministerial positions in the proposed Schüssel government and exacted that they be replaced was already an unusual, indeed unprecedented, step in Austria's postwar politics. Typically, heads of state in parliamentary democracies are merely titular and ceremonial figures who routinely approve cabinets which the heads of government propose to them. President Klestil fully realized the gravity of the situation and reacted accordingly. More important still, he had the two coalition partners sign an unprecedented document that he had drawn up in which the two coalition partners committed themselves in the most explicit of terms to respect human rights in full, to remain cognizant and mindful of Austria's heinous Nazi past and its continued responsibilities on account of this past, and to maintain all the policies that have stood in Austria's good stead through the entire postwar period and rendered the country one of the most stable and admired European democracies. This unique presidential act and document owe their existence solely to the pressure exerted by the 14 European governments on Austria.

Second, there is little doubt that Haider himself was completely surprised by the vehemence and seriousness of the EU's reaction. A very vain and publicity-conscious man, he suddenly found himself a complete persona non grata in the very world that was of paramount importance to him. While Haider's forced withdrawal from the national scene and his seeking refuge in his home base of Carinthia seemed merely a tactical move at the time—which it might very well have been—it, nevertheless, must have come at great cost to his ego and also to his political efficacy. And it would never have happened without the EU's strong measure. To be sure, Haider continues to exert complete Bolshevik-style control over the FPÖ as he did prior to the Europeans' step of ostracism. But the fact is that he had to cede the center of power; that he had been weakened in stature and immediate influence; that all politics, including Austria's, is potentially subject to the so-called "Brutus effect," in which absent leaders facilitate the emergence of vacua which then lend themselves to be filled by those who happen to be present or by other, less ostracized, rivals. The FPÖ has not been immune to such a development. New space permits the rise of potentially new stars as has indeed happened in the FPÖ's case in spite of Haider's iron grip over the party. That Haider had to cede the limelight was solely attributable to the EU's boycott.

Lastly, and perhaps most importantly, the European response helped confirm a resistance to Haider and the new government in Austria that has been truly unprecedented. More than in the case of any other development in the Second Republic, there developed an oppositional force, a critical public that engulfed all of Austrian life and that created a democratic discourse and an atmosphere of contestation never before experienced in Austria, and quite rare anywhere in most advanced industrial democracies. Be it the twice-weekly demonstrations in the streets of Vienna, or the regular public discussions among actors and audience that occurred after the conclusion of theater performances even in such staid loci of the established order like the venerable Burgtheater in Vienna, there developed a public space for debate and opposition that has surprised everyone, most of all the Austrians. There is no doubt that the vibrancy and viability of the Austrian opposition to the FPÖ's governmental role and to Jörg Haider's politics in particular derived much strength and stamina from the knowledge that Austria's European neighbors remain far from indifferent as to the fate of Austria and its continued liberal democracy. And if one reads the report of the "Three Wise Men," whom the EU empowered to assess the situation in Austria eight months after decreeing the boycott on January 31, 2000, one will find plenty of evidence that far from being a whitewash of the Austrian government and the Austrian situation and a face-saving device for the EU as many have alleged, this "white paper" contains matters of important substance. While complimenting the Austrian government (including its FPÖ members) for having taken particular care to maintain democratic discourse and to safeguard human rights, and absolving it of any wrongdoing, the "Three Wise Men" used emphatic language in their chastising the FPÖ as a party that they characterized as "right-wing populist with radical elements." In particular, the report blamed the FPÖ for having repeatedly used xenophobia in its political campaigns, thus rendering such discourse completely acceptable ("salonfähig" is the word used in the report) in contemporary Austria. The report concludes with perhaps the most important notion of all: that this unprecedented action by the EU lead to a routinized system of "preventive and monitoring measures" to guard against similar developments that violate "common European values" becoming part of any member country's government.

Structural and Cultural Antecedents

It is important to point out that one of the main reasons for the Europeans' unprecedented swift and vociferous reaction to the FPÖ's entering the Austrian government must be placed in the context of Austria's much less sincere, vocal, and serious attempts to come to terms with its Nazi past, particularly when compared to the efforts of *West* Germany (in stark contrast to East Germany, a comparison that, though highly relevant to the larger discussion here, is beyond the scope of this chapter).

Austria's exculpation began with the Moscow Declaration of 1943 which pronounced Austria as Nazi Germany's first victim. While certainly correct and appropriate in one sense, this categorization was far too flat and one-sided in terms of accounting for the other side of Austria's history, the one that welcomed the Anschluss and thus the Nazis' political rule over what had now become the Ostmark province in the larger Third Reich. After the war, Austrians could conveniently blame the "Piefkes" as the evil occupiers and the only ones responsible for National Socialist rule, especially its atrocities, since Austrians were occupied like everybody else in Europe and they, too, had become one of Hitler's victims like the Poles, Belgians, French, Norwegians, Czechs, etc. *"Anschluss—The Rape of Austria"* (to use the title of a book by a respected British historian) became a well-worn metaphor in the international discourse about Austria that helped decouple it from the Nazis and their crimes.

For however one can—and needs to—criticize the West Germans as to their inadequate confrontation with their Nazi past, one also needs to give credit where credit is due: No society in the world has ever tried to atone for a particularly heinous epoch of its history the way the West Germans have done concerning Germany's Nazi past. To be sure, this did not begin until the 1960s, and the silent 1950s provided more than their helpful cover-up in creating a smooth continuity between the Third Reich and important structures of the Federal Republic, but following the Auschwitz trial in 1963 in Frankfurt and the arrival of the '68-ers on the scene of West German politics, the Nazi past became an integral part of the Federal Republic's public discourse in virtually every aspect of life. Following is a brief—and incomplete—list of key events in which this past assumed center stage in West Germany's public debate to a degree unknown in Austria until the Waldheim Affair in 1986. There simply exists no comparable list for Austrian politics.

1963: Auschwitz trial
1969: First parliamentary debate about the expiration of the statute of limitation of murder committed by the Nazis
1972: Willy Brandt's impromptu knee fall at the Warsaw Ghetto memorial
1979: Second parliamentary debate about the expiration of the statute of limitation of murder committed by the Nazis
1979: The airing of the television series "Holocaust," which created a watershed in the public debate about the Nazi genocide of the Jews among virtually all groups in West Germany

1985: The Bitburg affair
1985: President Richard von Weizsaecker's legendary speech of May 8, perhaps, arguably, the most important public address in the Federal Republic's history
1985: Rainer Werner Fassbinder's play, "Garbage, the City and Death"
1986: The Historians' Debate
1988: Philip Jenninger's ill-fated speech in the Bundestag
1989: The fall of the Berlin Wall on November 9 and the ensuing public discussion about the proper commemoration of this day in German history
1996: The Goldhagen controversy
1998: The Walser-Bubis confrontation
1999: The Wehrmacht Exhibit
1986–1999—and continuing: The controversy over the Holocaust Memorial in Berlin: its very existence; its proper shape; its size; its location
2000: Compensation of slave labor under the Nazis
2001: The Finkelstein controversy

Whatever the causes, procedures, and eventual results of these issues might have been, all led to major debates in virtually all venues of Germany's public. Thus, however flawed Germany's coming to terms with its Nazi past might be judged, the attempt to do so most certainly created a public culture of awareness that rendered silence and complacency impossible. One simply could no longer be a thinking German without having the legacy of the Holocaust, in some way, shape or form, be part of one's identity. No matter how flawed one might gauge the German effort, it has been, comparatively speaking, far and away the most thorough in the world. Coming to terms with the Holocaust has in some manner become part of contemporary German identity. It had not been so in the case of its Austrian counterpart until very recently, if at all. Haider would still be unthinkable in Germany. Then again, the regular violence and constant intimidation exercised by the new German right on a daily basis, mainly—though far from exclusively—in the country's eastern Laender, are rather rare in Austria.

To be sure, Austria's Nazi past has also been covered up both consciously as well as structurally by that particular Austrian political arrangement known as consociationalism, a system of top-level elite

cooperation (critics would call it collusion) that derived its legitimation from a pre-Nazi Austrian trauma that was absent in Germany: The
Austrian Civil War of 1934. This war was merely the logical consum-
mation of a civil-war-like relationship between the Socialist "reds"
and the Catholic-conservative "blacks" that had plagued the entire
First Republic ("the republic that no one wanted" as it has been aptly
characterized) from its very beginnings, after the collapse of the
Habsburg Monarchy and the end of World War I, until its demise at
the hands of Austro-Fascism's "Fatherland Front" in 1934. In many
ways, this trauma defined Austria's postwar arrangement and political
life much more than the Nazi interlude. Lest 1934 re-appear once
again, the reds and the blacks set up a governmental system immediately following the conclusion of World War II in which both were
guaranteed constant inclusion regardless of electoral outcomes as long
as there was a rough numerical balance between the two. Thus emerged
a long-lasting system of red-black cooperation and collusion that consolidated Austria's postwar political stability and economic comfort to
the detriment of excluding those that did not quite fit the system. The
FPÖ and its followers were among the excluded. What is interesting—
and unique in the Austrian case—is that a governmental arrangement
that is usually designed to deal with exceptional situations demanding
the coalescence of society's major institutions (Germany's Grand Coalition featuring the SPD (Sozialdemokratische Partei Deutschlands)
and the CDU/CSU (Christlich Demokratische Union/Christlich Soziale
Union) between 1966 and 1969; Israel's Likud-Marach Coalition in
the late 1980s; and Britain's all-party coalition during World War II
come to mind) became the norm of government in Austria's Second
Republic. After all, for thirty-four of the Second Republic's fifty-five
years, Austria had been governed by a Grand Coalition of some kind
with the ÖVP furnishing the senior partnership in the coalition's first
installment until 1966 and the SPÖ assuming this role between 1986
and 2000 when the FPÖ under Haider's leadership joined with the
ÖVP to form a new coalition. There have been two major reasons for
this Austrian norm: to avoid the trauma of the 1930s—the battle between the reds and the blacks—and thus guarantee political stability
and economic prosperity; and to exclude—rather than confront—anything related to National Socialism by keeping the FPÖ at bay and
away from the government. Thus, the governmental arrangements most
common to the rest of Europe, so-called small coalitions, remained

beyond the acceptability and feasibility of much of Austria's postwar history. This "Austrian exceptionalism" remained fully intact until the Social Democrats formed a small coalition with the FPÖ in 1983. It is to the Social Democrats that I now turn my attention.

The Social Democrats/Socialists—the SPÖ

Key leaders of Austrian Socialism were active supporters of Austria's Anschluss with Nazi Germany. [To be sure, many Austrian socialists wanted an Anschluss with Germany as early as 1920 but for a very different reason: The SPÖ hoped that by Austria's joining Germany, the two jewels of the Second International—the SPD and the SPÖ— might in fact create a social democratic hegemony that neither could attain in their respective countries on their own.] Thus, for example, Karl Renner, one of the SPÖ's leading figures and later president of Austria in the postwar era, an intellectual with international contacts and experience, urged Austria's joining up with Nazi Germany. Approval of the Nazis' arrival in Austria in March 1938 was not confined to the country's middle class; many blue-collar workers, who had hoped that the "socialist" dimensions of the Nazis' policies would create jobs for them in the newly constituted Ostmark, also welcomed their arrival. Moreover, this wing of the party was always wary of what it perceived to be the inordinate presence of Jewish intellectuals in the SPÖ's policy-making apparatus and among its leaders.

Banned under the Nazis, the Austrian SPÖ reconstituted itself in 1945 under postwar circumstances. Adopting the November 1943 Moscow Declaration, the Socialists rebuilt the party on a very different foundation from the "Austro-Marxist" social democracy of the First Republic. Austria's two hundred thousand Jews, most of whom had voted for the Socialists because the Christian Social Party program contained a notorious Aryan paragraph, and the pan-German party was obviously not an option for them, were gone, either murdered or driven abroad. As Adolf Sturmthal, who had been an assistant to Friedrich Adler (head of the Labor and Socialist International) in the 1930s and returned to Austria in 1945 as the chairman of "Friends of Austrian Labor" in American exile, soon learned, the new SPÖ was not warmly disposed toward returning emigrés. Though a few well-known figures like Oskar Pollak, editor of the *Arbeiter-Zeitung*, did return to Vienna, the new Party chair, Adolf Schärf—later president of the Republic—made it clear that he regarded a flood of returning Jewish emigres as a potential problem for the Socialists in a country with a long anti-Semitic tradition. Some key leaders of postwar social democracy, such as Lower Austria's Heinrich Schneidmadl, had reputations as anti-Semites, and Schneidmadl's wing of the party had always been wary of what it perceived to be the inordinate presence of Jewish intellectuals in the SPÖ's top echelons. According to the British historian Rober Knight, when the subject of restitution of Jewish property was raised in postwar cabinet meetings, SPÖ interior minister Oskar Helmer said, "I am for dragging out the matter." It soon became clear that many of the exiles would not return to Austria. For example, Otto Leichter, who had been Otto Bauer's right-hand man before the war, and whose wife, Kaethe, had perished in Ravensbrueck, chose to remain in New York where his son Franz became a state senator.

Immediately following the war, the reconstituted SPÖ's emphasis on a pragmatism that was to fetishize neo-corporatist consociationalism as the only possible expression of political rule also meant a speedy accommodation with former Nazis whose past the party was willing to forget as long as they now proved to be its loyal supporters, followers, and functionaries. Particularly in Austria's southern province of Carinthia – Haider's home and his current bailiwick as this province's governor—the SPÖ openly wooed former Nazis to join its ranks and start a new life in a party whose pedigree, though far from innocent of complicity with the Nazis, was certainly the cleanest that this new republic could offer. Barring a complete integration of former Nazis into the postwar SPÖ, the party pursued a parallel track which was designed to weaken its only serious political rival (and consociational partner) until the meteoric rise of Jörg Haider, the conservative People's Party—ÖVP—successor to the Austro-Fascists of the 1930s. Rather than have the bulk of Austria's 680,000 registered members of the NSDAP (Nationalsozialistische Deutsche Arbeiterpartei) become supporters of the conservatives, the SPÖ openly advocated the creation of a third force which was to become the political home of Jörg Haider and his friends. Euphemistically labeled Verband der Unabhaengigen (League of Independents) and still disenfranchised for the 1945 parliamentary elections by dint of its members' active cooperation with National Socialism, this group conducted its first national poll under the new name of Wahlpartei der Unabhängigen (Party of the Independents) in 1949, garnering 11.7 percent of the popular vote. It is precisely this origin of what was to become the FPÖ in 1956 that has led Anton Pelinka, Austria's leading political scientist, to label the FPÖ not a Nazi party but, clearly, "a party founded by former Nazis for former Nazis" thus making it unique among all European parties, even among its cousins on the far right of the European political spectrum, like the Vlams Blok in Belgium, the Front National in France, the Allianza Nationale in Italy and the numerous small right-wing parties of the postwar period in Germany itself.

The SPÖ's tacit tolerance and quiet courting of former Nazis turned open and vocal under the leadership of Bruno Kreisky, beginning in 1970. Kreisky, an assimilated Viennese Jew of the educated middle class, who spent the war years in Sweden, returned to Austria to a successful career in politics which, among other things, openly and knowingly used anti-Semitism as a tool to further his own personal interests as well as those of his beloved SPÖ. Fascinated by the thirty-year hegemony of Swedish social democracy, as were so many continental emigrés (Willy Brandt and Rudolf Meidner, to name just two), Kreisky hoped that by weakening the conservative ÖVP and strengthening the right-radical FPÖ he, too, would be able to establish "Swedish" conditions in Austria where the bourgeois parties would be splintered, thus leaving a powerful social democracy as the permanent ruler of the country. The active pursuit of this Swedish strategy coincided quite conveniently with Kreisky's personal dislike of Jews, which he expressed to just about anyone willing to listen, such as the German weekly *Der Spiegel* to whom in a freewheeling interview he called the Jews "an old but ugly [*ein altes aber mieses*] people." From ostentatiously kissing and embracing Yasser Arafat and Muammar Qaddafy during their repeated meetings in Vienna and elsewhere, to denouncing some Israeli leaders, particularly Menahem Begin, in derogatory terms commonly used by German (and Austrian) Jews in their contemptuous references to East European Jews (the so-called Ostjuden); Kreisky's personal aversions happened to be superb politics in a country where in the 1970s well over 70 percent of the population still harbored deeply felt resentments towards Jews. When Kreisky and the SPÖ first came to power all by themselves in 1970, thereby breaking the traditional tandem of consociationalism in which they had to share power with the ÖVP as the latter's junior partner, the socialists formed a minority government, which meant that they had to rely on tacit parliamentary approval of their governance on the part of Austria's third party—the FPÖ, which was led at the time by Friedrich Peter, the party's second leader who, just like its first, had been a high-ranking member of the SS. Kreisky and Peter became not only political allies but actually personal friends. Kreisky defended Peter against Simon Wiesenthal's allegations that Peter's SS unit had been involved in mass killings of civilians in the Soviet Union: "The only thing that matters is the present, not the past," said Kreisky to the delight of millions of Austrians who loved hearing Kreisky's repeated utterances that Kreisky as a Jew could speak with abandon whereas it remained strictly taboo for "true Austrians," a sobriquet used by Kreisky's rival Josef Klaus in the 1970 election campaign (which Kreisky won) to differentiate himself from Kreisky who, by dint of his being Jewish, was presumably not a true Austrian. Studies by Austrian linguist Ruth Wodak and by other Austrian social scientists demonstrate quite clearly that in the wake of Kreisky's thinly veiled anti-Semitic attacks on Wiesenthal anti-Semitic discourse grew and became more legitimate in Austria's public domain. Four ministers of Kreisky's first cabinet and five of his second cabinet were card-carrying members of the National Socialist Party. Kreisky's agriculture minister, Hans Öllinger, had to resign after it was revealed that—unbeknownst to Kreisky—he had an "illegal" SS background. Unlike having been a member of the "illegal" SS, having belonged to the "legal" NSDAP bore no stigma in Austrian politics at all. Öllinger's successor then was a man who was a perfectly "legal" member of the NSDAP. In 1983, the Austrian socialists entered into an official coalition with the FPÖ, thus forming for the first time in the Second Republic's history a so-called "small coalition" which had become the governing norm in virtually all European democracies but remained impossible in Austria first and foremost by dint of the FPÖ's unique connection to the Nazi past but also by virtue of the entrenched consociationalism of the two big parties who, if they could not rule alone by themselves, preferred each other as coalition partners thus guaranteeing the smooth continuation of a well-oiled spoil system best-known under the term "Proporz." In fairness to Kreisky and the SPÖ, it should be mentioned that the FPÖ's debut at the helm of Austria's government occurred under the chancellorship of Fred Sinowatz, Kreisky's immediate successor, and during a brief hiatus in the FPÖ's postwar history when, in the course of the early 1980s, the party's liberal wing under Norbert Steger assumed a short-lived prominence only to be toppled by its current star Jörg

Haider later in the decade. While the small SPÖ-FPÖ coalition lasted only until 1986, the taboo had been broken: The Social Democrats had granted the FPÖ its first access to state power in Austria's postwar history.

The ugly collaboration between Austria's social democrats and former Nazis began to be aired for the first time in 2000 in what surely would have been Austria's last trial involving the Nazi past. The 83-year old psychiatrist Heinrich Gross was accused of having conducted under Nazi rule a euthanasia program in Vienna specializing in the multiple killing of children. Gross was a Nazi of the first hour: Member of the Hitler Youth as of 1932, member of the SA one year later, rapid career advancement as an active Nazi leader during a period when being a Nazi was illegal in Austria, joining the NSDAP in 1938 two days after the Anschluss in March—in short a Nazi by conviction not by opportunism. After the war he engaged in a straight-up trade: he relinquished his NSDAP party book (membership number 6335279) and acquired a socialist one instead (SPÖ membership number 011598). Under the full protection of the Socialist leadership, and as a special protégé of the former Trotzkyite Christian Broda, who served as Austria's minister of justice from 1960 until 1983 and, together with Kreisky, was one of the Second Republic's most prominent and re-spected Social Democratic politicians, Gross was accorded every pos-sible accolade, honor, and privilege that the Austrian Republic can bestow on an individual. Gross was merely an egregious example of a pattern that represents the still unwritten but all the more ugly side of postwar Austrian social democracy. Adding insult to injury, the trial—barely begun—was halted indefinitely on account of Gross's alleged physical and mental frailty. Yet another chance to come to terms with Austria's past was nipped in the bud.

The Austrian People's Party—ÖVP: Conservatism in the Postwar Era.

National Socialism helped in a way to make Austro-Fascism, the political regime of the ÖVP's predecessor, appear much less harshly than it would have been the case had National Socialism, first, not been a far more murderous regime than Austro-Fascism and, second, had it not been conveniently "foreign," which meant that the domestic evils of clerical fascism could conveniently be forgotten, indeed—as was the case in certain instances—even extolled, for example, by Kurt

Schuschnigg, who tried to resist Hitler's pressures as best he could only to succumb to a hopeless situation. These circumstances accorded Schuschnigg a position of prominence in the Second Republic as Austria's brave resister against Nazi might. His leadership of the "Fatherland Front" which, after all, was an openly fascist regime, was barely mentioned in public discourse of postwar Austria, and, if then, only in the world of the "red Lager." National Socialism's presence was strong enough to allow the ÖVP much leeway in dealing with its own fascist past. Yet, it was not strong enough to have the party stay clear of incorporating Nazis among its ranks and flirt with anti-Semitism when it suited the party's purpose. After all, in Austrian politics, harnessing the force of anti-Semitism has never been to any party's detriment. It has always been only a matter of how, never one of if.

Thus, the ÖVP, just like the SPÖ, had plenty of its own Nazi issues. Reinhard Kamitz, minister of finance in the 1950s, was a Nazi party member. The ÖVP was, of course, not above using subtle anti-Semitism in its electoral campaigns and other political events when it saw the expression of such sentiments as beneficial to its cause. Thus, as already briefly mentioned, in his campaign against Bruno Kreisky, the ÖVP's leader and chancellor's candidate Josef Klaus covered the country with posters that featured his face with the simple statement, "A True Austrian," clearly implying that Kreisky, a Jew, could not be a true Austrian. In 1965 Taras Borodajkewycz, an Austrian Catholic with a traditional background in the elite of political Catholicism, the Cartel-Verband (CV), the non-dueling student fraternity, made repeated and openly pro-Nazi and anti-Semitic remarks in his lectures at the School of Business (then Hochschule für Welthandel now rechristened Wirtschaftsuniversität) in Vienna. As a consequence of his anti-Semitic remarks, Borodajkewycz's lectures were among the most popular at the School where he became one of the students' heroes. Indeed, when his remarks appeared in public on account of the meticulous note-taking of a young socialist student named Heinz Fischer, who, subsequently became one of the SPÖ's most prominent politicians during the Kreisky years and beyond, and when on the basis of this publicity the government proceeded to censor Borodajkewycz and initiate his early retirement, his student followers by the thousands demonstrated on the professor's behalf and engaged in pitched battles with workers, who, trucked into Vienna's center from the city's "red" suburbs, protested against anti-Semitism and neo-Nazism at Austrian universities.

There were two huge demonstrations that turned seriously violent. In the course of one, Ernst Kirchweger, a survivor of Nazi persecution and a member of the Austrian resistance against Nazism, was beaten to death by members of the Burschenschaften, the right-wing student fraternities whose rituals continue to feature dueling. This, of course, was the milieu that spawned Jörg Haider and his associates. It was different and apart from the conservative student associations but these two worlds formed close alliances on issues pertaining to anti-Semitism, Jews, foreigners, and "reds." As testimony to the tremendous changes that have occurred in the development of Austrian social and political life, we now experience a complete role reversal as to the FPÖ's and the political right's supporters in the 1960s and now: Then, the bastion of the right (both radical and conservative) were the country's universities and its intelligentsia; today, it is the male, blue-collar working class that demonstrated against Borodajkewycz in 1965. Haider and his party have become anathema to Austrian universities and the country's intelligentsia. It would be unthinkable for Haider to deliver a lecture at an Austrian university. Wisely, he has never tried.

No discussion of the ÖVP would be complete without at least the mention of the Waldheim Affair. While even a superficial discussion of this controversy would be far beyond the scope of this chapter, three things need brief mention here. First, Kurt Waldheim was, of course, prominent member of the very milieu that tied this party in an indirect but far from insignificant way to Austria's entanglement with National Socialism. The relationship on Waldheim's part—and that of the ÖVP's—to the Nazis was never as clear cut, never as obvious in its complicity with National Socialism as was the case with the FPÖ. Still, a relationship there was. Second, most of the ÖVP, its members, voters, and supporters stood by Kurt Waldheim during the entire six years of his ill-fated presidency when, for the first time, an Austrian politician, indeed the country's head of state, was persona non grata in most European states. Thus, there existed a European precedent to the action that the EU initiated in the crisis surrounding the formation of the black/blue coalition in early 2000. Though far less coordinated than in the present situation, the fact then was that President Kurt Waldheim was unwelcome in most European capitals that he used to visit on a regular basis as former foreign minister of Austria, one of its most senior diplomats, and, most importantly, as two-term Secretary General of the United Nations. Third, it was the

Waldheim controversy that spawned two dialectically related developments that were to influence Austrian politics to this day: The first serious reckoning of the Austrian Nazi past on a major scale involving a public debate unprecedented in its intensity since the inception of the Second Republic; and the emergence of Jörg Haider as leader of a meteorically rising FPÖ. It is to a discussion of this entity that we now move.

The Freedom Party—FPÖ: Yet Another Austrian Exception?

There is no doubt that the last fifteen years have witnessed a re-emergence of the radical right in many European countries. The end of the Cold War, the break-up of old value structures, above all the creation of multicultural and multiethnic societies in countries that have been largely mono-cultural and mono-ethnic, at least in terms of being virtually all white and all "Western" by their self-understanding, have led to the emergence of a bevy of right-wing activities in almost all European countries. From Sweden in the north to Italy in the south, right-wing politics has emerged with a force (and violence) that was largely unknown in the first four decades of the postwar period. All of these movements—and one needs to consider them as such, not only as parties where their significance has been much less pronounced and seemingly less important than their actual existence has been in the political space of all these countries – share a number of commonalities: In terms of their social composition, they are disproportionately male; disproportionately young (15–30 years); disproportionately skewed towards the lesser educated segments of all their societies; and disproportionately dissatisfied with the trajectories of their societies and their futures in particular. (Interestingly, they have not hailed disproportionately from the unemployed as has been commonly reported.) As to their beliefs, they feature a heavy dosage of xenophobia, nationalism bordering on the chauvinist variety, racism, anti-Semitism, anti-feminism, anti-Europeanism and also anti-Americanism. Similar to its fascist predecessors of the interwar period with whom it shares many ideological and social similarities but from whom it is also quite different, this New Right disdains all aspects of weakness and remains skeptical towards the liberal democratic order of its respective countries.

The FPÖ fits this profile with a good measure of accuracy. Yet, it is also different in two key ways: First, as already stated, none of the other constructs of the New Right have been parties or movements for Nazis by Nazis; they all—without exception—include the crucial prefix "neo" in their self-identification and, more importantly, the identification by scholars and experts. In this essential manner, the FPÖ, in fact, is not a party of the New Right. It very much hails from an old Right that not only experienced the world of state power but also exerted such in the most brutal ways throughout much of the European continent. But second, the FPÖ is, indeed, new in terms of its leadership's age, its iconography, its habitus. Indeed, it is so new that its newness has also contributed to its immense success making it the most significant New Right phenomenon anywhere in Europe. This "newness" consists of all the elements that have become associated with the term "Boutique Fascism": young, dynamic, stylish – the antithesis to the fascists of yore who, by dint of their age and image, have simply lost most of their relevance and appeal at the beginning of the twenty-first century. Hobnail boots, goose stepping, one-arm saluting might still be attractive to a small fringe of right-radical young men who fancy themselves as the vanguard of a reborn fascist movement, but these symbols and the world that they represent remain unappealing to a large number of voters who are needed to bring a party like the FPÖ to political power.

The FPÖ, as has been already mentioned—started out as the VdU in 1945. This entity was the direct successor to the Grossdeutsche Volkspartei of the First Republic and to the pan-German "third Lager" of the Habsburg Empire, arguably one of the most virulently anti-Semitic and German-nationalist movements anywhere in the German-speaking world at the end of the nineteenth century and the beginning of the twentieth century. The VdU's associations were so identified with National Socialism that it did not even contest the postwar era's first parliamentary election in which the country's 680,000 Austrian members of the National Socialist party were disenfranchised of their voting rights. In the 1949 poll, the VdU, campaigning as WdU, attained 11.7 percent; in the 1953 poll it garnered 11.0 percent. This grouping was renamed FPÖ in 1956 and has maintained this name ever since. The party hovered between an electoral high of 7.7 percent in 1959 and a low of 5.0 percent in its brief liberal interlude in the early 1980s under Norbert Steger, Jörg Haider's immediate predecessor as party leader. That Steger's attempts at making the FPÖ something akin to the German FDP nearly cost the party its parliamentary representation (Austria's cut-off threshold for legislative representation lies at 4 percent of the tally, as opposed to 5 percent in Germany) and was an ill-fated course, is best demonstrated by the party's rapidly improving electoral fate under Haider, which can only be described as meteorically successful: 9.7 percent, 16.6 percent, 22.5 percent, 21.9 percent, and, in the last election of October 1999, 27.3 percent, a tally that has catapulted the FPÖ into becoming Austria's second largest party behind the rapidly slumping Social Democrats.

The FPÖ was different from the other two Austrian parties of the postwar era in that it was never really a membership party. Even during this meteoric rise at the polls since Haider's incumbency as party leader, the party membership has more or less held steady at circa 40,000. In stark opposition to the continuity on the membership dimension, there have occurred significant shifts in the social characteristics of the party's voters in the course of Jörg Haider's leadership: To be sure, the FPÖ had always attracted more male voters than female; but the gender gap has become significantly more pronounced since Haider's presence at the party's helm. But here, perhaps, are the three most important changes that amount to major shifts in the electoral topography of Austrian politics well beyond the FPÖ proper: Under Haider, the FPÖ has become especially popular among Austria's young voters in notable contrast to previous times when the party attracted older voters in disproportionate numbers. More telling still of the earth-quake-like shifts in Austrian politics, today's FPÖ attracts a majority of Austrian male, blue-collar workers, who—for one solid century—had been the immutable backbone of Austria's social democracy. A close corollary to the shift in class profile of the FPÖ's electorate is the one in education: If throughout the first four decades of the Second Republic the FPÖ's voters hailed disproportionately from those holding university degrees or equivalent professional credentials, and belonged to such elite professions as doctors and lawyers, the exact opposite has been the case in the course of Haider's meteoric rise: the FPÖ has become the party of choice for the least educated segments of Austrian society, while it has virtually disappeared among the country's intelligentsia and attained a minoritarian position among its professional sectors. Sociologically speaking, the party under Haider has assumed the profile of a traditional party of the Old Left.

Ideologically speaking, the FPÖ, until the 1970s, was basically a pro-German, indeed pan-German, right-wing party whose milieu over-lapped considerably with Austria's dueling university fraternities as well as, at least in the early 1960s, with those that committed terrorist attacks and bombings in Italy's Alto Adige province, which, as the South Tyrol, these people and the FPÖ wanted to see as part of Aus-tria by dint of a substantial majority of German speakers among its inhabitants. The first two leaders of the FPÖ were members of the SS; the party's leading politicians often expressed openly anti-Semitic sen-timents; and the party never drew a clear and decisive demarcation setting it unequivocally apart from the shadowy world of virulent neo-Nazism. It would not be an exceptional event in Austrian politics for various prominent FPÖ politicians constantly to test the waters of the permissible in terms of accepted discourse in the country's public culture. Thus, some remark that was clearly anti-Semitic, pro-Nazi, derisive of Austrian nationhood, anti-foreign or in whatever way part of the FPÖ's discourse, though only tenuously Austria's, would al-ways be retracted half-heartedly by an apology of sorts that—to the careful listener—merely confirmed that the original statement clearly reflected the person's actual intent and views. But a retraction had been made in a pro forma manner, thus making it possible for the FPÖ as a party and for the particular politician to have re-established their credentials as legitimate players in what had become officially ac-cepted language in postwar Austrian politics.

For fairness' sake, it is important to mention the small, but extant, liberal wing in the FPÖ that embodied all the values and views of a classical liberal party in the European sense: little state, lots of market, freedom of the individual, secularism. Only in the course of the first half of the 1980s, under the leadership of Norbert Steger, did this wing become hegemonic inside the FPÖ. Haider's successful putsch against Steger quickly eliminated this tradition from the party altogether, so much so that the victims of this purge departed from the FPÖ and formed the "Liberales Forum," a liberal party with the talented Heide Schmidt at its helm, whose personal charisma carried this new party into the Austrian parliament for two legislative periods. However, with liberalism never having played a significant role in Austrian poli-tics and the novelty factor having worn off, the Liberales Forum failed to pass the 4 percent threshold in October 1999, thus not making it into the current Austrian legislature.

Enter Jörg Haider, brilliant mixture of new and old; of young, hip post-modern and well-tanned androgyny espousing market liberalism in some areas and state protection in others, articulating Austro-chau vinism with a solid dosage of old-fashioned pan-Germanism, xeno phobia and racism, and launching relentless attacks on the red-black establishment that had run Austrian politics solidly since 1945. There can be absolutely no doubt that together with Bruno Kreisky, Jörg Haider has already become far and away the most important politician of Austria's Second Republic. Like Kreisky, Haider, too, has come to dominate Austrian domestic politics as no other politician ever has and in the process—also like Kreisky—has attained an international aura that has eluded all other public figures of the Second Republic.

Conclusion

There can be no doubt that Austrian postwar politics was foreve changed in the course of the last few months of 1999 and the begin ning of 2000. Haider's emergence as a political force has been part o a secularization process that has de-mystified and destroyed the old Lager. There will be no more automaticity in Austrian politics. In a country where politics was completely predictable for nearly fifty years where the ratio of party members to voters was the highest in any modern country (fully one-third of the electorate belonged to one o the three dominant political parties), including those of the Sovie bloc, where the SPÖ's membership in absolute numbers was nearly as large as the SPD's and the ÖVP's, in fact, larger than the CDU's in a country that contained one-tenth of the population of the Federal Re public of Germany, party politics has been indelibly altered. Writers such as Robert Menasse have rejoiced in this secularization of Aus trian politics and see the destruction of the old Lager as a welcome "Westernization" of a postwar Austria, which these critics have al ways regarded as merely semi-democratic at best. This "de Austrianization" of Austrian politics, to use Anton Pelinka's apt term once again, the end of "Austrian exceptionalism" means, of course, an opening of a hitherto blocked political space. This development cre ates new possibilities and opportunities but it also unveils the ugly underbelly of Austrian life, which had been safely tucked away under the firm cover of the old consociationalism of the Second Republic.

To be sure, this secularization of Austria, this pluralization of its political space allows access to all kinds of political expressions that are not to my liking. Yet, there is also something very welcoming in this secularization: It renders the ugly sentiments that have contributed to Haider's inordinate success much less dangerous than would have been the case in the previous era of de-secularized Austrian politics. Adherence to Haider and the FPÖ, no matter how sincere and heart-felt, is not a passion. This affinity has no religious overtones, no aspects of fanaticism. As such, these sentiments are expressions of a politics that will not vanquish liberal democracy in Austria. That welcome arrangement has become far too ensconced in the country's political culture to be displaced once again.

7

Haider–The New Symbolic Element of the Ongoing Discourse of the Past

Michal Krzyzanowski

*"...a nameless voice
has already been speaking long before me,
so that I should only have needed to join in."
—Michel Foucault*

Introduction

The outbreak of the political situation in Austria in late 1999 and early 2000 came as a shock to many countries and nations. The most significant part of "the Austrian crisis" occurred in early 2000, when it became apparent that the Freedom Party of Austria (FPÖ) had not only garnered a large percentage in elections, but it would also be a part of the newly created Austrian government. This situation met with international resistance and disapproval, since both the FPÖ and its leader Jörg Haider were widely known for expressing their approval for the times of National Socialism (NS) and for presenting a xenophobic attitude towards other nations, especially towards national and ethnic minorities. It was not anything very astonishing, since both Haider and the party he was leading come from the tradition of the Austrian "brown past" of the years 1933–45, which are the effect of what could be called "lack of reconciliation with the past" (Reisigl and Wodak forthcoming). The events in Austria of early 2000 were clearly a case of the past's influence on contemporary Austrian reality, and demonstrated that the problem of Austria had become an international problem. Most other European countries opposed the FPÖ's part in the Austrian government, and Austria suddenly found itself in the international limelight. Many official statements were issued about the Austrian situation, but very few were concerned with how the Austrian problems (including FPÖ) were received by other nations.

In February 2000, one of the Polish National Public-Opinion Research Departments (CBOS) conducted a poll, asking Polish people what they thought about and were afraid of in regard to the new political situation in Austria. Let me elaborate on the three most prevalent types of answers[1]:

- *Question*: What are you afraid of in connection with Jörg Haider's party coming to power?
- *Answers* (group 1): associations with fascism: fears of rebirth of fascism, nazism and hitlerism in Europe; anxiety about the neo-fascist policy of Haider's party, "this Haider is like a second Hitler"; all kinds of references to Hitler and to the return of history; "fear of repetition of what we had in Germany" (percentage: 44 percent, 14 percent of all).
- *Answers* (group 2): danger for the peace and stability in Europe and worldwide, anxiety about the outbreak of war or European conflict, fear of violence, turmoil and unrest in Europe, "we should not let the year of 1939 to be repeated"; "he should not have any agreement with the Germans, since it would be dangerous for Europe" (16 percent, 5 percent of all).
- *Answers* (group 3): associations with radical-right policy, nationalism; anxieties about the rebirth and spread of radical nationalism and radical right in Europe; anxieties about an intensification of the actions of nationalist parties and nationalist policy (14 percent, 5 percent of all). (*CBOS* "Omnibus" poll, February 18–22, 2000)[2,3]

The poll clearly shows that, as representatives of the past, Jörg Haider and his party have become the center of international attention. And it is not a good past, but a past that started in the times of National Socialism, the negative and sad past from which many European nations suffered a great deal. Haider's figure is more than clearly marked by the past: his political views and his party come from the past (tradition stemming from NS roots), he praises and trivializes the times of the past; he shows a xenophobic attitude (the same as was done in times of the NS past).

Thus, we should try to investigate the way in which Haider and his party have been perceived in the international context. In my study I will show how significant (in a negative sense) this symbol of the past, which I consider Haider to be, is for the opening of another stage of the discourse over the past. However, I will look at this discourse not from a national, but from a much wider, international point of view.

The national approach advocated in this chapter has been inspired mainly by many publications concerning the history by Austrian scholars, e.g., Wodak et al. (1990, 1994), on discourse-historical perspective, and Wodak et al. (1998) on national identity. It follows from these publications that the past and discourse of the past both possess national dimensions. However, they look at the Austrian problems from the "inside" perspective, whereas I would like to take here a clear, outside perspective, which, at the same time, would partially reflect an international point of view (see 2.3). The Polish perspective taken here might be significant since there is much that both Poles and Austrians have had and still have in common, especially as far as the near past is concerned. Poland and Austria were among those countries to first come under the influence of the effects of National Socialism. Obviously, it has to be remembered that Poland was one of the opponents of NS, also being one of its first victims, whereas Austria, despite the "Anschluss," was to a large extent an NS country itself with a strong Nazi movement. However, it can surely be said that the times of NS history left clear traces both in Polish and Austrian societies, shaping their histories for many years after World War II, due to these shared elements.

The interfaces of the shared past have been examined in many studies concerning the influence of the war period on contemporary reality, mainly from the subjective point of view of both nations. However, I will show that the perspective applied in this study can serve as a more objective alternative in approaching the Austrian issue. The purpose of this study is to make Austrians aware of how the situation in their country is perceived by other nations, especially those nations that have always remained in close relation to the Austrian people.

By means of a linguistic analysis of the discourse of the Polish media during the period of "the Austrian crisis" I will demonstrate that among many texts there exists a "new symbolic element." This element is Haider, since, as has been indicated above, Haider himself is the symbol of the past. This element serves as a connotative tool for the recognition of the new stage in the ongoing discourse of the past of one nation (Austria) in the eyes of another (Poland). Thus, my goal will be to show that, first, such a construct as symbolic element exists, and, second, that it can be shown not only as an element of linguistic representations, but also as an element present in collective national memory of the observing (Polish) nation.

In second part of this chapter I will explore some key ideas, which, in my opinion, are crucial for this study. The notions of the past, collective memory, or outside perspective are abstract and purely theoretical ones, and although they may seem too far-fetched from the core of linguistic investigation, I will show that those ideas are applicable to the theoretical account postulated in this chapter. A possible line of application of Teun A. van Dijk's socio-cognitive framework for the perception and interpretation on the international level (although van Dijk's approach originally concerned the intra-social context of ethnic groups, cf. van Dijk 1984) will be shown. The most crucial notion of discourse of the past, as a bridge from abstractness to continuity to linguistic representation, will also be analyzed. Finally, I will sketch general ideas standing behind the concept of symbolic elements, the existence and importance of which I will postulate in this study.

The analysis will be divided into three sections. Trying to anchor "site of production of texts" (van Dijk 1985, Wodak 1996a) within a specific cultural and social context, I will focus on socio-historical aspects of the text sources. The first part of the analysis will present topics and topic groups which could be observed in the Polish media discourse about the Austrian crisis. The second part will aim at showing how topics embedded within the "smaller" discourse (i.e., the discourse about the Austrian crisis) may contribute to thematic groups (aspects) of the continuous and ongoing discourse of the past. The third part will show possible ways of describing the symbolic element within propositions of analyzed discourses. As I will explain below, the second part may be called "horizontal," whereas the third one is "vertical." My analytical standpoint will be based chiefly on the concept of "discourse topic," stemming from Teun A. van Dijk's theory of macro-structures, hence both discourse-analytic, as well as, in a way, text-semantic in nature. Although the theoretical and analytical parts are presented separately, both form a unity, and the second part should be considered as a theoretical background for better understanding of the analyses presented in the third part.

In the methodology applied in this chapter, apart from the discourse-topical analysis which is well known from discourse-analytical approaches, most of the applied methods will be new, since the approach postulated in the study will also be none of the usual. Thus, a question arises as to whether the methodology applied here is adequate for our aims. I will attempt to show that that is, indeed, the case by trying to use various methods and demonstrating that they are not viable for the corroboration of the ideas postulated here. However, I am aware of the fact that there may be some other tools which might turn out to be even more suitable for this type of analysis.

What also needs to be mentioned here are the reasons for applying such a high degree of abstractness for a linguistic study such as this one, which is rather unusual. Linguistic analysis has to deal with a high degree of abstractness if we, the linguists, want to discover things which would not be seen or heard by the recipients of the analyzed texts. Most of the ideas and problems that will be postulated here merge with abstractness (i.e., symbolic elements) and hence "usual" analysis would only allow for the investigation of phenomena that are to be seen at the very surface level of linguistic manifestations. Since we would like to investigate here certain phenomena that have linguistic character, but are deeper and far more abstract than their representations in language, we have to account for much deeper analysis, as well as for a high degree of abstractness in both theoretical background and analytical practice.

Another important point about my analysis should be mentioned here. It goes without saying that if we were to examine how the texts analyzed were, indeed, comprehended within a society, we would have to undertake a much broader study following the line of various concepts of text and discourse comprehension (e.g., van Dijk and Kintsch 1983). Although some cognitive concepts, mainly from the domain of social cognition, will be touched upon in this study, I would, however, like to leave my analysis somewhat "midway through," thus only examining texts and showing active discourses without further insights into ways in which these texts and discourses were comprehended. I believe that the main factor in an analysis of perception and comprehension of media texts among members of such a disseminated perceptive group as one society would require a much larger time scope than the one which passed from the moment of production of the texts until the moment of my analysis. This would also require another perspective as well as somewhat different methodological tools. However, my approach makes my study, in a way, open, and I hope that the topic of the reception of the analyzed texts, in the contexts described here, will be worth an examination from a more distant perspective in the future.

We have to bear in mind that the perspective presented in this study is far from typical. First, I am not using typical tools for the analysis of my data, i.e., media texts. Second, I want to see media texts in a light somewhat different than usual, chiefly by making them a means of "interaction through messages" (Gerbner 1985) on the international level, and by seeing them as a tool for better international understanding. In my perspective, I aim at remaining as objective as possible and I will show a critical attitude only at those points that require my personal interference, for example, my negative attitude to World War II, to the NS past, or any possibility of their return.

Exploring Key Notions

The ideas presented below are ones I believe to be crucial for the perspective implied in this study. First, the past as an abstract concept that is reflected in many phenomena we touch upon. Second, discourse of the past is a continuum which lets the past extend further and thematically projects it into the present and future. Third, the outside perspective is the perspective reflecting the standpoint of the author of this study, that is, the perspective in which we want to see a nation from the outside. Finally, the socio-cognitive model applied here is a possible framework for an analysis of cognitive processes involved in international, mutual perception.

The Past

The vision of the past which I would like to adopt here will be based mainly on the concept of "memory-forgetting-history," as sketched by Paul Ricoeur (cf. Ricoeur 1995), following Kosseleck (1979). Ricoeur claims, that there is a direct "polarisation" between the past and the future, between the "space of experience" and the "horizon of expectations" and, that "all constitutive parts of the triadic construct [MK: memory, forgetting and history] are closely bound with the past, and the past itself gains somewhat doubled meaning in the light of what once was or could have been and what would be impossible without clear links with the future," cf. Ricoeur (1995). I share the point of Ricoeur's in seeing a direct link, or polarization, between the past and the future. My approach will emphasize the problem of the past with respect to the extent in which present events may become constitutive of the past (hence the discussion of discourse of the past below), since they are opening another stage in the certain, discursive order of events. The polarization between past and future gives almost no significance to the present, since "the present as such cannot be considered as a clear point on the ongoing path of time,…it is the dialectic mediation between space of experience and horizon of expectations" (Ricoeur 1995: 24). Thus, present events do not have significance as such, and they gain their meaning only in relation to the future or past. However, since future events cannot be determined, but only predicted, it is only the past that remains as a determinant of everything that occurs. This is the way in which I would like to approach the analyzed texts, so that once they occur, they immediately become constitutive elements of the past. The texts which I will analyse in this study are marked by the past in many possible ways, most obvious of which is the meaning shared by the topics of discourse with the thematic aspects of the ongoing discourse of the past. However, future should not be neglected here either, since, according to Ricoeur's "polarisation," it is of the same importance as the past. Although future itself is not the focus of this study, it is worth mentioning that continuity between what once was and what comes may sometimes be seen in the analyzed texts (e.g., texts about the future Polish EU membership described in the international context, with reference to the European past). Thus, I will postulate that aspects of the future might be seen in the texts too, however, I will still ascribe the predominant role to the past, and hence, I would like to place my study somewhere midway through the scope of mediation as sketched by Ricoeur.

There are certain stages of the past which are discursively ordered on the line of time and which all consist of certain events. There are also certain symbols (e.g., important social actors) which may be crucial for the recognition of some of these stages. We have to bear in mind, however, that I'm not speaking here about the past in general, but about its specific kind. Thus, we should consider the times of National Socialism as the "moment of beginning placed in time"

(Kolakowski 1995), since the type of the past we will consider here will be marked "brown" and will remain negative in character.

Discourse of the Past

Discourse of the past should be understood here in the Foucauldian sense of continuum, hence, as a "continuous voice" (Foucault 1970). The notions of continuum and continuity are the ones which we should see as basic properties of the discourse with which we will be dealing. Discourse of the past remains prominent and the most important one within analyzed texts. Discourse of the past is the discursive order of events that shares its meaning with the events and texts, which are marked by past events. In the case of the texts analyzed below, we will look for propositions with the symbolic element of HAIDER in them. One could ask why it is impossible to speak about the discourse over Haider, if that is the existing element in many texts, and instead why it is the discourse of the past that remains as prominent here. The problem of national perspective (or outside perspective, cf. below) is most crucial here. The national perspective is the one that determines both a creation and perception of certain discourses, and hence, one nation can be seen as one "discourse community." The national perspective in the analyzed texts is the Polish one. The texts were written by members of the Polish society (i.e., journalists), "distributed" among the Polish society (newspaper readers, radio listeners), and their reception also took place among the Polish society. It is also the Polish perspective that makes it impossible to speak about the "discourse about Haider." Haider as an element of discourse (in Polish texts) was first introduced on a larger scale at the moment of the crisis, so there was no discursive continuity that would allow for the existence of such a discourse within this particularly national context. However, such a discourse occurred in the Austrian context, where Haider was part of discursive events since the very beginnings of his political career at the local level in the south of Austria. It continued throughout his various activities at the national level (e.g., the ones analyzed by Reisigl and Wodak 2000), until the moment of his entering the international "scene of perception and recognition," at the moment of "the crisis." The Polish discourse perspective does not allow for the recognition of "discourse about Haider" or any other discursive order with this particular element. We should thus look for an active dis-

Figure 7.1
Stages of Events and Their Link to the Continuum of the
Discourse of the Past

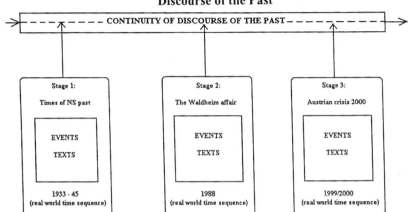

course which will either show the feature of continuity, or which will be "ongoing," thus allowing for the existence of a symbolic element. It is my contention that the only discourse which might remain relevant and be considered as ongoing in this context is the discourse of the past. Calling a discourse ongoing is somewhat tautological, since all discourses are, by definition, continuous in nature. The term "ongoing" is used in this study to signify that the "old" discourse has regained its aspect of continuity by means of new events. Discourse of the past is not being revived by any kind of events, but rather by some specific events marked by the same aspect of the past whose occurrence along with texts will initiate another stage of the discourse. This could be presented as in figure 7.1.

The events in figure 7.1 are precisely those (i.e., "the crisis") which contributed to a re-activation of discourse of the past, thus the continuity (the act of ongoing events) moved again in the direction of the future. It should be stated that besides the aspects discussed, the discourse of the past might have its specific form, i.e., the Austrian past seen from the Polish, outside perspective. The Austrian past seen from the inside, Austrian perspective would have a much more detailed form since the Austrian national perception of the discourse community is able to recognize many more discursive orders of certain stages.

Moreover, it has to be mentioned here that the projection of meaning does not take place only in one direction, hence it is not only the events that are contributing to the overall meaning of the continuum. By means of the shared thematization, stages can project the meaning between themselves, hence, for example, the unclear NS past will be not only contributing to the meaning of the continuum, but also, by way of continuum it will influence another stages. However, this projection may take place only according to the direction of the continuum. Earlier stages can thematically mark the following ones, and hence project their meaning. This follows from principles of continuity of the discourse of the past that abstractly run towards the future, but remain past in character due to the meaning projection of the earlier stages. The thematic projection of a certain period, which due to its important characteristics of meaning, viz. shared topics, marks other periods, divides the ongoing discourse into various dimensions (e.g., the dimension of the past begun with NS times with which we are dealing in this study). Discourse of the past can also be divided into forms which are built along sites of reception of that discourse. Thus, Polish discourse about Austrians will be a different form of discourse of the past than the Austrian discourse about Austrians, due to obvious differences in perceiving the reality and, what I postulate here, due to the existence of certain symbolic elements (which are much more possible for the outside discourse).

The Outside Perspective

As has already been stated, the creation of outside perspective of Austrian problems is one of the basic aims of this chapter.

The inside-outside dialectics to which I refer here, is well known within the scope of linguistics in general, and discourse studies[4] in particular. Within this dialectical framework many linguistic studies concerning national problems have been done. In these studies we can distinguish two major trends.

First of the trends is what might be called an inside perspective, hence, an approach aiming at describing problems of a certain nation from inside, with the researcher being preferably a member of the national group, and a native speaker of its language. The approach focuses on the problems of the inside nation as a group, without using reference to other nations or ways in which they might perceive the inside nation. This method is well known from the ethnographic discourse-historical approach developed by Ruth Wodak and her co-operators within the framework of Critical Discourse Analysis. In the studies within this approach (e.g., Wodak 1996, Wodak and Van Leeuven 1999, Wodak et al. 1990, 1994) it might clearly be seen that Austrian problems (existence of the racist and anti-Semitic discourse in Austria) are described from an inside perspective.

The second trend is the one in which the outside, hence, international perspective is created. Thus, from such an approach, perception of certain nations, or national groups, is described from the standpoint of "others," viz. the outside nations. Out of that framework we have to mention here the study concerning constructions of national self—and foreign images (*Selbst—und Fremdbilder*) of certain nations and their manifestations in discourse (cf. Czyzewski, Gülich, Hausendorf, Kastner 1995). In this study, the above-mentioned images and their discourse manifestations are investigated in the light of the significant social and national changes that took place in Europe in late 1980s and early 1990s (i.e., the unification of Germany, fall of communism in Central and East Europe). As the study shows those social changes profoundly influenced the ways in which certain nations were perceived by other nations.

In this chapter we aim at creating the outside perspective, thus, we will obviously follow here the ideas of the second of above approaches. However, it should be mentioned that the texts and methodology used in the study concerning self- and foreign images were much different than the ones presented and applied here. The study of Czyzewski, Gülich, Hausendorf, and Kastner was based on methodology stemming from ethnographic conversational analysis, and the texts examined were those of the everyday talks.

In our study the media texts, which are different from everyday talks in various respects (i.e., degree of formality, influence of institutional setting, aims of the editorial, etc.), are being examined. Second, the method applied here is that of the discourse-analytic perspective, thus, it will focus mainly on discovering thematic interfaces shared by texts and discourses examined here.

Memory, Collective Memory

One of the basic characteristics of the past is that it is stored and somehow remembered. The past shared by a group of people is stored in "symbols, ways of expression, old buildings, temples and tombs"

(Kolakowski 1995: 49). The collective memory of a nation[5] (or national memory), lets the nation store both the past in general, as well as its own past. Kolakowski's vision finds memory as the constitutive factor in determining any continuity.[6] Collective memory of a certain nation allows for continuity of remembering certain crucial events which would reinforce its collective identity, since "no nation can exist without being conscious of the fact that its existence is the continuity of existence in the past" (Kolakowski 1995: 49). Thus, events crucial for a certain nation would be stored in its collective memory. However, those events do not have to be nation-specific, they can also be ones which were much more significant to other nations, or were generally significant in international terms. The significance of those shared events rises, as long as they are able to bring something important of "ourselves," i.e., of each of the sharing nations, to collective identity. In my opinion the most important are those events that could be shared by two (or more) nations because then they would reinforce the collective identities of each of those nations, they would create a shared past of those nations, as well as help to understand troublesome moments of their common past. However, a problem arises if we ask how much we (as one nation) can remember about events that did not concern us in a direct way. Paul Ricoeur claims: "memory is selective...memory without any gaps would be too much of a burden" (Ricoeur 1995: 25). That is also why I would postulate that nations cannot remember everything about their own past, thus even less about the past of other nations. There has to be some collectively shared way of storing the memory about certain events in the entities much smaller than whole texts, or let us say, than descriptions of events. Certain symbols might come as solutions to this problem, since "past is being stored in various symbols" (Kolakowski 1995: 49). I would also add here in regard to the collective view of the past that it is known by everyone that the elements of the past are not perceived in the same way by everyone and that this perception may differ even among members of one nation (*es gibt warscheinlich mehrere, mögliche Vergangenheiten*, Wodak et al. 1994: 12). That is why we can only hypothetically assume here that there would be no differentiation, at least initially, within Polish memory with regard to collective attitudes towards Austrians.

The Socio-Cognitive Model

Van Dijk's socio-cognitive model (van Dijk 1984) gives primary importance to group schemata as a "specific form of attitude structures" (p.33). However, attitudes are not only kinds of evaluation about things or events, but they are "complex, organised memory systems" (p.33). This immediately brings to mind our previously sketched ideas concerning collective memory, which, in this respect, could be conjoined with "collective" attitudes. We can see collective memory of one nation not only as the one storing information about itself, but also storing stereotypical information about attitudes towards other nations. According to van Dijk, attitudes consist of "hierarchical cluster of social beliefs (p.33)," that is, "beliefs about social objects, such as other persons, groups, social structures and social phenomena" (p.33). The beliefs are further divided into epistemic, thus "factual beliefs shared by groups" (p.33) and evaluative ones. Attitudes are also seen as general and abstract in nature because "beliefs they organise are also general" (p.33). Attitudes, as the ones with a "social basis" (p.34) are contrary in their nature to models (or situation models) that are strictly subjective, personal, and cannot be applied to collective entities such as groups or societies. What is then the foundation of attitudes is their social nature, and the fact that "people would form attitudes only if they are useful for their social life, that is, for the interpretation of social events or for participation in interaction" (p.33). Hence, according to van Dijk, that point of view depends entirely on eventual, future interaction. What can be postulated here is that group schemata will still be the process of creation even with respect to past events, with respect to such elements of the past that were common to both nations. This may be considered an "abstract interaction," which will be taking place at the level of national collective memories of both nations, and not necessarily at the level of members of particular nations. This also emphasizes, first, what has already been said about polarization between the past and the future (cf. above), and, second, what the reasons for selecting "non-interactive" texts for the investigation here were.

In what follows, I would like to move away from this intra-societal perspective, and try to apply the concepts of attitudes and schemas to whole societies or nations. Although nation has already been described in the context of group schemata (cf. Wodak et al. 1990), it is viewed in the same light as in van Dijk's original, i.e., with respect to ethnic minorities. Thus, I would like to see nations and societies as van Dijk saw groups because I believe that his theory about group schemas and attitudes formation is applicable to any collective body, providing that there is a process of perception and interpretation of actions of one group by the other group. Hence, Polish national attitudes towards Austrians may be described in the framework of group schemata, since the Polish nation certainly shares certain beliefs about the Austrian nation as a whole. In an attempt to remain objective, I will tackle only "factual-epistemic" Polish beliefs, since there will be no evaluative elements of beliefs to be dealt with here, assuming that there was no intention among the quoted authors of socially received texts to evaluate Austria and put it in a bad light. However, a problem arises when we consider the fact that van Dijk's models were basically interactive in nature, assuming that models and frames are created mostly in the "ingroup"–"outgroup" participant situation. We deal here with attitudes and groups, but there is no direct interaction between participants of both national groups, since the only mediation that takes place occurs by means of texts, which are only interactive at the level of intercultural communication. Thus, distant or outside perspective should also be taken into consideration when we speak about attitude creation. It has to be considered here that the medium which carries the texts analyzed here might be adding evaluative elements in their presentation, and hence not allowing for the formation of factual-epistemic, but instead, only evaluative attitudes. Thus, we can apply this model only if we theoretically assume that medium, viz. mass media: press and radio, has not deformed information about other nations' events. However, the medium may also be seen from a more positive point of view. It might demonstrate that some abstract contact between the two nations still exists, as long as one of them wants to know something about the other. This abstract contact may also be reinforcing links between the two nations which stem from elements of the shared past.

The notion of "schema transfer"(van Dijk 1984:24) or "the acquisition process for new attitude schemata (ibid.)" applied to this study shows that certain dangerous socio-cognitive processes may take place at the moment of opening a new stage of discourse of the past. If, in the texts received and interpreted by one nation (in this case Polish), there is too much reference to the past with its load of negative elements, the whole schema which exists among the Polish society and concerns the negative past, might be transferred to the newly created attitudes concerning Austria, and change the overall perception of the Austrian problems in the eyes of the Polish society, with an obvious and collectively undeserved harm to the Austrians.

Symbolic Elements

Symbolic figures, be they significant social actors or who/whatever else, may serve in a certain nation as a kind of general "entry" to sub-branches of memory about more specific groups of events, sets of attitudes which would be associated with the symbol. In this respect, we can see symbols metaphorically, as a kind of door which might be opened, whenever another stage of discursively ordered events is or needs to be opened. The tool that comes to mind, and which could serve as such a "door to memory" could be the one of symbolic element.[7] Symbolic elements may certainly be seen as factors active in collective memories of various nations. These are symbols that work as triggers evoking certain memories, hence also attitudes, stored by the nation, and concerning events of its own or other nations' past. Symbolic elements are linguistically represented mostly as lexical items (e.g., HITLER), which are sometimes substituted with definite descriptions, e.g., "leader of Nazi Germans," "initiator of World War II," etc. Those lexical items are embedded within propositions that state a certain kind of attitude (be it epistemic-factual or evaluative), thus demonstrating that "attitudes are represented as propositional structures" (van Dijk 1984: 35). The basic condition for an occurrence of symbolic elements originates from discourse. Topics of discourse within which a proposition is embedded have to be interfaced with aspects (abstract thematic units larger than text topics) of a continuous discourse (e.g., ongoing discourse of the past). This creates semantic agreement among a symbolic element, a proposition, the macro-structure of the text and the ongoing discourse, hence allowing the symbolic element to become a representation of social memory or any of its representations, for example, attitudes (cf. below).

Social attitudes may easily be detected among linguistic forms of everyday speech, for example, sayings, which are loaded with certain set of beliefs about an event, person, etc. In such linguistic constructions, symbolic elements, along with their connotative load, may also

Figure 7.2
Symbolic Element(s) in a Proposition

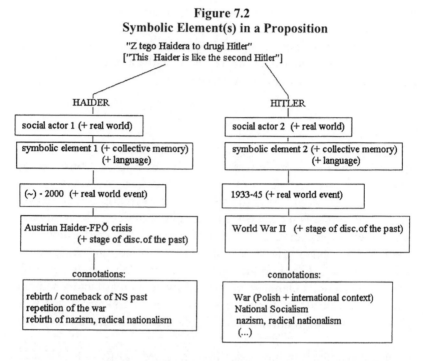

"Z tego Haidera to drugi Hitler"
["This Haider is like the second Hitler"]

HAIDER

social actor 1 (+ real world)

symbolic element 1 (+ collective memory)
(+ language)

(~) - 2000 (+ real world event)

Austrian Haider-FPÖ crisis
(+ stage of disc.of the past)

connotations:

rebirth / comeback of NS past
repetition of the war
rebirth of nazism, radical nationalism

HITLER

social actor 2 (+ real world)

symbolic element 2 (+ collective memory)
(+ language)

1933-45 (+ real world event)

World War II (+ stage of disc.of the past)

connotations:

War (Polish + international context)
National Socialism
nazism, radical nationalism
(...)

be seen pretty clearly. This type of analysis is exemplified below, in an analysis of the Polish saying (taken from the *CBOS* "Omnibus" poll, February 18–22, 2000, cf.1) "Z tego Haidera to drugi Hitler" ("This Haider is like the second Hitler"). In this proposition certain symbolic elements (e.g., lexical items: HAIDER, HITLER) stand as representatives for whole stages of events, which were stored within collective memory by use of those symbols. Parallel to that, those symbols stand for particular periods of the discourse of the past. A graphic representation of this proposition is suggested in figure 7.2.

The existence of symbolic elements, which stems from group schemata and attitudes, may also be demonstrated in the linguistic characteristics of everyday speech of various speech communities , thus making our concept much more universal in nature. Let us consider the German saying that arose in the context of the Austrian case and which can be heard in Germany in talks concerning the Austrian situation: "Wir brauchen ja nicht noch einen Österreicher" ("We do not need, though, another Austrian"). Although this time the result of the evaluative attitude (prejudice) is much clearer, the existence of the symbolic element "ÖSTERREICHER" ("Austrian") is still seen. In this example the symbolic element that we indicated as a possibility before is methonimically substituted. We can also assume that the structure of the analysis of this proposition would be exactly the same as above (figure 7.1), since there are actually two elements ("noch einen" ("another one"), the second is only presupposed).

A problem arises if we try to find symbolic elements in linguistic forms other than the ones analyzed here, i.e., other than expressions coming from everyday speech. There is one basic condition: linguistic forms in which symbolic elements can be found have to be ones that show a direct link to social reality, mostly by means of describing and reflecting common, social attitudes and group schemata shared by the society. Media texts (cf. below), produced by members of a society (journalists), describing social reality and consumed by the society (readers, listeners) will, thus, also be the ones allowing for the existence of symbolic elements, since they would directly constitute a reflection of group schemata and attitudes towards members of a given society and towards other societies.

Analytical Approach

In my analysis I will try to show analyzed discourses from a constructive point of view, thus, attempting to analyze them from the point of view of those units of discourse which may further be "functionally used, understood and analyzed as elements of larger ones" (van Dijk 1997: 7). The analysis will reveal that there are, indeed, numerous levels of discourse, both in the linguistic and abstract sense. Joining the gap between abstractness and concrete texts will be discourse topics (in the macro-, and super-structural sense, cf. mainly van Dijk 1984, also van Dijk 1977, 1980). Topics will be thus analyzed as the most significant properties of discourse, following the idea that "the most obvious property of discourse is its overall meaning or topic" (van Dijk et al. 1997: 149). Hence meaning, like discourse, should be understood here in a twofold way. First, meaning will be seen as the property of texts, with the inference being based on macropropositional properties of discourses. Second, it should be understood as an abstract term, showing properties of meaning which are shared within the international, sociocultural perception of the continuous discourse. Although the scope of this study does not allow me to investigate all issues concerning intercultural perception, I hope that the present analysis will contribute to a better understanding of this discipline.

Another approach included here is studying discourse as "a constitutive part of its local and global, social and cultural contexts" (van Dijk 1997: 2) As we will see below, our texts are relevant to this type of analysis in that they are anchored to social, cultural, and historical conditions of the community from which they come.

The present analysis can be seen as having many possible uses. An exploration of discourse about the Austrian crisis can surely be treated as a discourse-analytic overview of the reception of the Austrian crisis in the Polish media. It is more than obvious that the Polish perspective is just one of many possible views outside Austria, but its role in creating an objective view may be quite significant. An analysis concerning both discourse of the past and the role of symbolic elements might serve as one of the tools for looking at the Polish perception of Austrian problems in the context of ideas such as, for example, the past.

Description of the News Sources

Gazeta Wyborcza (*GW*) is a daily newspaper, which was created just before the first free elections in Poland, early in the year 1989. Today it is the most widely read Polish newspaper with over 40 percent of all Polish readers. It is also worth mentioning that since the paper has a liberal profile and deals extensively with international problems, its readership includes well-educated and well-to-do people (mainly secondary school and university graduates). Moreover, the paper is considered to be relatively objective.

GW was created and supported by the intellectual circles of the Solidarity movement. However, in the course of time, most of those intellectuals, presenting too much of a pro-capitalist and liberal way of thinking left the Solidarity (which still remains a trade union), and created their own party *UW* (Freedom Party), which is now the party being closely identified with *GW*. Both the newspaper and *UW* are of the same liberal and pro-European orientation (many *UW* members are also working for the paper). The intellectual character of the paper seems to be crucial here, especially in the context of the past, since most of the above-mentioned intellectuals were and still are closely bound to Polish intellectual traditions of the so-called "Second Republic" (Poland in the years 1918–39). That is also the reason why *GW* puts so much emphasis on the problems of the past, especially on the issues concerning World War II. Almost in every weekend edition the paper deals with issues concerning the past, be it the past of Europe, Poland, or ethnic minorities. In the last category, especially, the Jewish people are included, since they were also members of the Polish national past. The opinion that the paper is sometimes too concerned with the past is relatively common, but in response to this critique *GW* always emphasizes the importance of understanding and remembering the past for the better and wiser creation of a Polish future, without losing our identity. *GW* also puts much emphasis on the European problems, very often linking them with and describing them in a historical context. Europe and the EU are, thus, almost the most common issues described in the newspaper, especially from the perspective of the Polish bid for EU membership.

BBC Polish Section radio stems from similar intellectual traditions as *GW*, and its links with Polish "Second Republic" intellectuals are even closer and clearer than those of the newspaper. The radio, which is a part of the BBC World Service, was created back in 1939, mostly by Polish intellectuals coming to Great Britain as war emigrants. The radio's main goal was to provide Polish people in the occupied country, and later in the country governed by communists, objective information concerning events from all over the world. The status of the radio has always been high due to its contacts with great Polish intellectuals such as writers (e.g., G. Herling-Grudzinski, W. Gombrowicz, C. Milosz) and scholars (e.g., L. Kolakowski). For the renowned intellectuals it was also the only possibility "to come back to the country by means of radio waves during the time when communist censorship condemned them to non-existence" (Smolar 1999: 39). However, nowadays, more than ten years after media censorship was abolished, the BBC has lost part of its popularity as the interests of radio listeners have turned to various kinds of commercial stations. The BBC Polish Section is no longer broadcast independently, its programs being transmitted by numerous, regional radio-stations in Poland. Nevertheless, the station "is still known to be a balanced and reliable source of information" (Smolar 1999), and, especially in the eyes of intellectual circles, it still plays a crucial role in creating opinions, based on objective views about facts and events.

Both sources might be considered as representing pretty much the same way of thinking, and in this light, they also represent a similar view on issues concerning the past (e.g., the times of World War II), and they share the same vision of the Polish future (free market, joining the EU). This is the kind of mediation, or polarization that I will look for in the texts coming from the two sources. I intend to analyze texts that will show clearly the importance of the past and its possible effects for the future, and hence, they will demonstrate discursive continuity of both the past and discourse of the past. That is why my description of the sources, as the ones shaping form and content of texts according to the traditions from which they come, plays an important role in my analysis. Consequently, if both *GW*, and the *BBC Polish Section* present a high level of historical and international awareness, it can be assumed that their publications and broadcasts concerning the "Austrian crisis," which will be examined below, stem from an analogous context and mood, and thus represent an analogous orientation.

The corpus was collected in January and February 2000, and altogether it consists of over twenty press reports (of various forms) and almost thirty radio broadcasts (including ten longer broadcasts and over twenty short reports). The two-month period of my collecting the corpus was the time-span in which the number of broadcasts and articles concerning Austria was especially high. After that time, roughly speaking about the end of February, the number of editorials concerning Austria suddenly dropped, and practically since the beginning of March there was little to be heard or read about Austria and its problems (which was parallel to the lack of any events that would put Austria once again in the international limelight).

I am aware of the fact that genre differences among the analyzed texts had an impact both on their form and content. I am also aware of the totality of textual strategies and properties (e.g., intertextuality,) which can clearly be seen among the texts. However, since the approach taken in this study differs markedly from a text-analytic one focusing on, e.g., text-properties,[8] these undoubtedly highly interesting issues will be ignored here as being beyond the scope of my analysis.

Exploring the Topics of "Discourse about the Austrian Crisis"

What we should understand as the discourse about the Austrian crisis is the totality of texts produced by the Polish media during the time of the crisis. These included various types of discourse about the Austrians and about numerous issues that were brought up in the descriptions of the Austrian situation in early 2000. We do not mean here all Polish media sources, but following the inductive way of generalization, we will consider the discourse of the sources analyzed below as representative of most of the Polish "thinking" (i.e., upmarket) media.

We will try to identify most prevalent topics of the discourse about the Austrian crisis, by trying to find sequences of sentences, or propositions, that share the same topics. Looking at the topics from our media discourses, we are able to group them under three larger categories: Austria, international affairs, and Haider. Below we will try to explore these topic groups, following each of the topics by examples of propositions (which also might be called here sentences or excerpts) taken from the texts. It is worth noting that the exemplified sentences have been selected according to two types of characteristics. First, their meaning should make them constitutive of certain topics. Second, they should include the lexical item HAIDER (or any of its substitutions, e.g., JÖRG[9]), which will be useful in the third part of our analysis exploring the notion of symbolic element.

Discourse about the Austrian Crisis

The topics of the discourse about the Austrian crisis are indicated as follows. Since many of them have much in common they will be joined in larger thematic groups called topic groups. For reasons of brevity, the corpus of the Polish texts analyzed below will be given in my English translation.

Topic Group 1: Austria

Topic 1: Support for Haider/FPÖ in Austria

1. "According to 60 percent of (Austrian) citizens, it was a great mistake of President Klestil's to insist on creating a minority government of the Social Democrats, since the Christian Democrats and HAIDER's party have a majority in the Parliament."— "Chcemy Haidera" ("We Want Haider") *GW*, 28 January 2000, p. 9

2. "And this year the occasion to celebrate seems to be pretty unique since JÖRG's advocates have many reasons to be happy: soon they will be celebrating the first anniversary of his (MK: Haider's) taking over the power in Carynthia, and two days ago, the government with members of his party was sworn in." –"Bal u Haidera" ("A Ball at Haider's") *GW*, 7 February 2000, p. 5

3. "We can conclude from last official polls that 70 percent of Austrian society is for this coalition, and supports HAIDER."— BBC "Reflektorem po swiecie" ("Spotlight on the World")[10] *BBC Polish Section*, 4 February 2000

Topic 2: Opposition against Haider/FPÖ in Austria

4. "The new government of the populists and Christian Democrats was harshly criticised yesterday by both Social Democrats and the Green Party members from the opposition, as well as the Trade Unions and artists, who are afraid of Jörg HAIDER's censorious influence."—"Oceniajcie po czynach" ("Assess According to Actions") *GW*, 5–6 February 2000, p. 9

5. "Young Austrians say that HAIDER took advantage of xenophobia, they also talk about/mention the opposition to his program."—BBC "Reflektorem po swiecie" ("Spotlight on the World") *BBC Polish Section*, 4 February 2000

Topic 3: Austrian Politics/New Austrian Government

6. "Although Chancellor Schüssel excludes the possibility of eventually allowing the Freedom Party leader to take part in the government, the vice-chancellor's seat as well as five other ministerial offices will be taken by HAIDER's people...who, contrary to what HAIDER promised, will be no experts, but loyal party comrades."—BBC "Reflektorem po swiecie" ("Spotlight on the World") *BBC Polish Section*, 4 February 2000

Topic 4: Austrian Past is Responsible for Current Situation

7. "The episode of HAIDER, if it is really just an episode, is in fact a continuity of the Austrian schizophrenia which started with the Anschluss and Hitler, followed by a long hibernation broken by the Waldheim's farce, and now revived by opening

the door to power in Vienna for the extreme right."—
"Schizofrenia" ("Schizophrenia") *GW*, 28 January 2000, p. 9

8. "Due to boredom and its deeply rooted racism Austria faces the
Haider problem now."—"Emocje opadaja" ("Emotions are subsiding") *GW*, 10 February 2000, p. 6

The topics of this first thematic group show clearly that both the
events of the Austrian crisis, as well as social actors such as Haider,
are subject to large social interest. Both Haider and his party are
perceived in quite contradictory ways in Austria, since attitudes vary
from support to very strong opposition. We see the fact that the Austrian past is viewed as being, to a large extent, responsible for the
current problems, while we also see the eventual significance that
current problems may have for Austrian future.

Topic Group 2: Haider/FPÖ

Topic 1: Haider's Influence on Austrian Politics

9. "And although under international pressure HAIDER will not
get into the government, he will be still guiding it from the
most privileged position: he will stay in opposition while having his own people in the government."—"Widma na salonach"
("Phantoms in the Rooms") *GW*, 5–6 February 2000, p. 12

Topic 2: Haider's/FPÖ's Roots in NS Past

10. "HAIDER's father was one of the first Nazi activists in town,
his mother was an active member of a female fascist movement, quite similar were the credentials of the teacher of
HAIDER junior."—BBC "Reflektorem po swiecie" ("Spotlight
on the World") *BBC Polish Section,* 4 February 2000

11. "In the year of 1963 a son of the Nazis from Carynthia, Jörg
HAIDER, was only 13 and brought up in the spirit of
Hitlerjugend. He could not have been active anywhere else but
in the FPÖ."—"Widma na salonach" ("Phantoms in the
Rooms") *GW*, 5–6 February 2000, p. 12

12. "But as regards HAIDER, we are talking here about the greatest
crime that has ever been committed against another nation,
against children, women and old people, who were killed not
for what they had done, but because of their ethnic ancestry."—

BBC "Reflektorem po swiecie" ("Spotlight on the World") *BBC Polish Section,* 4 February 2000

Topic 3: Haider's/FPÖ's Xenophobia and Nationalism

13. "It is the racist and xenophobic elements of HAIDER's policy that he (MK: the writer Doron Rabinovici) is mostly afraid of."—"Emocje opadaja" ("Emotions are Subsiding ") *GW,* 10 February 2000, p. 6
14. "Jörg HAIDER was leading his campaign under xenophobic slogans, he was talking about the necessity of stopping 'foreignization of Austria,' which is a Nazi term."—"Haider budzi Unie" ("Haider Wakes Up the EU") *GW,* 9 February 2000, p. 9
15. "Austrian children cannot learn their native language properly because the number of foreign children at schools is too high— said Haider to the *Hürriyet* newspaper."—"Lodowaty bojkot" ("Ice-Cold Boycott") *GW,* 12–13 February 2000, p.7

Topic 4: Haider as a Controversial Speaker, Constantly Changing IIis Opinions

16. "The world has just noticed another of HAIDER's controversial statement, i.e., that Churchill had been one of Europe's greatest criminals."—"Sluchali, ale nie posluchali" ("They listened, but they did not follow") *GW,* 15 February 2000, p. 7

"And we remember what HAIDER used to say, so we could ask the following question: Is what HAIDER is saying today his new strategy, what he has not yet proved, is it a kind of tactics (?)"—BBC "Reflektorem po swiecie" ("Spotlight on the World") *BBC Polish Section* ,4 February 2000

The sizeable thematic group on Haider results from the attempts of the Polish media to present the Haider problem from many possible angles, mostly, however, with a focus on the international significance of this phenomenon. Haider and his party are seen here as significant phenomena of both Austrian social and political reality, as well as an element significant for international affairs.

Topic Group 3: International Affairs

Topic 1: International Opposition against Haider and against the FPÖ's Part in the Austrian Government

"Yesterday in a couple of European cities, including Vienna, Berlin and Paris, HAIDER's opponents continued their street-protests against Freedom Party's (MK: FPÖ's) coming into the Austrian government."— "Spusccie z tonu" ("Ease the Tension") *GW*, 7 February 2000, p.7
"A suggestion which was enforced by the French, Belgian and Italian Christian-Democrats to expel Austrian People's Party (MK: ÖVP) from the EPP, for allowing the populist and extremist Jörg Haider's party to come into power in Vienna, is to be voted on April the sixth."— "Glosowanie w kwietniu" ["To Be Voted in April"] *GW*, 11 February 2000, p. 6
"And then again, during the EU summit in Helsinki he (MK: Chirac) was warning Wolfgang Schüssel, then Austrian foreign minister, against the union of his Conservatists, ÖVP, with FPÖ which is openly xenophobic and suspiciously revisionist, mostly due to all HAIDER's statements about the Third Reich."—"Chirac kontra Haider" ("Chirac against Haider") *GW*, 16 February 2000, p. 6
"After the new, coalition government had been created in Austria, the Czech foreign ministry expressed its anxiety, bearing in mind widely known, controversial statements of Jörg HAIDER, including his criticisms of the EU and the Czech Republic, which he spared no use of during the election campaign."—"My, Czesi mamy prawo sie obawiac" ["We, the Czechs, We Have Reasons To Be Afraid"] *GW*, 17 February 2000, p. 7

Topic 2: Opposition against Haider and against the FPÖ's part in the Austrian Government in the Context of the European Union

"This week the European Council expressed its concern about the election successes of extremists movements, having in mind also HAIDER's party."—"Bede gwarantem" ("I Will Be a Guarantee") *GW*, 28 January 2000, p. 9
"The European Parliament warned Vienna about the consequences of forming a government with Jörg HAIDER's party (the violation of rudimentary EU rules, e.g., human rights) which would result in

Austria's suspension as an EU member."—"Ekstremy nie chcemy" ("We Want No Extreme") *GW*, 4 February 2000, p. 8

Topic 3: Opposition against Haider and against the FPÖ's part in the Austrian Government in the Context of the Expansion of the EU

"And here I would like to come back to Austria, namely HAIDER. He is a politician, who is against *the expansion* (MK: of the EU), that is why I believe that the Polish government is carefully following everything that happens in Austria, since that might be of crucial importance to our membership, this change of government in Austria."—BBC "Reflektorem po swiecie" ("Spotlight on the World") *BBC Polish Section,* 3 February 2000

Topic 4: The Opposition of the Internatoinal Jewish Community to Haider and the FPÖ

"The management of the Holocaust Centre in Montreal did not allow Jörg HAIDER, the leader of the Austrian populist movcmcnt, to visit its (MK: The Centre's) museum. '–We advised the management not to agree to the request of this cynic manipulator, who brings the heritage of Hitler wherever he (MK: Haider) goes' said Moshe Ronen, President of the Canadian Jewish Congress."—
"Ani muzeum, ani wesele" ("Neither a Museum, nor a Wedding") *GW*, 18 February 2000, p. 11

The third and largest thematic group is that of international affairs. The size of this group emphasizes once again what we said about the properties of our sources (cf.3.1), and the attention they pay to international affairs. It is interesting that out of the numerous topics presented in this third group, only one concerns Poland, i.e., future Polish EU membership. However, the data quoted above do not clearly reflect the heated discussions going on both in the Polish media and in everyday conversations about the Austrian problems and about Haider himself. What Polish people were mostly interested in (which I believe is quite understandable) was whether all the turmoil caused by Haider, the FPÖ, and the new Austrian government would not slow down the process of the EU's expansion, which is what Poland has been looking forward to for a very long time now.

Exploring Another Stage of Discourse of the Past

Discourse of the past should be seen from our analytic perspective as a set of large, social meanings built up in the sequence of time, the sequence being that which allows for their anchorage to the past. Thus, as we said before, meanings from particular discourses, or stages of events, will always be bringing new meaning to this always open and constructing discourse, but only if they will be bound thematically to the continuous, overall meaning of that discourse. One cannot claim that discourse of the past has any particular beginning; perhaps the only possible moment of the beginning of this discourse was the first occurrence of any texts, which were interwoven within various stages of human history. However, since there are as many perspectives of the past as there are sites of its perception (for example, nations or societies) the discourse of the past might be entering various dimensions. Its stages can be ordered according to events that were crucial for "recent history," or what sometimes might be called the immediate past. The dimension of the past and discourse of the past, which we have been touching upon in this study, has been one of the negative type, and we have claimed that this particular dimension has its opening point at the stage that might discursively be termed as NS past or, historically, as times of the NS past and World War II. This particular stage, although it is also one of many stages in the general discourse of the past, became prominent because of the influence it had on later stages.

In previous parts of this chapter we have called this section a horizontal analysis. Thus, this analysis will show how topics of texts analyzed above, texts embedded within certain stage of events, can contribute to the overall meaning of discourse of the past. The horizontal dimension follows from the fact that discourse of the past is a continuum, and thus can be placed on a time axis towards the future in the horizontal dimension (cf. above). We also have to account for the above-mentioned aspects of the discourse of the past. [Aspects or thematic aspect are therefore groups of meaning which are parts of continuous discourse.] The thematic aspects might be understood in semantic analyses as groups of meaning. The meaning of aspects is the joint of meanings of discourses, hence topics, which are contributing to the overall meaning of discourse of the past. Thematic aspects can also be seen as larger, abstract, semantic categories under which social meanings, hence meanings in a way adopted from various texts, can be grouped. We still have to bear in mind that discourse of the past has various forms that depend on the receptive standpoint, the standpoint of a certain culture, society, or nation. Since thematic aspects of the ongoing discourse are abstract entities, the division into thematic aspects can also take place by means of inference and inductive thinking, which must be based on the analysis of thematic units, viz. topics, of texts. These texts may come from various stages of continuous discourse. Let us describe briefly those thematic aspects of discourse of the past to which the texts analyzed above have contributed.

- *NS Past*: this is a thematic aspect of discourse of the past which came into existence with the events and texts of the times of the National Socialism Past (see 2.2). The topics subordinated under this thematic aspect will reflect the influence of the NS Past on contemporary reality (e.g., social phenomena: xenophobia and racism of the FPÖ)
- *Europe/Austria*: this thematic aspect has been split into two areas, since all meanings concerning Austria will be contributing to the overall ongoing thematic aspect of Europe (Austrian discourse as one of the parts of discourse about Europe). The topics within this aspect will show how elements of the past in a particular Austrian context can influence Austrian reality (e.g., it is the Austrian, and not any other nation's, past that influences Austrian reality)

The proposed division may seem somewhat vague, but we should bear in mind that since we are speaking here about abstract entities, our approach cannot escape a certain degree of tentativeness and subjectivity.

Let us sketch the topics of texts embedded in the discourse about the Austrian crisis of 2000 in light of their links to the discourse of the past:

Looking closer at certain topics, in order to better understand why they are subsumed under particular thematic aspects, we can take one of the topics from each aspect and show the way of thinking that led us to a given generalization. Topic 4 of topic group 3, "Opposition of international Jewish community against Haider," was placed under the thematic aspect of the NS past, because we can claim that there probably would not have been any opposition of the Jewish people and other ethnic groups to the xenophobic and nationalist groups if the Jewish people and ethnic minorities had not suffered so much during times of the NS past, which were marked by such social attitudes. Topic 1 from topic group 1 "Support for Haider/FPÖ in Austria" can

Figure 7.3
Topics of Texts in Their Contributions to Thematic Aspects of
Discourse of the Past

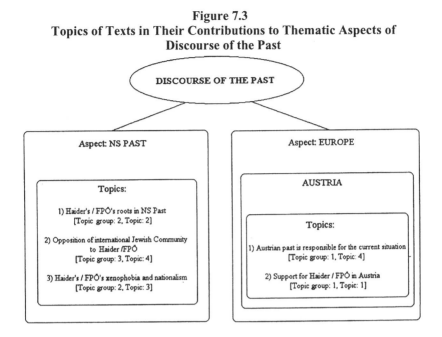

be placed in the thematic aspect, "Austria," because we can also infer that the support for Haider and the FPÖ is the effect of the racist and nationalist tendencies still existent (fortunately, to a certain extent only) among Austrian society.

Exploring the Symbolic Element

As has already been mentioned in the first part of this analysis, the propositions chosen as representative of certain topics were supposed to fulfil two requirements, first by being thematically bound to the topic and, second, by including in them the lexical item HAIDER. This was a preliminary step necessary for the analytic approach proposed in this section where we will attempt to create a "model semantic field" built around a lexical item ("symbolic element": SE). Thus, this semantic field would be the sum total of possible connotations that are or could be related to SE. These connotations will be created in the comprehensive process of the texts (and propositions within). The connotations of SE will be activated when a lexical item standing for SE is identified within the propositions.

We may also put forth a general hypothesis that the created connotations will be, to a large extent, similar to the ones that could have been stored in the collective memory of outside-group members (Poles).

First, however, we should explain the way in which we understand certain notions. In this part of the chapter, we will go somewhat deeper into our analysis, i.e., to the level of propositions, and by getting more "local semantic" (van Dijk et al. 1997), we will attempt to draw certain general conclusions from the analysis of certain properties of propositions. The term "proposition" should be understood in our approach as "meaning of declarative sentence" (van Dijk and Kintsch 1983) and should be taken as the joining of all loads of meaning brought to the propositions by every word. It is unusual to focus on words here since normally a sentence is considered the basic constitutive part of discourse (see van Dijk 1977, 1980). However, since we have already shown how meanings can be joined in an abstract sense, we can also infer that the same phenomenon of "building up the meaning" takes place from the lowest possible units of discourse (following the line: lexical item—proposition–sequence of proposition—topic—...). The reason to sketch out the above notions is to describe briefly our idea and understanding of "local meaning," on which we will base our further analysis.

Since the propositions have already been discussed previously, we will not repeat them here, and we will only try to sketch the field of possible connotations built around SE.

We can see in figure 7.4 that connotations grouped in the semantic field around the SE very much order the field itself since this field can further be divided into smaller ones, which would still carry a relatively heavy connotative load. Thus, the connotations in figure 7.4 are not grouped at random, but are placed in groups that would allow for creating smaller semantic fields.

We should once again mention that we are dealing here with a hypothetical inference, and the connotations following will be ones coming from the propositions of particular texts. We can thus generalize that this inference might be a model one for exploring our notion of symbolic element. Surely, the sketched connotations are only a fraction of all the possible connotations of the symbolic element, which is as broad in its semantic load as the HAIDER element is.

Going back to what we said before about the idea of symbolic elements, most important for us will be those connotations that bring

Figure 7.4
Connotations of Symbolic Element HAIDER Inferred
from Propositions

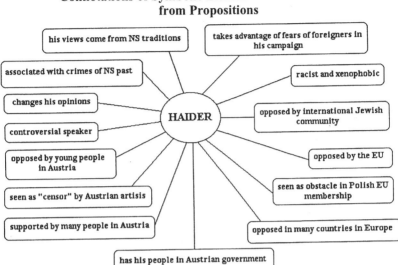

elements of the past with them. According to our division of the thematic aspects of the discourse of the past, there would be six such connotations within the sketched model. The problem remains as to how representative media texts are for the reflection of collective memory and the way of thinking of representatives of certain groups, such as nations. We have already shown that one of the most reliable sources of such elements is everyday discourse, e.g., sayings. However, in this study we are dealing with media texts as also representative of the Polish way of thinking. Thus, if we assume that the authors and readers/listeners of the texts were Polish, we can conclude that all connotative processes have been the same as in the case of sayings.

It should be emphasized again that the notion of symbolic element is purely hypothetical and we do not have at our disposal any analytical tool to tackle it. The only inference following from the poll on Austria (cf.1) and from a large connotative load carried by the element of Haider is that it may be claimed to exist within the Polish collective perception and, possibly also in Polish collective memory.

Conclusions

As we have mentioned before, the ideas postulated and discussed in this study constitute a somewhat new look at the problems and phenomena of our national and international reality. The ideas presented in this study will certainly have to be revisited and reshaped. We have been operating here on a relatively abstract level and dealing with a great many ideas that each of us, be it linguist, sociologist, or philosopher, perceives in his/her own subjective way. Moreover, many social concepts dealt with here, e.g., memory or identity, are hard to explain on an individual level, not to mention collective terms.

Symbolic elements are entities undoubtedly present in both our individual and collective memories. The only problem that remains is how we can approach the analysis of those elements from a linguistic, social, or other perspective in order to investigate them thoroughly and to show solid evidence for their development and existence. It is my contention that media, which are social in nature, certainly reflect the memories and ideas of the societies from which they come.

The stage in which the symbolic element HAIDER came to existence has not yet ended, and we cannot now predict the future course of events. This is why one must bear in mind that the stage of events which we have been discussing here, hence the one which eventually would be ascribed as belonging to the past, is not yet completed and still remains open. We cannot project now what social actors will say or do in the future, we cannot predict much about the events to come. Nations live close to one another and should view one another in the best light. Thus, we can only regret that there are still elements in our memory which are negative and still revive the negative past, although they should have been long ago reconciled so no one could or would need to return to them again.

Notes

1.   The answers in the analysis of the poll were grouped in the same way as presented here. These are the first three groups of answers to appear out of twelve that were presented. The question was one of many asked in that poll. The first number (e.g., 44 percent in answer group 1) shows how large a percentage of respondents of the investigated representative group answered in such and such way, whereas the second (e.g., 14 percent in answer group 1) shows how many of the foreseen

percentage of the Polish people would answer that way if the inference would be generalized.

2. The CBOS (The Centre for the Analysis of Public Opinion) Omnibus Poll was conducted between February 18, 22, 2000, under the auspices of KIE ([the governmental] "Committee for the European Integration").

3. All translations from Polish in this chapter are mine.

4. The inside-outside perspective is known, for example, from the critical-analytic approach to racism and ideology: creating ingroup "we" vs. outgroup "them," see e.g., van Dijk (1984). The discourse-historical perspective (cf. 2.4) features also the idea of dividing the discourse in a similar way, e.g., by creating *we-discourse* "wir-diskurs" (Wodak et al. 1994).

5. Nation is understood here as an abstract construct of "imagined community" (Wodak 1997, following Anderson 1988). The properties of a nation accounted for in that study are to a large extent followed here. The national identity perspective was also developed from the Greek standpoint by Chouliaraki (1999).

6. We can understand continuity as in Wodak 1997, Wodak et al. 1998, hence nations should be seen as having "discursive construction" (ibid.).

7. My term.

8. For further insights, see, for example, deBeaugrande and Dressler (1981).

9. I am aware of the stylistic changes such substitution may bring. However, due to obvious delimitation of space, I did not take up the issue of influence of stylistic variation here.

10. In order to avoid misunderstanding, or claims that our analysis is based on one broadcast only, we should mention that "Reflektorem po swiecie" ("Spotlight on the World") is a daily, one-hour long broadcast of the BBC World Service Polish Section in which most important events from Poland and around the world are described and commented on.

Acknowledgments

My many thanks go to Professor Ruth Wodak, University of Vienna and Research Centre "Discourse, Politics, Identity," for the inspiration that her work has been to me, as well as for her great scholarly help and support shown to me over the last year. I am also thankful to Professor Wodak for inviting me to participate in this project. I am grateful to Professor Barbara Kryk-Kastovsky, Adam Mickiewicz University, Poznan, and University of Vienna, for her great scholarly help and support, as well as her comments on the early draft of this paper. Many thanks to Professor Elisabeth Gülich, University of Bielefeld, for her comments on an early draft of this paper. I would like also to thank Professor Helmuth Feilke, University of Bielefeld, for his time and scholarly help during my developing of the concept of this paper, and for his comments on an early draft. Many thanks to Mr. Eugeniusz Smolar, vice-president of the Board of Polskie Radio S.A., for his help with this paper. Last, but not least, I would like to thank my brother, Wiktor Krzyzanowski, M.Sc., and Wojciech Lubowiecki, both of the BBC World Service Polish Section, London, for their help with the data used in this paper.

154   The Haider Phenomenon in Austria

References

Anderson, Benedikt (1988).*Erfindung der Nation*. Frankfurt a.M.: Campus.
Chouliaraki, Lilie (1999). "Media Discourse and National Identity: Death and Myth in a News Broadcast," in: R. Wodak., C. Ludwig (eds.), *Challenges in a Changing World: Issues in Critical Discourse Analysis*. Vienna: Passagen Verlag.
Czyzewski Marek, Elisabeth Gülich, Heiko Hausendorf, Manfred Kastner (eds.). (1995). *Nationale Selbst—und Fremdbilder im Gespräch*. Opladen: Westdeutscher Verlag.
De Beaugrande, Robert, Wolfgang Dressler (1981). *Introduction to Text Linguistics*. London: Longmans.
Dijk Teun A. van (1977). *Text and Context*. London: Longman.
_____. (1980). *Macrostructures*. Hillsdale, NJ: Erlbaum.
_____. (1984). *Prejudice in Discourse*. Amsterdam: John Benjamins.
_____. (1985). "Introduction: Discourse Analysis in (Mass) Communication Research," in: T. A. van Dijk (ed), *Discourse and Communication*.. Berlin: Walter de Gruyter.
_____. (1985a). "Structures of News in the Press," in T.A van Dijk.(ed), *Discourse and Communication*. Berlin: Walter de Gruyter.
_____ (ed.). (1985). *Handbook of Discourse Analysis*, 4 vols. London: Academic Press.
_____ (ed.). (1985b. *Discourse and Communication*. Berlin: Walter de Gruyter.
_____. (1997). "The Study of Discourse," in T.A van Dijk (ed.), *Discourse as Structure and Process*. London: Sage.
Dijk Teun A. van et al. (1997). "Discourse, Ethnicity, Culture and Racism" in T.A van Dijk (ed.). *Discourse as Structure and Process*. London: Sage.
_____. (ed.). (1997). *Discourse as Social Interaction*. London: Sage.
Dijk Teun A. van, and Walter Kintsch (1983). *Strategies of Discourse Comprehension*. New York: Academic Press.
Foucault, Michel (1970). "The Order of Discourse," in M. Shapiro (ed.). (1984) *Language and Politics*. Oxford: Blackwell.
Gerbner, Gerd (1985). "Mass Media Discourse," in T.A van Dijk (ed.), *Discourse and Communication*. Berlin: Walter de Gruyter.
Kolakowski, Leszek (1995). "O tozsamosci zbiorowej," (orig: *Über kollektive Identität*), in K. Michalski (ed.), *Tozsamosc w czasach zmiany: Rozmowy w Castelgandolfo* (orig. Identität im Wandel: Castelgandolfo Gespräche). Cracow: Znak.
Kosseleck, Reinhard (1979). *Vergangene Zukunft*. Frankfurt a.M.: Suhrkamp.
Michalski, Karl (ed.). (1995). *Tozsamosc w czasach zmiany: Rozmowy w Castelgandolfo*, (orig: *Identität im Wandel: Castelgandolfo Gespräche*). Cracow: Znak.
Reisigl, Martin, and Ruth Wodak *Discourse and Discrimination* NEEDPUBLISHER/CITY (forthcoming).
Ricoeur, Paul (1995). "Pamiec—zapomnienie—historia," (orig: *Gedächtnis-Vergessen-Geschichte*) in K. Michalski (ed.), *Tozsamosc w czasach zmiany: Rozmowy w Castelgandolfo*, (orig: *Identität im Wandel: Castelgandolfo Gespräche*). Cracow: Znak.
Smolar, Ernst (1999). "Glos polski spoza Polski," in *Media w Polsce XX wieku*, Poznan: Press.
Wodak, Ruth (1991). "Turning the Tables: Anti-Semitic Discourse in Post-war Austria." *Discourse and Society* 2 (1):65–83.

_____. (1996). "The Genesis of Racist Discourse in Austria Since 1989," in C. R. Caldas-Coulthard and M. Coulthard (eds.) *Texts and Practices: Readings in Critical Discourse Analysis*. London: Routledge

_____. (1996a). *Disorders of Discourse*. London: Longmans.

_____. (1997). *The Discursive Construction of National Identities*. Paper presented at: "Discourse and Politics" conference, University of Aston, Birmingham, July 17, 1997.

Wodak, Ruth et. al. (1990). *Wir sind alle unschuldige Täter*. Frankfurt a.M.: Suhrkamp.

_____. (1994). *Die Sprachen der Vergangenheiten*. Frankfurt a.M.: Suhrkamp.

_____. (1998). *Zur diskursiven Konstruktion nationaler Identität*. Frankfurt a.M.: Suhrkamp.

Wodak, Ruth, Theo Van Leeuven (1999). *Legitimizing Immigration Control: A Discourse-Historical Analysis*. *Discourse Studies* 1 (1): 83–118.

8

Anti-Foreigner Campaigns in the Austrian Freedom Party and Italian Northern League: The Discursive Construction of Identity*

Jessika ter Wal

Introduction

Walking through the historical center of Vienna during the national election campaign in September 1999, on each street corner one was struck by posters of the Austrian Freedom Party asking for a stop to "over-foreignization" and "asylum abuse." During the same period in Northern Italy's towns and cities, groups of Northern League activists distributed material against the "invasion" of illegal immigrants, and collected signatures for a referendum against the "savage immigration" produced by the existing foreigners' law. This chapter aims to elucidate some of the backgrounds of the Freedom Party and Northern League discourses on immigration. More precisely, the objective is to examine the ideologies[1] and linguistic patterns that signify their talk about in-and-out-group identity in terms of nation, ethnicity, and "race."

* The research project of which this article forms a part was conducted at the Institute for Applied Linguistics at Vienna University between 1998 and 2000 with a Marie Curie Fellowship grant from the European Commission DGXII, contract no. ERBFMBICT983312.

Since the early 1990s, in many European countries, support for the extreme Right and radical right-wing populist[2] parties[3] has increased. The *Front National* in France, the *Republikaner* in Germany, the Belgian *Vlaams Blok* used to be among the more familiar examples of parties that did not hesitate to use racist and xenophobic discourse to increase their support. However, while in most European countries these parties have remained in the opposition, and are consciously placed outside the mainstream, in Austria and Italy they have instead obtained again a leading position in national politics. The emergence and success of these parties reveals the tension between the construction of a European identity, on the one hand, and a widespread insecurity and concern with the preservation and protection of national and local identities, on the other. In their primary slogans, these parties reveal a populist ultra-nationalism[4] by claiming to put "their own people first" through policy solutions that thrive on the physical, social, and economic exclusion of migrants. The rise of these parties should thus be seen as a European phenomenon.

Reasons for Success

In political science literature, three major explanations have been given for the success of the extreme or radical-populist right. First, processes of socioeconomic transformation, social fragmentation and the individualization of risk in contemporary society are claimed to have produced a new type of politics that aims at constituting new forms of collective identity. For example, the *Lega* and the FPÖ are skeptical towards the process of European integration and propose the formation of a "Europe of regions," in which regional identity is marked. They appeal to working-class voters by fuelling among them a fear for unemployment and competition from a new "underclass" of migrant laborers.[5]

As a second reason for success are mentioned the conditions and transformation of the political system, such as the existence of a political culture based on clientelism, patronage, and a "blocked democracy" with high levels of voter distrust. Countries such as Italy, Austria, and Belgium share these political conditions. In Italy, the electoral success of the *Lega* has been attributed to the parties' anti-establishment (anti-party-system) message in a climate of general voter distrust and disaffection with the old party system. This system was composed mainly of Christian Democrats and Socialists, who in the beginning of the 1990s went on trial for corruption and finally were submerged in the scandals deriving from it. During the first years of success, the *Lega* gained support in those areas that had been traditional strongholds of the Christian Democratic party, in particular, the smaller centers in the industrialized North-East where private enterprise was strong (Diamanti 1995). In Austria, the FPÖ has represented itself as the alternative to political corruption and the spoils system of the Socialist and People's Party that dominated Austrian political and socioeconomic life for decades.

Finally, various scholars have mentioned the decision of the party *not* to present itself as openly racist, and as having ties with fascist ideology (Betz 1996) as a condition for success. However, surveys and studies have shown that anti-immigrant politics is a major motor behind either supporting or joining these movements.[6] The potential for public support of racist positions may depend on conditions of political culture, including the collective imagery of (national) history, and the possibilities for critical dialogue taken up by the media as well as the specific attitudes toward recent immigration.[7]

Background

Although the levels of support for the FPÖ and the Northern League differ, they are comparable in their orientation on the immigration issue.[8] The Northern League was formed in the early 1980s as a grouping of regional movements with a secessionist program aimed at the autonomy and self-determination of the people of Northern Italy, the so-called "*Padania*" region.[9] Until the early 1990s racist discourse was primarily directed at the people from Southern Italy and Rome. From 1990 on, the *Lega* launched several campaigns against immigration, in particular petition campaigns to abolish the existing legislation on immigration through referendum (Constantini 1993). During the campaign for regional elections in Italy in April 2000, the Northern League's leader Umberto Bossi, together with media-tycoon and leader of the center-right party *Forza Italia*, Silvio Berlusconi, launched a proposal for harsh legislation against illegal immigration. An appeal to Christian and nationalistic values was used to justify these measures. At the regional elections, the center-right coalition led by Berlusconi gained the majority in eight of the most populated regions that represented almost two thirds of the electorate. In the elections of May 2001 this coalition seized power. Berlusconi became Italy's prime minister, and Lega leader Bossi, Minister of Institutional Reform and Devolution.

The FPÖ has also initiated numerous anti-foreigner campaigns.[10] During the 1999 election campaign nationalist and xenophobic rhetoric, which has always been at the core of the FPÖ discourse since the advent of Haider, appeared prominently. Slogans about "Austria first" and "right to our homeland" were repeated and arguments were advanced to avoid the contamination of Austrian culture and economy by undesired foreign elements (ter Wal 2000b).

Overview

The analysis in this chapter deals with the foundations of the anti-foreigner campaign discourses, and their function in the construction of in-group and out-group identities. Firstly, I examine the traces of typical ideological positions of the FPÖ and *Lega Nord* in their discourse on identity and migration. The point that I will try to make is that in order to understand racist discourse it is necessary to take into account the configuration of populist, anti-system and anti-globalization ideologies that monitor and provide legitimacy to this discourse. Indeed, examining these general ideological orientations that inform the discourse about "race" and identity can increase understanding of the type of party to which the FPÖ and Northern League belong.[11]

Secondly, I aim to discuss the way in which ideologies of ethnic nationalism and specific notions of nation, race, and economic relations sustain the construction of in-group and out-group identities and the representation of immigrants as a threat. Here I will also illustrate the linguistic transformation of meaning of ideologically charged words. This transformation, so I will argue, changes the meaning of crucial terms in the political debate, with the function of legitimizing questionable positions and precluding possibilities for dialogue in the political arena. In this way the FPÖ constructs a language of its own with interpretations that fit its ideological framework.

Populist and Anti-System Attitude Discourse Markers

One of the main ideological elements that characterizes the radical right is populism. The populist ideology is revealed by an anti-establishment stance and by claims to represent the ordinary man. Both the *Lega* and the FPÖ advocate forms of direct democracy, as practiced in petition campaigns and referenda. They appeal to latent public feelings of dissatisfaction, resentment or fear, and legitimate their political claims with reference to the common sense of the "silent majority" (Betz 1996:363–64). Populism is among the predominant elements in the FPÖ campaign discourse, expressed in frequent appeals to the "common man" and anti-establishment positions. In his public speeches and television interventions, Haider aims to articulate the views of the ordinary Austrian, while acting as the guardian of the national identity and interests. The underlying claim is that only those who actually experience it locally can judge "reality." By taking their perspective, Haider stages himself as the exclusive representative of the people and their wishes. Also through his use of language Haider apparently excludes himself from the political class and thus reinforces anti-elitarian and anti-establishment positions.

A combination of populist and racist discourse is found in the use of narrative evidence, i.e., reporting a case from the field, to provide "facts" that support claims, which confer credibility and persuasiveness. Such narrative, when used to support racist talk, is also referred to as "anecdotal racism" (Brown 1999).

(1) "Austria first" [slogan appearing on screens behind podium]. In Graz we...Susana Ries[12] met a mother, who has given birth to eleven children, has raised them and lives today with 3.792 Shilling. How should this mother understand the world in Austria, when she reads in the newspaper that in St. Pölten an illegal Albanian, who lives there with his two children and his wife, receives per month 12.700 Schillings from the social service? How should this woman understand that? This is what we want to tell the people. It is not the issue, so to say, to forbid the foreigners a payment, but the issue is finally to think about the Austrians. First we have to take our own people seriously; first we have to pay due respect to our people. And therefore one can only say to the future government, whatever it may look like: worry more about the own people, otherwise the voter will not worry about you anymore, otherwise democracy will slowly become a farce. (Jörg Haider, speech at the launch of the election campaign, 11.9.99, Klagenfurt)

In this fragment we see, apart from the devices of populist discourse, the positive representation of the Austrian mother apposed to the negative stereotype of the illegal Eastern-European immigrant who cheats the Austrian system and who is unrightfully privileged with respect to the Austrian people, who are commiserated with. The argument used to justify the exclusion of immigrants is precisely that the "own people" are discriminated against and disadvantaged.

Anti-system attitudes typical of populist parties are expressed by a general distrust towards individual representation and parliamentary agreements, a rejection of the traditional parties, and the proposal of fundamental changes in the existing socioeconomic or socio-political system. This orientation was prevalent in the campaign discourse of the *Lega Nord*. In its petition campaign against illegal immigrants, the party profiled itself as anti-capitalist, anti-American, and anti-EU. Its anti-globalization stance is related to the appeal to a sense of community, which has been lost. The United States and global culture are associated with individualism. Instead, the *Lega* envisions a "Europe of the people," a "Europe of autonomous regions/homelands," against the image of the European Union as a new supranational state body, representative of large economic interest groups, which produce an unacceptable multiracial and free-market-oriented society.

In the text that introduces the Bossi/Berlusconi law proposal, the proponents claim that theirs is a "Christian" model of society based on an "equilibrium between local and global, between in and out, between new forces that push from the outside and historical values rooted in tradition."[13] The universalism and multiculturalism of the other societal model is seen as detrimental, and instrumental in gathering votes from the new "*lumpenproletariat*" of immigrants. In the discourse of the *Lega Nord*, xenophobia is thus articulated not only as a fear against foreigners but specifically more as an anti-American stance, which requires the defense of the "own" culture. A conspiracy theory identifies the United States and other forces of globalization as enemies responsible for the assault of different cultures and populations on Europe's citizens' freedom, economic structures, and the preservation of traditions and cultures of the own population.

(2) We are mobilizing against the attempt of the international bankers and freemasons who bring the ideology of the free flow of goods not only within the economic reality (bringing about a crisis in the national production system), but also within the social and cultural reality, blowing up the family ties, causing a mixture and "free-flow" of religions, reducing them to a mishmash without meaning and roots (syncretism)"…we are facing an apocalyptic invasion, not just of a few hundred people. One hears talk of the 13 million immigrants that will assail us in the next ten years. To help those in need should not mean to destroy all values, identities, and traditions, so that all is reduced to money making. There are always those who manage to take real advantage of chaos of this kind. (Umberto Bossi, la Padania,[14] 15.1.99)

This use of conspiracy theories would seem to classify the *Lega Nord* as a representative of ideological extremism or radicalism, as it shows similarities with the discourse of traditional extreme right-wing parties that have mobilized these theories to propagate anti-Semitism.[15] The question whether this should be taken for a fundamental trait or rather as a part of its eclectic approach shows the difficulty in classifying the nature of the *Lega*.

The FPÖ has directed most of its rhetoric against the established parties and the system of political patronage in Austria (the so-called *Proporz* system). Anti-liberalist stances are also articulated in Haider's (1995) "The Freedom that I mean." Here the party's leader enumerates the destructive consequences of hedonism, consumerism, and individualism, which derive from American culture. However, in the campaigns of 1999 anti-Americanism is not found. The major responsibilities for uncontrolled immigration are attributed to the Austrian Socialist Party and to the EU-enlargement program to Eastern Europe. The discursive style of the FPÖ is marked by contempt towards the political establishment. Derision and sarcasm, accusations, and the expression of cultural commonplace, are used to verbalize anti-politics and anti-elitarianism. This language leads to a polarization between "us" and "them," also revealed through the use of violent language (verbal attacks), mocking, and the use of conspiracy theories.

Ethnic Nationalism, Identity Construction, and Racist Discourse Markers

In addition to the populist and anti-system orientations, the FPÖ and *Lega Nord* emphasize the position of the own people as a traditional natural community by mobilizing ideologies of *ethnic nationalism/regionalism* and *racism*. The concern with issues of identity and territory, and positions on the theme of immigration are intertwined with these ideologies. This can be revealed through the analysis of various linguistic phenomena. A thematic clustering can be observed, which establishes implicit forms of causal reasoning, i.e., attribution of causes and responsibilities.

To illustrate the main elements of the racist discourse thus articulated, I use the social psychological notion of in-group-out-group differentiation. In discourse on ethnic minority groups the out-group is categorized as different on the basis of origin, appearance, socioeconomic, cultural, or personal characteristics, and evaluated negatively as a threat. Particularly in more subtle expressions of ethnic prejudice, immigrants are represented as a threat to in-group economy and social relations (e.g., labor and housing market). In more blatant expressions of negative prejudice, immigrants are represented as a threat to public order due to their deviant personal characteristics. In the discourse of the FPÖ and *Lega Nord* we also find more traditional forms of racism and blatant expressions of racial prejudice through the dehumanization of immigrants, and their representation as a threat to ethnic integrity and identity because of their cultural differences.

Public Order Threat: Illegal Immigrants, Deviants, and Criminals

The theme of security and public order, which has a highly populist appeal, recurs frequently in interventions about immigration. In the speeches and slogans of the FPÖ, one sees the negative representation of migrants as lawless, merciless deviants who threaten the well being of Austrians as opposed to the commiseration with innocent young Austrian people who fall victim to drugs. The FPÖ argues that rather than protecting the foreign perpetrators the victims should be protected. Themes of children cheques, child abuse, drug dealing, and foreigners are juxtaposed in vague and implicit argumentative chains.

(3) What kind of responsibility is it when an expulsion of an illegal foreigner, who deals drugs in our country, who dies, that is tragic [*sic*].[16] But then for weeks we have a discussion in the Austrian media what kind of impossible Republic it is, how terribly the poor drug dealers are treated who have been expelled here and die. I would wish that the discussion be conducted in a different way. And say: how poor are the victims, who have become victims of these drug dealers, our children, our youth—We protect the victims and not the perpetrators (slogan appearing on screen)—who are put on a wrong track, who die, who are permanently damaged. And therefore it is completely clear: we do not want to make a politics of polarisation between nationals and non-nationals. But someone who comes to us, who stays here illegally, who becomes criminal here in Austria has not even for a minute the right to be in Austria, and is to be expelled, my dear friends! And that with all consequences! Therefore it is humane to think first about the own people instead of letting the eyes drift somewhere else. And it is profoundly humane to protect the children instead of exposing them to c.., eh, criminal deeds. (Jörg Haider, Klagenfurt (Carinthia), speech launching the election campaign, 11 September 1999)

This statement contains the stereotype of the illegal immigrant and drug dealer, and suggests that deviance is an inalienable feature of this group. It also uses the well-known apposition between a negative out-group of criminals and a positive in-group of innocent vulnerable children. Other strategies occur at the lexical and semantic level, such as the reversal from victim to perpetrator and the change of perspective from the out-group onto the interests of the in-group. Because the FPÖ is accused of violating humanitarian norms and rights, it has created a new definition of humanitarian politics (*menschliche Politik*). The FPÖ defines its policy of protecting its "own people first" as "humane," thus reversing the conventional meaning of the fundamental ideological concepts of humanitarianism. This reversal strategy is used to externalize negative characteristics: "our policy is not anti-humanitarian, the other policies are."[17] The FPÖ thus redefines the meaning of politically charged concepts to its own advantage. Haider employs the same strategy in fore-grounding talk about *Familien— and Kinderfreundlichkeit* (friendliness towards families and children) as opposed to the *Fremdenfeindlichkeit* (hostility towards foreigners) of which he is accused.

In the discourse of the *Lega*, immigrants are mainly represented as potential criminals, juxtaposed *tout court* to criminals, or held responsible for the expansion of crime. This is combined with a discourse about territorial domination (thus signifying the threat of immigration in spatial terms) and the construction of disaster scenarios, as in the following example:

> (4) Who could have imagined only 15 years ago that entire neighbourhoods of cities like Turin or Milan would be dominated territorially by clans of extra-communitarian (non-EU) criminals? If we continue this way where will we be in 15 years from now? (Padania, identity and multiracial society, December 1998, p. 4)

In its discourse about the threat of immigrants the *Lega* often uses generalizations and causal reasoning that presents rules of history in order to provide the apparent "evidence" for claims that, for example, immigration "always" tends to produce an increase in crime.

Threat to Ethnic Identity and Integrity

In the discourse of the FPÖ the right to preserve the identity of the own people (language, values, culture) and to feel at home among one's own people is rendered concrete by standing up to protect Austrian families and children. They have to be protected, that is, from the threat of foreign disruption of traditional ways of life, of societal structures and ethnic integrity. This argumentation also draws on the collective identification with a great national destiny that has to be preserved, an idea that is also based on a re-interpretation of Austrian and European twentieth-century history that challenges "official" interpretations.[18]

Among the children-friendly and humanitarian policies that the FPÖ advocated during its 1999 election campaign was the issuing of special allowances for Austrian families with small children. In an election-time television interview Haider defined this policy as a *"Wiedergutmachung,"* a reparation of damage.[19] This completely transforms the most well-known meaning of this concept, which is that of reparation of damages to Holocaust survivors and families of Holocaust victims. On the basis of other Haider statements, it cannot be misunderstood that this reversal of the conventional lexical meaning of a politically and historically charged concept is done purposefully to redesign the reading of Austrian history. With this wordplay, the historical memory of a large number of people is mocked, whereas the memory of the generation of former SS officers who hideously opposed the *"Wiedergutmachung"* is defended. At the same time, the wordplay and its intention of historical reversal is done in such a veiled way that it can always be denied. In addition, the new *Wiedergutmachung à la* Haider is a form of historical revenge in favor of the preservation of the Austrian people as a deterrent against the "trauma" of immigration. Indeed, the proposed children's cheque to support families is to be given only to Austrian parents, and Austrian identity is only given by birthright.[20] The insistence to constantly change perspective from the out-group to the interests of the in-group further supports the ultra-nationalist and racist discourse of the FPÖ.

A particular defense of traditional community ties and ways of life is expressed in the opposition to integration policies. This position is expressed very bluntly: immigrants are dehumanised and only represented as a disruptive force for natural communities, and their exclusion is justified by means of a reference to humanitarian and environmentalist ideologies, typical of the new right. At the same time, however, the preoccupation with these themes recalls an ideology of control of "race" and territory, which was also found in the National Socialist program.

(5) Millions of economic refugees/nomads will not only destroy the population structures that have grown for centuries and bring about the biggest social tensions, but they will also represent an environmental burden that should not be underestimated....In areas, which are already overpopulated, either enormous slum cities will emerge or under the heaviest environmental burden one would have to create infrastructures for many millions of people. In this sense the preservation of different people and cultures is a humanitarian protection and a protection of natural resources. (FPÖ Abg Niederösterreich Ilse Hans, Völkerfreund 2/1990)

Another interesting strategy is Haider's comparison of the position of labor migrants with the positive example of how Austrian citizens rebuilt after World War II and did not leave the country. In this way, with the claim that immigrants should rather rebuild their own country, the rejection of immigrants is justified and used as a further occasion to disqualify them. The opposition between a positive in-group and a negative out-group thus created is furthermore used to boost nationalist pride and appeal to populist sentiment. Hereby the in-group of Austrians is categorized and evaluated as good-minded and fatherland-loving, whereas less positive personality characteristics (such as treason and instability) are implicitly attributed to the out-group of immigrants. In addition, the cultural relativist belief that every population should best prosper in its own "territory" is implicit in this statement.

Also from the discourse of the *Lega* emerges the belief that immigration is a form of domination by other peoples, and that this has to be prevented by stimulating the formation of "indigenous" families. In the introduction to the recent proposal, immigration is defined as "a quantum that has to be calculated essentially in relation to the survival of the nation." Hereby the nation is compared to a human organism, which needs optimal conditions for survival. *Lega Nord* and *Forza Italia* build their proposal on the necessity of maintaining *national belonging* (for the sake of the *Lega*'s regionalist politics also expressed as nations) as a basis for citizenship. They justify their anti-immigrant measures with the belief in "the supremacy of the nation in a romantic sense, as the core and basis of values and religion, culture and language, customs and traditions."[21] In the document issued with *Forza Italia*, the nation is defined as "the safeguard of European civilization." The individual, the historical memory, and the nation are fundamental to social order, as they "form integrative parts of a social structure which in the new global geopolitics is the only antidote to chaos." Order and the values that support this would be established through the protection of the authenticity and historical roots of the peoples.

However, herewith immigration is not a priori excluded or banned altogether. Despite the blatant racism expressed, the *Lega* has, and has to have, a higher level of compromise to other political forces and the public debate culture. For example, the following statement shows that the *Lega* does not hold responsible or attack immigration per se, but rather the political and economic forces causing immigration, i.e., the "pro-immigration lobby." Immigration is represented as an inevitable "substitution of a population." The statement also features the exaggerations and disaster scenarios typical of the *Lega* discourse and its conspiracy theories.

> (6) "An argument which the pro-immigration lobby brings in support of the arrival of extra-Europeans, is that this phenomenon would resolve the problem of our ageing population and the demographic downfall in which Padania is the largest in the world. Incredibly, they think they can resolve the problem by substituting one population with another! Why instead are motherhood and family not protected?" (Padania, identity and multiracial society, December 1998, p. 5)

The claim that with further entries of immigrants "our" ways of life will be irremediably broken up and overrun further justifies exclusion and the preservation of the own identity. In this discourse it is presupposed that an aggressive and disruptive force is inherent to immigration, and that "we" do not have any force to react. It is also presupposed that the only possible reaction is one of defense, which indicates the rejection in the ideology of the *Lega* of any model of true equality in the treatment of immigrants. Interestingly, the defense of "our" way of life and interests against that of the immigrants includes in the "we" group not only the *Padanians* but any Italian citizens: they apparently share the same aims in this matter. This confirms the identification of *Padania* as a primarily economically, but not necessarily culturally, superior "people" with respect to the rest of Italy.[22]

What makes the discourse of the *Lega* stand out against that of the FPÖ is that it adopts disclaimers either to avoid or to deny biological racism, by dismissing evaluations of particular cultures as being better or worse. These disclaimers, which indicate some degree of constraint by anti-racist norms, introduce statements about the irreconcilable cultural differences of immigrants. It is assumed that the only way to avoid the disruption and suppression of community values is for differences to be kept separate, an assumption which is typical of the cultural relativism found in the racism of the new Right.[23]

Furthermore, both parties' discourse implies that migrants' deviance is linked with their incompatible cultural and religious identity. The representation of immigration as a threat to "our" religious values is found in frequent use of anti-Islamist stereotypes that, in the *Lega Nord* discourse, are combined with conspiracy theories. In generalizing statements, the *Lega* claims that Islamist terrorism and fundamentalism are a direct and inevitable consequence of further immigration. This leads to the representation of the difference of immigrants in the form of traits that are inalienable and essential to any immigrant's identity.

Socioeconomic Threat

The negative representation of immigrants as causing economic damage is another vital element in the discourse, which has already emerged from some of the examples reported above. Although the *Lega* and the FPÖ are against the loss of values produced by consumerism, on the other hand they wish to protect the own population against the economic threat of competition by immigrants. The *Lega* frequently represents immigrants as being responsible for tax evasion.[24] Moreover, it claims that labor standards will be lowered as a result of migrant workers, who are attracted by the forces of global economy and who accept lower wages. The *Lega Nord*, however, signifies the fear of immigration as a fear for a class struggle initiated by the left-wing parties. By contrast, in Austria it is the "too hasty" enlargement of the EU to the East, which is expected to produce a loss of jobs and labor standards for the "national" population. The FPÖ's exclusionary discourse is defended with a reversal strategy by which the vocabulary of anti-discrimination is employed to claim that the Austrian population is disadvantaged and discriminated against and that a truly "humane politics" should look after "the own people first" (see also example [1]).

Concluding Remarks

While the representation of immigrants as a threat to the public, order, economic interests, and ethnic integrity represent three core elements of racist discourse; other categorizations would clearly deserve further attention as well. My aim was to focus on the way in which racist beliefs are embedded in a complex configuration of ideologies of populism and cultural relativism. Rejection and scapegoating of those perceived as inferior or weaker, i.e., immigrants, are complemented by an opposition to those at the top, i.e., the elites, the EU, the established parties, and, in the case of the *Lega Nord*, the United States. I have also tried to show the strength of rhetoric and language in the communication of stereotypical beliefs and images of "otherness" and in the re-interpretation of ideological values. The change of meanings of ideologically charged concepts of humanitarianism and discrimination into their opposite, a discursive practice of reversal central to the anti-foreigners discourse of the FPÖ,[25] indicates the attempt to redefine and dismiss widely accepted anti-racist norms and to challenge references to racism and Nationalism Socialism that are considered taboo.

In this respect, the FPÖ seems to be more explicit in its populist and racist claims than the *Lega,* which favors a discourse monitored by anti-system positions. In the 2000 election campaign debates and preceding documents, at least the *Lega*'s leader Umberto Bossi has emphasized a theoretical discourse in which anti-immigration positions are embedded in an anti-capitalist and anti-globalization discourse. Similarly, anti-racist norms seem to be at times more integrated and not so overtly challenged in the discourse of the *Lega Nord*, as for example in its dismissal of biological racism and the avoidance of blaming-the-victim strategies. These differences between Italy and Austria can be explained by the different political, cultural, and historical configuration, which determines not only the uniqueness of both the *Lega* and the FPÖ, but also the way in which their discourse can tune in to and resonate within the public and political debate culture. From the analysis also emerges that the role of history in the discursive construction of identity needs more investigation.

On the other hand, both the *Lega* and the FPÖ use every available argument to portray immigrants as (potential) criminals. They also share the defense of ethnic integrity and the cultural relativism typical of new Right ideologies. Overall, their constructions of identity classify immigrants and foreigners as "outsiders" who, without further explanation, are considered "not human." It is this unquestioned dehumanization that, in my view, represents one of the most worrying aspects of their discourse.

Notes

1. Hereby ideology is understood as a complex organizing and monitoring system of socially shared beliefs, attitudes and opinions (van Dijk 1998). Van Dijk's approach links discourse analysis, i.e., the analysis of language use in its social and political context, to the analysis of ideology, intended as a form of social cognition, and as the basis of the social representations shared by a group.

2. The discussion on classification of these parties as either extreme right or radical right-wing populist is influenced by different national research traditions with different theoretical views and interests. The North American literature has focused on radical right and populist right (Betz 1994; Betz and Immerfall 1998; Kitschelt and McGann 1995), whereas in several European countries the literature on these parties has used the terminology of right-wing extremism (Eatwell 1998; Mayer 1998; Mudde 1996). Similarly, within the Austrian scholarly debate, voices that defend the extreme right classification of the FPÖ, because of its continuous identifications with or half-hearted withdrawal from National Socialism and anti-Semitism (Bailer-Galande and Neugebauer 1997, *http://www.doew.at/ fpoeenglbn.html;* Schedler 1995), are contrasted by the opinion of a large number of Austrian political scientists that Haider would rather represent a right-wing populist party (e.g., Riedlsperger 1998; Pelinka and Rosenberger 2000; Plasser and Ulram 1994).

3. The term "party" may seem inappropriate to designate these political formations, while they themselves also tend to emphasize their movement-like character, which derives from anti-establishment positioning and the aim to bring about a fundamental change in the political system. In the case of the FPÖ the aim to present itself as a movement exists despite the fact of its coming from the position of a political block ("Lager"), which forms part of twentieth-century Austrian political history (Riedlsperger 1992). A further contradiction inherent to the project of these "movements" becomes apparent with their participation in government, as in Austria. Similarly, from the activist bases of the Northern League to its government representatives and media speakers, the discourse may shift considerably in content and style. Since both FPÖ and *Lega* are full participants in the settings of political decision-making and debate, and are active in the political scene after many years, I have decided to use the party label here. This is also done in order not to mitigate their influence on mainstream politics.

4. Populist ultra-nationalism is a term coined by Roger Griffin (1991) to describe "political forces which...depend on 'people power' as the basis of their legitimacy" (p. 36), and "forms of nationalism which 'go beyond' and hence reject anything compatible with liberal institutions or with the tradition of Enlightenment humanism which underpins them." "It tends to be associated with a concept of the nation as a 'higher' racial, historical, spiritual or organic reality which embraces all the members of the ethical community who belong to it. Such a community is regarded by its protagonists as a natural order which can be contaminated by miscegenation and immigration, by the anarchic, unpatriotic mentality encouraged by liberal individualism, internationalist socialism and by a number of 'alien' forces allegedly unleashed by 'modern' society, for example the rise of the 'masses,' the decay of moral values, the 'levelling of society, cosmopolitanism, feminism and consumerism.'" (ibid., p. 37)

5. Different kinds of claims against immigrants prevail in different type of socioeconomic systems. According to Gächter (1999), in welfare-oriented societies such as

Austria the perception of foreigners as a threat is signified prevalently as a fear of competition in access to services and abuse of welfare system services. In Italy, a society with a weaker social security system, and high levels of anomie, the threat of foreigners to property would be signified primarily in a fear of illegality and crime (ibid.). However, also in Austria the crime theme was very prominent in the FPÖ discourse. Conversely, the claims made by the Italian *Lega* and other right-wing parties resonate well with the feelings of disadvantage experienced by a proportion of working or middle-class people in the larger cities in Northern Italy, who express social malcontent by claiming that the left has privileged the immigrants. It is important to note that this is not so much perceived as a disadvantage for access to social services or material welfare. Instead, people express the threat of a differential access to political attention and mediation, an asset that characterizes the organization of Italian political culture (i.e., of replacing services with "favors" by those in powerful positions).

6. A survey conducted by Fritz Plasser (Plasser et al. 2000b) showed that in the 1999 national elections in Austria the first motivations to vote for the FPÖ were the party's anti-corruption stance (65 percent), its promise of change (63 percent), and the representation of interests and tradition (48 percent). But xenophobia followed suit: 47 percent of votes given to the FPÖ were motivated by xenophobia, literally, by reason that "the FPÖ stands up against immigration of foreigners" (reported in Pelinka 2000).

7. Although it is, in my opinion, dangerous to suggest a direct causal relation between immigration and racism, it is, of course, observable that one of the reasons behind an increase in anti-foreigner attitudes is the *visibility* of migration. This visibility is, in turn, related to the amount and type of media and political attention given to the theme (ter Wal 1996).

8. The FPÖ gained 26.0 percent of the votes in elections held in October 1999 and the *Lega Nord* held 10.1 percent of the votes in national elections held in 1996, but dropped to 3.9 percent of the votes in the national elections in May 2001. Under the new electoral system based on proportional vote, in 2001, thirty Lega candidates were voted in the House of Representatives (total seats 630) and seventeen in the Senate (total seats 315). In the previous legislation, they were forty-six and twenty-seven, respectively. The Italian *Alleanza Nazionale* (AN), especially after its transformation from the former traditional extreme right-wing *Movimento Sociale Italiano* (MSI), is less comparable to the FPÖ because it has used a far less overtly anti-immigrant discourse (Cheles 1995; Griffin 1998). Nevertheless, an analysis of Italian parliamentary debates has shown that ideologies of ethnic nationalism, cultural relativism and defense of the "right to difference" to justify a refusal of equal treatment of migrants do characterize the discourse of individual members of AN (ter Wal 1999, 2000a, 2000c). The typical populist style of the *Lega Nord* is however lacking; instead we find a "theory-driven" party with an elitist appeal (Betz 1996:364). This means that ideological statements often build on the intellectual tradition within the former MSI.

9. In most North-American studies, the *Lega Nord* is claimed to be part of a new type of radical right-wing party (Betz 1994; Kitschelt 1995). The *Lega* is not considered extreme right, because of its appeal to a center-positioned electorate and the absence of fascist ideological elements (Betz 1996; Merkl 1997).

10. Wodak and Reisigl (2001) analyze the discourse of the anti-foreigners petition campaign organized by the FPÖ in 1992–93, which caused a split in the party and the foundation of the Liberal Forum by then former-FPÖ member Heide Schmidt.

The background of this campaign is also reconstructed in Mitten (1994). A detailed analysis of the 1999 national election campaign discourse on foreigners is given in ter Wal (2000b).

11. See note 2 for the debate on classification. This plays a crucial role in understanding and also in devising instruments for intervention against the racist elements in the discourse.

12. Susana Ries was elected successor of Jörg Haider as party leader in the national party assembly in May 2000 and represents the Austrian government as vice-prime minister.

13. The document is available in Italian at http://www.lapadania.com/2000/aprile/09/09042000p02a1.htm.

14. *La Padania* is the Lega Nord's newspaper, which is distributed to party followers and is available also on the Internet at http://www.lapadania.com.

15. A detailed analysis of this discourse based on conspiracy theories for the anti-Semitism of the British National Front is found in Billig (1978). See also Dal Lago (1999:126) on the parallelism between fascist propaganda, the style and contents of the classical anti-Semitic literature and the discourses of the *Lega Nord*.

16. This refers to the case of an asylum seeker who was expelled from Austria under police escort in May 1999 and died on the plane due to lack of air because the police had taped his mouth. The FPÖ and also large circulation newspapers immediately suggested (without sustaining this with concrete evidence) that the victim was a common criminal, while at the same time they tried to absolve the police officers who were involved in the incident.

17. This is only one of many possible strategies aimed at the "denial of racism" that are practiced in different types of elite discourse (for a categorization, see van Dijk 1993).

18. For example, Haider (1995), chapter 4.

19. Jörg Haider, Pressestunde, Austrian television, 12 September 1999.

20. Haider in Sommergespräche, Austrian television, ORF2, 8 August 1999.

21. In the discourse of the *Lega Nord*, the crisis of the nation-state is used as a starting point to detach the notion of nation from state. The nation is conceptualized as the imagined community of belonging, which is fundamental to identity. The state instead is defined as an economic interest group, with economic and cultural hegemony. The present European states are defined as defenders of the global economy that deny the existence of peoples, nations and states, their history, origin and traditions.

22. Eatwell (1998) and Ruzza and Schmidtke (1996) also emphasize the economic motivations of the *Lega*'s xenophobia. However, my analysis in the section on ethnic identity does show that xenophobia is also based on nationalistic and racist grounds.

23. The new Right ideology as developed by the "*Nouvelle Droite*" of Alain de Benoiste in France is one of the inspirers of this cultural relativism, which, however, has multiple roots.

24. This is typical of ethnic prejudice in which causes for negative behavior are attributed to personal dispositions (abuse) rather than situational factors, which would in this case be the demand for foreign black labor in the Italian informal economy (Duckitt 1992).

25. As already observed in the seminal work of Wodak et al (1990), this strategy of "turning the tables" is certainly common for many discourse types on anti-Semitism and racial discrimination in Austria.

References

Bailer, B., and Neugebauer, W. (1999). The FPÖ of Jörg Haider—Populist or Extreme Right-Winger? *http://www.doew.at/fpoeenglbn.html*.

Bailer-Galanda, B., and Neugebauer, W. (1997). *Haider und die Freiheitlichen in Österreich*. Berlin: Elefanten Press.

Betz, H.-G. (1994). *Radical Right-Wing Populism in Western Europe*. New York: St. Martin's Press.

_____. (1996). "Radikaler Rechtspopulismus in Westeuropa," in J. W. Falter, H.-G. Jaschke, and J. R. Winkler (eds.), *Rechstextremismus. Ergebnisse und Perspektiven der Forschung*. Opladen: Westdeutscher Verlag.

Betz, H.-G., and Immerfall, S. (eds). (1998). *The New Politics of the Right. Neo-Populist Parties and Movements in Established Democracies*. New York: St. Martin's Press.

Billig, M. (1978). *Fascists. A Social Psychological View of the National Front*. London: Harcourt Brace Jovanovich.

Brown, A. R. (1999). "The Other Day I Met a Constituent of Mine": A Theory of Anecdotal Racism. *Ethnic and Racial Studies* 22(1): 23–55.

Cheles, L. (1995). "The Italian Far Right: Nationalist Attitudes and Views on Ethnicity and Immigration," in A. G. Hargreaves and J. Leaman (eds.), *Racism, Ethnicity and Politics in Contemporary Europe*. Cheltenham: Edwar Elgar.

Costantini, L. (1993). *Dentro la Lega*. Roma: Koiné.

Dal Lago, A. (1999). *Non Persone*. Milano:Feltrinelli.

Diamanti, I. (1995). *La Lega. Geografia, storia e sociologia di un soggetto politico*. Roma: Donzelli editore (2ᵃ edition).

Duckitt, J. (1992). *The Social Psychology of Prejudice*. New York: Praeger.

Eatwell, R. (1998). "The Dynamics of Right-Wing Electoral Breakthrough." *Patterns of Prejudice* 32(3): 3–31.

Gächter, A. (1999). "Daten und Fakten zu Integration und Einwanderung." Vienna: Institute for Higher Studies, manuscript.

Griffin, R. (1991). *The Nature of Fascism*. London: Pinters.

_____. (1998). "Ce n"est pas Le Pen. The MSI's Estrangement from the Politics of Xenophobia," in C. Westin (ed.) *Racism, Ideology and Political Organisation*. Stockholm: CEIFO.

Haider, J. (1995). *The Freedom I Mean*. New York: Swan Books.

Kitschelt, H. (1995). "Blending New Right Appeals into a Broad Populist Anti-Estab-lishment Strategy: Austria and Italy," in H. Kitschelt and A. J. McGann (eds.), *The Radical Right in Western Europe. A Comparative Analysis*. Ann Arbor: University of Michigan Press.

Kitschelt, H., and McGann, A. J. (1995). *TheRadical Right in Western Europe. A Comparative Analysis*. Ann Arbor: University of Michigan Press.

Koopmans, R., and Statham, P. (1999). "Ethnic and Civic Conceptions of Nationhood and the Differential Success of the Extreme Right in Germany and Italy," in M. Giugni, D. McAdam, and C. Tilly (eds.), *How Social Movements Matter: Theoretical and Comparative Studies on the Consequences of Social Movements*. Minneapolis: University of Minnesota Press.

Mayer, N. (1998). "The French National Front," in H.-G. Betz, and S. Immerfall (eds.), *The New Politics of theRight: Neo-Populist Parties and Movements in Established Democracies*. New York: St. Martin's Press.

Merkl, P. H. (1997). "Why are They So Strong Now? Comparative Reflections on the

Revival of the Radical Right in Europe," in P. H. Merkl and L. Weinberg (eds.), *The Revival of Right-Wing Extremism in theNnineties.* London: Frank Cass.

Mitten, R. (1994). "Jörg Haider, the Anti-immigrant Petition and Immigration Policy in Austria." *Patterns of Prejudice* 28(2):27–47.

Mudde, C. (1996). "The War of Words. The Defining of the Extreme Right Party Family. *West European Politics* 19(2):225–248.

Pelinka, A. (2000). "Die Rechte Versuchung. SPÖ, ÖVP und die Folgen eines falschen-Tabus," in H. Scharsach (ed.). *Haider. Österreich und die rechte Versuchung.* Hamburg: Rowohlt.

Pelinka, A., and Rosenberger, S. (2000). *Österreichische Politik. Grundlagen, Strukturen, Trends.* Wien: WUV Verlag.

Plasser, F., and Ulram, P. A. (1994). *Radikaler Rechtspopulismus in Österreich: die FPÖ unter Jörg Haider.* Vienna: Institut für Marktforschung/Aentrum für Angewandte Politikforschung.

_____. (2000) The Changing Austrian Voter. Vienna: Center for Applied Political Research (http://www.zap.or.at/e202006.html).

Plasser, F., Ulram, P.A., and Sommer, F. (eds.). (2000a). *Das Österreichische Wahlverhalten.* Vienna: Center for Applied Political Research, vol. no. 21, (*http://www.zap.or.at/201021.html*).

_____. (2000b). *Analysis of the 1999 Parliamentary Elections in Austria.* Vienna: Center for Applied Political Research (*http://www.zap.or.at/e202005.html*).

Riedlsperger, M. (1992). "Heil Haider! The Revitalization of the Austrian Freedom Party since 1986." *Politics and Society in Germany, Austria and Switzerland* 4(3):18–47.

Riedlsperger, M. (1998). "The Freedom Party of Austria: From Protest to Radical Right Populism," in H.-G. Betz and S. Immerfal (eds.), *The New Politics of the Right. Neo-Populist Parties and Movements in Established Democracies.* New York: St. Martin's Press.

Ruzza, C., and Schmidtke, O. (1996). "The Northern League. Changing Friends and Foes, and Its Political Opportunity Structure," in D. Cesarini and M. Fulbrook (eds.). *Citizenship, Nationality and Migration in Europe.* New York: Routledge.

Schedler, A. (1996). Die antipolitischen stereotypen Jörg Haiders. *Journal Für Sozialforschung,* 35(3/4):283–306.

Ter Wal, J. (1996). "The Social Representation of Immigrants: The *Pantanella* Issue in the Pages of *La Repubblica. New Community,* 22(1):39–66.

_____. (1999). "New Right, New Racism? Alleanza Nazionale and the Lega Nord in Debates on Immigration in Italian Parliament." Paper presented at the 22ª International Society of Political Psychology Conference, Amsterdam, July 1999.

_____. (2000a). "Italy: sicurezza e solidarietà," in R. Wodak and T.A. van Dijk (eds.), *Racism at the Top: Parliamentary Discourses on Ethnic Issues in Six European States.* Klagenfurt: Drava.

_____. (2000b). "Racism and Xenophobia. The Discourse of the Freedom Party in the 1999 Election Campaign." Vienna: internal report for the European Monitoring Centre on Racism and Xenophobia.

_____. (2000c). "Extreme Right-Wing Discourse and Its Ideological Implications: Alleanza Nazionale on Immigration." *Patterns of Prejudice* 34(4):37–51.

Van Dijk, T.A. (1993). *Elite Discourse and Racism.* London: Sage.

_____. (1998). *Ideology. A Multidisciplinary Study.* London: Sage.

Wodak, R., Nowak, P., Pelikan, J., Gruber, H., De Cilia, R., and Mitten, R. (1990). *"Wir sind alle unschuldige Täter." Diskurshistorische Studien zum Nachkriegsantisemitismus.* Frankfurt am Main: Suhrkamp.

Wodak, R., and Reisigl, M. (2001). "Aliens' and 'foreigners': the political and media discourse about the Austria First petition of Jörg Haider and the Austrian Freedom Party in 1992 and 1993," in M. Reisigl, and R. Wodak (2001), *Discourse and discrimination. Rhetorics of Racism and anti-Semitism.* London: Routledge.

Part 3

9

Austria all Black and Blue:[1]
Jörg Haider, the European Sanctions,
and the Political Crisis in Austria

Richard Mitten

The New Specter Haunting Europe

The October 1999 parliamentary elections in Austria, in which the Freedom Party (FPÖ) led by Jörg Haider won nearly 27 percent of the votes, was the occasion of much editorial hand-wringing in Europe. If the *Financial Times'* description of Haider as a "dangerous chameleon" seemed almost charitable, the Milan daily *Corriere della Sera's* headline "Sieg Haider"[2] more accurately reflected the anxiety which Haider's latest electoral success had elicited. On February 4, 2000, these critics' worst nightmare seemed to have come true: Haider's party had become the junior partner in a coalition led by the Christian Democratic Austrian People's Party.

In response, fourteen members of the European Union—marching separately, but striking together, as it were—imposed on the Union's fifteenth member, Austria, the diplomatic sanctions they had threatened before the government had been formed. There have been virtually no voices of outright praise for the ÖVP-FPÖ coalition, and press commentary in both Europe and the United States on Haider and the new Austrian government has remained overwhelmingly hostile, even if sometimes of dubious factual reliability. To mention a few notable

179

examples: if for Thomas Friedmann, writing in the *New York Times,* Haider was simply a "neo-Nazi," and the Austrians were unflatteringly similar to the. . . Syrians,[3] the editors of the *New Republic,* convinced that Haider "is not Adolf Hitler," merely a "slick and sickening fascist," also claimed—erroneously—that Haider was a member of the government.[4] Still others, such as conservative columnist George Will, seemed to view Haider as little more than a tanned, athletic, and incomparably more successful version of Republican presidential candidate Steve Forbes.[5]

As the recent effusion of such reporting amply confirms, since the Waldheim Affair in 1986, when the hidden biography of the former U.N. Secretary General came to be viewed as a symbol of Austrians' ambiguous relationship to their National Socialist past, people who do not follow winter sports would scarcely hear about Austria were it not for racist bombings, the debate over compensation for victims of the Holocaust, and Jörg Haider. That the information readers do receive about Austria tends to be disproportionately devoted to the fears engendered by Haider's string of electoral successes is not, of course, unrelated to the images of Austria generated by the Waldheim Affair, to Haider's provocative allusions to the Third Reich, nor to the idiom in which Haider is portrayed by his opponents in Austria.[6] The growth in extreme rightist violence directed against foreigners and their political advocates in Austria in the 1990s also appeared to correlate strongly with Haider's political ascendancy.

Yet what makes the recent promises of the FPÖ to "Stop the inundation by foreign elements (*Überfremdung,*)"[7] seem so much uglier than, say, the Willie Horten ads broadcast by George P. Bush's 1988 presidential election campaign,[8] is traceable not only to the inferences we draw from the more detailed knowledge we have acquired since the Waldheim Affair of many Austrians' involvement in Nazi policies of racial persecution and mass murder. This reaction also reflects deeply embedded political-cultural assumptions, particularly widespread in the United States, which tend to associate things Germanic with more or less distinct, but unfailingly negative, images of Nazism, and which influence how we perceive news about Austria in general, and about Haider in particular. Exemplary of this kind of thinking was a *Time* magazine article devoted to the killings at Columbine High School in Littleton, Colorado. Included among the "Nazi paraphernalia" which the so-called "trench coat mafia" embraced "to spook their classmates,"

Time reported without irony, was the fact that its members "spoke German in the halls."[9] It is, therefore, not surprising that permeating most commentary on Austria is the unspoken assumption that there is something culturally or ethnically distinctive about Austrians that makes pandering to racism there so much more menacing than elsewhere.

If a lack of detailed knowledge of Austrian affairs has led many commentators to see in Haider's success a recrudesence of Nazi beliefs which were never successfully expunged in Austria,[10] there is also a tendency to see Haider's FPÖ as the advance guard of a pan-European movement of far right parties on the march.[11] With Haider cast as a kind of xenophobic Everyman, "Haiderism" has become the new specter haunting Europe, while the FPÖ's entry into the Austrian government has come to be viewed as the precedent which would transform Le Pen's National Front, Filip Dewinter's Flemish Block, or Pia Kjaersgaard's Danish People's Party into legitimate contenders for national governmental office.

Such perceptions of Austrian politics in general, and of Haider and what he represents in particular, are less mistaken than merely incomplete. The political provenance of the FPÖ and many of its former leaders, as well as Haider's oft-quoted positive allusions to aspects of the Third Reich, indeed raise questions about the party's commitment to the postwar Austrian consensus condemnation of the Nazi period. Moreover, the rise of the FPÖ in Austria since 1986 does share features with other similar xenophobic currents in other countries. However, in my view analyses that emphasize the specifically neo-Nazi danger to Austria tend to underestimate the non-ideological bases of much of Haider's electoral appeal, while others, less attentive to the specific domestic sources of Haider's success, exaggerate the (causal) significance of Haider's rise for Europe as a whole.

The prospect of the National Front, the Flemish Block, the Danish People's Party, and the FPÖ all serving in European governments is a depressing scenario. However, in this essay I will argue that, should this come to pass, its explanation will not be found primarily in Haider's political rise in Austria. If, indeed, there is a more general European lesson to be learned from the Austrian case, it is that any strategy for combating the populist right which depends primarily on the talismanic invocation of democratic values against what are described as these parties' atavistic ideological impulses, hoping that by doing so these groups can be kept in political quarantine and hence out of power, will probably fail. The specific *domestic* factors, and the *multiplicity* of these, which have been so important to Haider's political success in Austria, suggest that, if these far right parties are prevented from assuming, or resuming, national office in Belgium, Denmark, France or Italy, it will be because more traditional democratic parties prove capable of responding to the fears and grievances created by the international economic, and domestic social and political developments in their respective countries more creatively than the SPÖ and ÖVP in Austria were willing or able to do.

While I believe that Haider's success in Austria should be viewed with alarm in Europe, I also view most conventional diagnoses of the problem in Austria as incomplete, and in this essay wish to offer my own analysis of Haider's political success, and what the formation of the ÖVP-FPÖ government might imply for politics in Austria. I will also argue that the diplomatic sanctions imposed on Austria by the fourteen other European Union governments are misguided, hypocritical, and will prove ineffective. Most of the arguments advanced in this essay are not new;[12] they do seem, alas, more urgent.

Haider's Freedom Party of Austria

From its inception as an uneasy alliance between former Nazis and European-style liberals of a German nationalist bent, the Freedom Party is a peculiarly Austrian phenomenon. Historically, liberals in the German-speaking areas of the Habsburg empire were among the most ardent German nationalists: one of the cardinal principles of the liberal "camp" (*Lager*) in nineteenth-century Habsburg Austria was the preservation of German cultural predominance in the multinational empire. The successor parties of the so-called third *Lager* (the other two being the Christian Socials and Social Democrats) in the Austrian First Republic (1918–34), the *Grossdeutsche Volkspartei* (Pan-German People's Party) and the *Landbund* (Agrarian League) were thoroughly German nationalist and anti-Semitic, thus scarcely liberal in any but the most narrowly construed economic sense (even here they were not consistent). During the final years of the First Republic, German nationalist constitutional parties increasingly ceded influence to Austrian National Socialists among the core Pan-Germanist constituencies, and under the "Austro-fascist" dictatorships of Dollfuss and Schuschnigg (together with ideologically similar elements of the fascist *Heimwehr* formations), went over en masse to the Nazis, severing altogether the tenuous link between Liberalism and German nationalism. After the Second World War, for lack of a viable alternative, voters who felt they could not support the Socialist Party on economic grounds or the People's Party on secular grounds gravitated towards the Union of Independents (*Verband der Unabhängigen*), which was founded in 1949. Though its original leaders wished it to be a liberal democratic alternative to the two major parties, the League predictably became the principal electoral home for the former Nazis who had been disfranchised in the 1945 elections as part of "de-Nazification," but whose franchise was restored in a 1948 amnesty. The FPÖ was founded in 1956 as the successor to the League, and while the FPÖ's programmatic affirmation of the "German cultural community" alluded to a tradition easily reconciled with the German nationalism of the former Nazis, its liberalism had to be reinvented.[13]

It was into such a world that Jörg Haider was born in 1950. Growing up in a family deeply imbued with values of the German *Volksgemeinschaft,* Haider earned his political spurs in the German nationalist student milieu, and in 1966 won an oratorical contest with a speech entitled "Are We Austrians Germans?" (He answered yes.) Haider set his sights on power early and has enjoyed a spectacular career in the FPÖ. Already national youth leader by the age of 20, Haider became party secretary in his adoptive province of Carinthia in 1977.[14] Augmenting his youthful hubris with uncommon rhetorical skills, both in Carinthia and in the Austrian parliament, Haider has given voice to inchoate resentments in sections of the Austrian population bred, among other things, by over forty years of domination of the national spoils system by the Socialist and People's parties. Although in the 1970s and early 1980s FPÖ leaders attempted to strengthen the party's liberal credentials, Jörg Haider's election to the leadership of the FPÖ in September 1986 returned the nationalist wing to predominance. During the early years of his leadership, Haider did promote some of the party's showpiece liberals like Heide Schmidt, who, although from a Nazi family, was more notable for her aggressive advocacy of the FPÖ's liberal agenda. However, political conflicts between the remaining liberals and the Haider leadership intensified to the point that in February 1993 Schmidt and a few other FPÖ members of parliament resigned from the party and formed the Liberal Forum.[15]

The Waldheim Affair in 1986 demonstrated the potential electoral gains of pandering to ethnic (then anti-Semitic) prejudices. Waldheim's repudiation of his critics' alleged attempt to "criminalize the wartime generation" played not only to deeply held beliefs about the moral uprightness of the Wehrmacht, but also to resentments among Austrians at being forced to critically re-examine the assumptions of victimhood which had remained largely uncontested for forty years. Haider learned these lessons well, and he, rather than the ÖVP, which had nominated Waldheim as its presidential candidate, was able to reap the principal political benefits of the Waldheim controversy.[16]

In the late 1980s and early 1990s, the FPÖ under Haider made an opening to the extreme right. This policy, which combined a deft linguistic coquetry about the Third Reich—ranging from praise of Waffen-SS veterans as "spiritually (geistig) superior" men "who have character and who remain true to their convictions against strong head winds, and who have remained true to them until today," to the belief, which Haider expressed in 1985, that convicted war criminal Walter Reder merely "did his duty, as his oath as a soldier required," to his endorsement of the Nazis' "sound employment policies"[17]—with verbal attacks on "foreigners" that were laced with ethnic stereotypes of the crudest sort, enabled Haider to consolidate his base among the traditional German nationalists in Carinthia and had the effect of reducing much of the political space between the FPÖ and the far right.[18] Haider's rhetoric has thus adroitly played on several ambiguities of postwar Austrian identity: he has chipped away at the reigning consensus of unconditional condemnation of the Nazi regime and other cherished values of the Austrian Second Republic, while his party has succeeded in further raising the public tolerance threshold for ethnic prejudice.

This was reflected in the anti-immigrant initiative petition Haider launched in late 1992. The petition contained twelve points altogether. Stripped of the provocative excesses of their presentation, in fact many of the substantive proposals contained in the FPÖ petition did not diverge markedly from the series of immigration laws the Austrian government itself had enacted in the early 1990s. The provisions to limit to 30 percent the number of school pupils in a given classroom whose native language was not German (point 6), however, would have resulted in open discrimination against ethnically non-"Germanic" Austrians (the criterion was not proficiency in German, but German as a native language). The claims advanced in support of the various provisions of the initiative petition presented in the official brochure circulated by the FPÖ, moreover, employed argumentative strategies that included apodictic (but arguably false) assertions and an especially stereotypical vocabulary that encouraged or justified hostility towards foreigners. Though the FPÖ cleverly (and not entirely unwarrantedly) attempted to portray the arguments on the "foreigner problem" as fully within the prevailing boundaries of political discourse, the SPÖ and the ÖVP condemned the planned initiative petition as irresponsible incitement of xenophobia, while stressing the restrictiveness and efficiency of their government's own Asylum and Residence Acts. The FPÖ-initiated petition received far fewer signatures than Haider had hoped for or than his opponents had feared. However, 417,000 registered voters (in a country of 8 million) were prepared to sign a petition that contained one explicitly discriminatory provision. Nonetheless, Haider's anti-foreigner agitation seems to have been undermined less by arguments preaching tolerance than by the governing parties' corollary emphasis on the restrictive nature of their own immigration policies. The mere perception of the government as having the "foreigner problem" more or less under control, of course, has done little to undermine the ethnic stereotyping of "foreigners" itself among Austrian voters.[19]

Haider's supporters have consistently considered immigration to be an important issue, and believe the FPÖ to be the most effective party to address the issue. According to exit poll interviews conducted during the October 1999 election, for example, 47 percent of Austrians who voted for Haider said that the FPÖ's immigration policies influenced their choice. However, a significantly higher percentage (66) said they voted for the Freedom Party because of its campaigns against corruption and entrenched power. Haider's political appeal for voters beyond the core German nationalist and overtly xenophobic constituencies has thus lain in his ability both to identify and to capitalize on the disillusionment with Austrian political institutions, and to channel a wide-ranging but inchoate mixture of social anxieties among certain groups of voters into hostility towards immigrants and "foreigners." In order to explain Haider's politics and his success, it is, I believe, necessary to understand both the salience and resilience of voter dissatisfaction with some of the seamier side effects of the postwar SPÖ-ÖVP oligopoly, and Austrian voters' willingness to vote for Haider despite, as well as because of, his controversial references to Nazism and the racist appeals of his party. I would like to address each of these aspects in turn.

The Decline of "Consociationalism" and the Rise of Haider's FPÖ

One way of visualizing Austrian political culture since 1945 is as a kind of catamaran, with twin hulls of power supporting, as it were, a relatively stable Austrian "ship of state" navigating the troubled waters of international and domestic politics.[20] One hull represents electoral politics as they are conventionally played out, the other the uniquely Austrian exemplar of "neo-corporatist" cooperation, the "social partnership." Both have been indispensable to Austrian political stability and economic prosperity. More recently, however, this Alpine "catamaran"—to keep to our metaphor—which had proved extremely seaworthy in the past, began to show signs of wear just as it was entering waters less suitable for a twin-hulled vessel.

Throughout most of the postwar years, the two major political parties, the SPÖ and the ÖVP, have together exercised power as a condominium which extended well beyond the state into the deepest crevices of "civil society." Until 1966, this arrangement was embodied governmentally in the "grand coalition." In the arena of electoral politics, each party staked out and defended its ideological territory, hurled partisan propaganda at its opponent(s), and competed for government office. Though never reducible simply to this, parliamentary elections in postwar Austria in fact determined little more than the specific relationship of forces within this condominium. For the extent of the spoils to be had was vast (reaching from government ministries down to primary school teaching positions), and were apportioned strictly according to the party's relative strength at the polls. This system, known as *Proporz*, predictably gave rise to what is known as the "party-card economy" (*Parteibuchwirtschaft*) and all manner of petty political corruption.

The so-called "social partnership" originated in a series of ad hoc national wage and price agreements struck between the heads of the Chamber of Commerce and Austrian Trades Union Confederation (*Österreichischer Gewerkschaftsbund,* or ÖGB), but has proved to be more durable. The basic institutions of the social partnership are the three "chambers," of labor, commerce, and agriculture, in which membership is mandatory, and the trade unions, in which it is voluntary. Since the memberships of the chambers of commerce and of agriculture overlapped with the core constituencies of the ÖVP, and the chamber of labor and ÖGB with those of the SPÖ, and many officials of all four of these associations also sat in parliament, in government, or in party leadership bodies, the division of power in the social partnership paralleled that of the grand coalition.

The advantages Austria has derived from this political-institutional configuration and the closely related "Austro-Keynesian" economic policies successive governments followed—sustained growth, low unemployment, a stable currency, industrial peace, increasing productivity—have been much studied and admired. Naturally, the cozy arrangements of this ÖVP-SPÖ oligopoly bred complacency and corruption, both of which were on occasion targets of the parliamentary opposition (primarily the FPÖ before its Haiderian reincarnation). Nonetheless, such corruption was grudgingly tolerated because of the benefits this arrangement provided. Indeed, as late as 1983 the Socialists and People's Party between them could count on the support of over 90 percent of the electorate. At the same time, the degree of actual power that the inordinate personal and institutional imbrication of government coalition and social partnership conferred on its leading members made the Austrian parliament chiefly into a body that merely endorsed decisions that had been taken elsewhere. During the period between 1966 and 1983, for example, when there was either an ÖVP or SPÖ single party government, 72 percent of all laws were adopted unanimously by the Austrian parliament.

The relatively frictionless arrangement between government, social partners, and parliament began to break down with the end of coalition government in 1966, with first the Socialists and then the People's Party assuming the traditional role of parliamentary opposition. In this context the social partnership itself took on additional significance, and the SPÖ-ÖVP condominium was never seriously in danger. Still, the period of one-party governments did serve to stengthen the institutions of parliament, which have given new openings for the opposition parties since the return of the grand coalition in 1986.

Many of Austria's postwar social and political institutions have been slow to adapt to the new economic and demographic exigencies of the 1980s and 1990s. Indeed, into the 1990s the leaders of the Social Democrats and the Christian Democratic People's Party seemed unable or unwilling to adapt their policies and institutions to changed economic and demographic circumstances and as a consequence had forfeited much of the political consensus which had kept them in office. As a consequence, the hyper-stable party system in Austria has been subjected to continual erosion, reflected in declining voter allegiance to any political party. If in the 1960s, for example, three-fourths of all Austrians identified with a party, by 1994 only about 50 percent did so, a trend especially strong among young voters. The combination of voter mobility, institutions perceived as inert, and increasing media boldness created a situation propitious for the growth of Haider's brand of right-wing populism. And though in the years since the Waldheim Affair in 1986 prominent politicians have learned to articulate a notion of "historical responsibility" for Austrians' share in the Holocaust, their endeavors could not recompense the ambiguities at the heart of Austrian postwar historical "memory" for over forty years, a memory centered on the notion of victimhood. Haider's successful exploitation of several dilemmas of Austrian identity brought him unprecedented electoral success, made government policies on a range of issues hostage to Haider's political initiative, and culminated in the FPÖ under his leadership entering government at the national level. He has exploited these openings with consummate political skill.[21]

Receptivity and Inurement to Xenophobic Politics in Austria

There have been two overriding elements of Haider's electoral strategy since he first became leader of the FPÖ in September 1986: (1) to attack the corruption in the Austrian political system while (2) posing as someone not afraid to break political taboos, in particular by playing the "foreigner" and "Nazi" cards. The political rhetoric of the FPÖ since 1986, but especially after 1989, has consistently promoted "ethnic" explanations for real or imagined social and economic problems, wagering that the prejudice which exists in contemporary Austria towards ethnic minorities as well as "foreigners" from eastern and southern Europe, and more recently, from Africa, could be tapped to increase its vote.[22] While it is difficult to determine how many of those who vote for the FPÖ do so primarily out of xenophobic or racist motives,[23] it is obvious that significant numbers of Austrians at least have not viewed Haider's revisionist views on National Socialism and the FPÖ's inflammatory anti-foreigner rhetoric as a reason *not* to vote for it or him. At least part of the explanation of Austrian voters' seeming inurement to the FPÖ's explicit or coded xenophobic and racist appeals would thus seem to lie in the extent of ethnic prejudice among the population as a whole. Prejudice is notoriously difficult to measure accurately, and public opinion surveys are a far from perfect tool for gauging the attitudes, beliefs, and potential tolerance of discrimination. Nevertheless, such polls can provide evidence of what might be called the reservoir of prejudice in Austria, which, in my view, has been a necessary, though not sufficient, condition for Haider's electoral success. The specific political objectives that appeals to prejudice are designed to achieve, and those which the FPÖ has promoted, may, but need not, have a specifically ethnic inflection (i.e., discrimination against a target group), but the very existence of this reservoir in Austria (but not, of course, in Austria alone: think of the Willie Horten ads again) seems to have limited or neutralized potential opposition to xenophobic and racist politics per se.[24]

The most recent data on ethnic prejudice in Austria were collected in polls in the 1990s.[25] Although designed primarily to determine Austrians' attitudes towards Jews and the Holocaust, these surveys also contained questions that yielded information on Austrians' feeling about other ethnic minorities. On the whole, not only did the polls suggest that FPÖ voters were more likely than other Austrians to hold negative views about Jews; they also indicated a significantly higher prevalence of ethnic hostility among declared Haider supporters than among all Austrians. Yet the results also show that the levels of prejudice and ethnic hostility among supporters of the ÖVP and SPÖ, as well as in the Austrian population as a whole, remain quite high.

The results of the two polls conducted for the American Jewish Committee (AJC) in 1991 and 1995 suggest that a noticeably higher percentage of FPÖ supporters than other Austrians hold negative attitudes towards Jews. Yet the difference between FPÖ supporters and supporters of the SPÖ and the ÖVP was not as great as one might have wished. Moreover, the percentage of FPÖ supporters exhibiting a negative orientation towards Jews declined in every one of the relevant categories between 1991 and 1995, in some cases by more than the Austrian average (though the figures from 1991 frequently revealed exceptionally hostile attitudes towards Jews among FPÖ supporters). For example, while 29 percent of the total sample in 1995 agreed[26] with the statement "Now, as in the past, Jews exert too much influence on world events," (down from 37 percent in 1991), a much higher percentage (41) of FPÖ supporters did so. Yet this 41 percent represented a 20 percent reduction compared to 1991! Moreover, according to the 1995 poll, 36 percent of FPÖ supporters said they would "prefer not" to have Jews as neighbors (down from 40 percent in 1991), as against 26 percent of other Austrians (down from 31 percent in 1991). And while in the 1995 poll 28 percent of FPÖ supporters, as compared to 19 percent of other Austrians, believed that Jews had "too much influence" in Austrian society (the figures for SPÖ and ÖVP supporters were 19 and 21 percent, respectively), this represented a decline of over 21 percent for the FPÖ compared to 1991, but of only 9 percent for Austrians as a whole.

A similar pattern was discernible in the Holocaust-related items in these two surveys. Asked whether "Now, 50 years after the end of the Second World War, it is time to put the memory of the Holocaust behind us," in 1991 an astounding 70 percent of FPÖ supporters agreed; by 1995, this number had dropped to 41 percent, with the number of those who "strongly agreed" falling from 52 to 17 percent. Thirty-three percent of Austrians as a whole (a decline of 20 percent from 1991) agreed with this statement. Forty-one percent of FPÖ supporters (down from 55 percent in 1991) also agreed that Jews were "exploiting the Nazi Holocaust for their own purposes," compared to 28 percent of other Austrians (down from 31 percent in 1991). Finally, while the not inconsiderable figure of 7 percent of the total sample in 1995 believed it "possible that the Nazi extermination of the Jews never happened," a full 17 percent of FPÖ supporters did so (this question was not asked in the 1991 survey).

Several questions in the 1991 poll relating specifically to the range and intensity of anti-Jewish prejudice and potential tolerance for discrimination against Jews were inexplicably not repeated in the 1995 study. We know, for example, that in 1991, 19 percent of all those surveyed believed it would better to have no Jews in the country; 39 percent endorsed the statement "Jews have caused much harm in the course of history"; 50 percent agreed that the Jews "themselves are at least partly to blame" for the persecution they have suffered; 6 percent said they experienced "a feeling of revulsion" when shaking hands with a Jew (and 37 percent could not decide whether they did or not!); 20 percent agreed that Jews' access to specific (influential) positions should be restricted (and an additional 27 percent had "no response" to this question of basic civil equality); 15 percent concurred that the acquisition of capital and land by Jews should be legally limited (31 percent gave no answer); and 24 percent of Austrian respondents endorsed the hoary canard that "the Jews must still assume responsibility for the death of Jesus Christ."[27] Unfortunately, it was not possible to chart the evolution of Austrians' beliefs on these questions further.

While the results of the 1995 survey showed Austrians as a whole to be more open to historical memory about the Holocaust than they had been in 1991 (perhaps not unrelated to the series of commemorations marking the liberation of Auschwitz, the founding of the Austrian Second Republic, etc., which took place that year), a substantial number of respondents still remained indifferent or hostile. Thus, 28 percent of those polled agreed that "the Holocaust is not relevant because it happened about 50 years ago," and 22 percent considered it either "only somewhat important" or "not important" for "all Austrians to know about and understand the Holocaust." The 33 percent of Austrians surveyed in 1995 who believed that "it is time to put the memory of the Holocaust behind us," while still high, nonetheless represented a drop of 20 percent compared to 1991.

Although the two AJC opinion surveys revealed a disquieting resilience of certain anti-Jewish stereotypes in contemporary Austria, they also suggested that attitudes towards Jews had improved in the four years between the two surveys. Thus, in 1991, 28 percent agreed that Jews had too much influence in Austria, but in 1995 only 19 percent did so. On the other hand, while in 1995, 28 percent of all Austrians still believed that "Jews exert too much influence on world events," 37 percent had so believed in 1991. The 1995 poll also reinforced another trend noticeable in the 1991 survey: although 26 percent of those polled in 1995 still preferred not to have Jews as neighbors, on this question Jews scored "better" than Poles, Serbs, Slovenes, Croats, Turks, Rumanians or Gypsies (better, indeed, than any group listed apart from Germans).

Over the same period, however, with some minor exceptions, the data collected for the AJC studies suggested that hostility of Austrians in general towards other ethnic minorities and foreigners had increased (if in some cases only slightly) from an already high level. Thus, 33 percent of the total sample in 1995 stated that they would "prefer not" to have Croats as neighbors (up from 31 percent in 1991), and 44 would rather not have Serbs as neighbors (up from 43 percent in

192   The Haider Phenomenon in Austria

1991). Forty-two percent gave the same reply for Turks (41 percent in 1991), and 35 percent for Rumanians (34 percent in 1991). Austrians' antipathy towards some other ethnic groups (as measured by a respondent's stated desire not to have them as neighbors), however, has declined slightly since 1991. Thus, if in 1991, Slovenes were spurned as neighbors by 30 percent of all Austrians, in 1995 it was down to 27 percent. The comparable figures for Poles were 34 percent (1991) and 29 percent (1995), and for Gypsies 49 percent (1991) and 45 percent (1995). With one exception (Gypsies), moreover, the same general tendency was evident in the responses to the question of which ethnic groups "behave in a manner which provokes hostility" in Austria. Thus, while the behavior of Croats, Serbs, Turks, and Gypsies was found to be provocative by more Austrians in 1995 than in 1991 (in numbers ranging from 26 to 39 percent), fewer Austrians found the behavior of Poles, Slovenes, Rumanians and Jews similarly provocative.

The 1995 survey's findings confirmed that FPÖ supporters were also consistently more hostile than other Austrians towards ethnic minorities. Moreover, the relative increase in enmity compared to 1991 also tended to be greater among FPÖ supporters, and there were fewer cases where the animosity of FPÖ supporters towards ethnic groups had abated since 1991. Thus, for example, the 56 percent of FPÖ supporters who "prefer[ed] not" to have Turks for neighbors in 1995 (compared to 42 percent of other Austrians) represented a 6 percent increase compared to 1991. In 1995, 43 percent of FPÖ supporters (as against 33 percent of other Austrians) were averse to having Croats as neighbors, up from 35 percent in 1991; and, in contrast to the trend for Austrians as a whole, the percentage of FPÖ supporters who would rather not have Slovenes as neighbors increased from 27 percent in 1991 to 35 percent in 1995. Similarly, according to the 1995 AJC survey, 51 percent of FPÖ supporters (compared to 39 percent of other Austrians) believed that Serbs "behave in a manner which provokes hostility" in Austria, up from 45 percent in 1991, and 27 percent felt the same about Rumanians (up from 24 percent in 1991). Apart from the Jews, only the Poles (among those included in the survey) were considered by a smaller percentage of FPÖ supporters in 1995 (22 percent) than in 1991 (34 percent) to provoke hostility through their behavior.

The overall results of the AJC survey thus do not yield any simple conclusions. In general, both the extent and the intensity of negative attitudes towards Jews have tended to decline in the Austrian population as a whole, though the aggregate Austrian figures remain fairly high. And while supporters of the FPÖ exhibited hostility towards Jews to a higher degree than Austrians as a whole, and a decidedly higher percentage of their supporters were open to Holocaust denial, in most of the relevant categories the figures for FPÖ supporters did not diverge strikingly from those for supporters of the coalition parties SPÖ and ÖVP. Moreover, the results showed a noticeable decline in the percentage of FPÖ supporters who expressed hostile sentiments towards Jews and Holocaust remembrance compared to 1991. At the same time, negative attitudes towards many other ethnic minorities had increased both among Austrians as a whole and most notably among FPÖ supporters from figures that were disturbingly high to begin with. Expressed differently, if the political climate in Austria after 1991—as measured by such opinion surveys—had become increasingly less tolerant towards ethnic minorities in general, Jews, nonetheless, seem to have represented an exception to the pattern.

Allowing for the caveats that apply to all such studies,[28] I would like to suggest how the results of these opinion surveys might help us understand the electoral advances of the FPÖ under Jörg Haider. Against the backdrop of, and taking skillful advantage of the breakdown of traditional voter loyalties; a high degree of disillusionment among a wide spectrum of the population as a whole with the reigning political system in Austria; the sense of economic, social, and cultural insecurity felt by those most directly affected by recent changes in the economy and the welfare state; and the transformations in Central and Eastern Europe, the FPÖ under Haider has been able to increase its share of the votes in parliamentary elections three-fold since 1986, most recently registering 26.9 percent in the October 1999 elections. The FPÖ has long been the home of authoritarian German nationalism and an attendant visceral anti-Semitism. Although all evidence suggests that this old guard and its younger co-thinkers continue to support Haider loyally, their relative numbers inside the party have, nonetheless, declined. Thus, while the FPÖ was never simply coterminous with Nazi nostalgia, it is even less so today. Yet saying that Haider and his party are not Nazis, or neo-Nazis, merely inaugurates, rather than concludes, the discussion of him and his policies.

One important element of such a discussion is the evidence offered principally by Austrian political scientists Fritz Plasser and Peter Ulram, which suggests that the profile of FPÖ voters is far from one-dimensional.[29] On the basis of exit-poll interviews made with voters in parliamentary elections between 1989 and 1999, Plasser and Ulram found that the motive for voting for the FPÖ most frequently given over the years was that the FPÖ fights against the "party-card" economy of the major parties, (i.e., against the privileges that members of the SPÖ and ÖVP receive, or are believed to receive, in areas like employment and job promotion), and because the FPÖ mercilessly exposes abuses of power and scandals. To take the figures from the 1994 election, which are fairly typical, 44 percent voted for the FPÖ because it fought against the "party-card" economy (up from 35 percent in 1989). Other motivations which were considered less important by FPÖ voters were: that the FPÖ fought against immigration (32 percent); that the FPÖ was thought to bring "fresh air into Austrian politics" (31 percent, a decline from 40 percent in 1989); and that the FPÖ was seen to fight "against too much state and bureaucracy" (24 percent, down from 27 percent in 1989).

The comparable figures from the 1995 and 1999 elections corroborate these earlier results. For example, in the 1995 elections, 81 percent of "old" FPÖ voters (i.e., those who had voted for the FPÖ in previous elections) and 79 percent of first-time FPÖ voters supported the party because it exposed corruption and abuses of power. The FPÖ's stand on immigration was a reason given by 49 percent of previous, but 51 percent of first-time FPÖ voters. The FPÖ's attack on welfare fraud was mentioned by 49 percent of previous and 52 percent of first-time FPÖ voters as a major reason for their support. In the 1999 elections, among both FPÖ voters as a whole and first-time voters (65 percent each), the highest single motivation for voting for Haider's party remained its exposure of corruption and abuses. Forty-seven percent of all FPÖ voters, and 39 percent of first-time FPÖ voters, claimed that the party's stand against immigration had been important in their decision to vote FPÖ, while "sending a message" to the big parties was a reason for voting for the FPÖ offered by 36 percent of all FPÖ voters and 49 percent of first-time FPÖ voters.[30]

These results suggest that a great deal of Haider's political success relates directly to a diffuse dissatisfaction with the two major political parties and these parties' failure to address issues of corruption and the overweening influence of the state and bureaucracy. A poll from the

1990s on voter disaffection with the political system more generally also confirms the importance of Haider's "anti-politics" appeal to potential FPÖ voters. Asked whether they believed that "members of parliament lose touch with the people rather quickly," for example, 46 percent of all Austrian respondents, but 60 percent of FPÖ voters agreed. Similarly, 41 percent of all Austrians, but 75 percent of FPÖ supporters believed that "the parties only want the votes of the people, but their views don't interest them." Fully 60 percent of FPÖ supporters indicated their intention to "send the parties in power a message" at the next election, compared to 28 percent of Austrians as a whole.[31]

Despite the prominence of the "foreigner" issue in FPÖ electoral propaganda, therefore, voter preferences for the FPÖ do not seem to represent either a knee-jerk xenophobic reflex, or necessarily an endorsement of far-right ideology. Indeed, according to the results obtained by Plasser and Ulram, in most cases voters cast their ballots for the FPÖ despite, rather than because of, the party's ambivalent attitude towards German nationalism and the Nazi past, and even despite its xenophobic and racist propaganda. FPÖ voters, they suggest, revealed a cluster of motives, including (1) a thoroughgoing disillusionment with politics and politicians, traceable to and crystallized around the issues of corruption, scandals, and unearned privileges; (2) criticism of the penetration of partisan political influence into too many aspects of Austrian society, which condensed around the slogans against the "party-card economy"; (3) the issue of immigration, which served as a focus for amalgamating a broad spectrum of prejudices and social anxieties (fears of loss of job or de-skilling, insufficient housing, crime, problems of cultural conflict, including in the area of schools), not all of which are traceable to ethnic hostility, but which find their easiest and most salient expression in the "foreigner problem"; (4) fears of the consequences of social developments which are seen to threaten one's social position or identity, coupled with the loss of confidence in traditional parties and interest groups to reverse the decline; (5) reflexive opposition to the entrenched power of the dominant coalition nationally and the concentration of power on the provincial level; (6) actual support of FPÖ positions on specific issues, or support of its criticism of personalities in the parties themselves, as well as support for Haider's attacks on government performance.

The results of the two AJC surveys cited earlier reinforce Plasser and Ulram's analysis of the varied motivations of FPÖ voters. For example, the polls showed a proportionately much larger decrease in anti-Jewish sentiment and attitudes towards the Holocaust among FPÖ supporters than among Austrian voters as a whole. In the first instance this is clearly a question of absolute numbers. As their support extended beyond their traditional German nationalist constituencies and included voters who were attracted to the FPÖ by reasons other than xenophobia, a fairly stable and consistent quantity of xenophobes and/ or racists would represent a smaller percentage of FPÖ voters as a whole.

What these and other similar polls also suggest is that while hostility towards Jews and prejudice towards other ethnic minorities are disproportionately high among FPÖ voters, these negative stereotypes continue to be fairly widespread among the Austrian population as a whole. It would seem to follow that this reservoir of prejudice acts as a kind of political anesthetic in Austrian political culture, in two distinct ways. On the one hand, voters who are not primarily motivated by xenophobia, and who might even find this aspect of the FPÖ mildly distasteful, become inured to that party's racist rhetoric. Indifferent to this rhetoric, they vote for Haider's party because they view it alone as capable of consistently and effectively exposing scandals and corruption, the issue about which they feel most strongly. On the other hand, this reservoir, and the "anesthetic" effect it has, limits the impact of attacks on the FPÖ that focus on exposing and denouncing the party's xenophobic and racist propaganda. Of course, this reservoir of prejudice can be exploited for political ends, for, given a favorable constellation of political circumstances (such as during the Waldheim Affair in 1986, or the opening of the borders between Western and Eastern Europe after 1989), politicians who openly pander to, or attempt even to reinforce this fairly widely distributed prejudice towards ethnic groups could increase the tolerance for the kind of utterances and measures that previously existing taboos had enjoined.

Towards the 1999 Election

Haider has been especially adept at exploiting such opportunities. He has always used explicit and allusive language to speak to his multiple constituencies on various levels simultaneously. Not only has this ability enabled him to weather a number of political storms over the years; by focusing on the corruption in the political system, and by challenging the political taboos on National Socialism and immigration, Haider took, and has retained, the political initiative in determining the issues that have been debated, and largely the terms in which they have been debated.

It is important to emphasize that Haider's electoral success would almost certainly not be nearly so impressive were it not for the support he receives from the Austrian daily *Neue Kronen Zeitung,* which, relative to its potential readership, is the most widely read newspaper in the world. In 1986, the *Kronen-Zeitung* acted as a kind of pro-Waldheim journalistic hit-squad and was instrumental in helping promote what amounted to an international Jewish conspiracy theory to defend Waldheim against his critics.[32] Since Haider became leader of the FPÖ, the paper has editorially consistently endorsed Haider's views on the "foreigner problem," and it supported his anti-immigration initiative petition, though it has differed with him on some specific policy issues, and recently argued in favor of continuing the grand coalition.[33] One particularly glaring example of the symbiosis between the sensationalist reporting of Austrian newspapers (which is not limited to the *Kronen-Zeitung*) and the FPÖ's campaign against "foreigners" is a full-page ad taken out by the Vienna FPÖ in May 1999. This ad, which called on the Social Democratic interior minister to crack down on Black African drug dealers, pictured Vienna FPÖ chairman Hilmar Kabas surrounded by newspaper articles from the *Kronen-Zeitung* and *Kurier* with headlines such as "Powerless against 1000 Nigerians" (which was followed by the lead "Thanks to the absurd legal situation, as illegal immigrants [*U-Boote*] they deal drugs nearly with impunity"), "Colored Dealers have the Vienna Drug Scene Firmly in their Hands," and "Black Africans as Dealers."[34]

Inasmuch as it is not simply what Haider declares it to be on any given day, the FPÖ's full electoral platform amalgamates several diverse items, some more extreme and further right than others. Apart from his continued verbal support for Austria's welfare provisions and the party's promise to provide every Austrian mother with money so that she might stay home with her children (the famous *"Kinderscheck"*), virtually every individual plank of the FPÖ's electoral platform, from its stubborn economic liberalism, its proposals to introduce more extensive use of plebiscites, to its calls for streamlining government, would be familiar to voters in the United States or other countries in the European Union. Indeed, Haider (who has attended summer school at Harvard the past few years) has been quite explicit that his "contract for Austria" and call for a "flat tax" were taken directly from Republican politicians in the United States. His attacks on "welfare cheats," his party's appeals to ethnic hostility, even his party's invention of "facts," are not unknown in local, and even national, election campaigns in the United States and other countries of the European Union.

At the same time, one should harbor no illusions either about the odiousness of the Freedom Party's racist appeals or of Haider's cynicism. In 1998, for example, while discussing the increase in foreign doctors in Vienna, Haider stated that, "In the future every Jungle Bunny [*Buschneger*] will be able to treat his kind in Austria."[35] Another party leader, Helene Partik-Pablé, was quoted in an Austrian paper as saying that "Black Africans not only look different, . . . they are different; in particular, [they are] especially aggressive."[36] The municipal election campaigns of the FPÖ in Vienna, moreover, have become increasingly less abashed in their xenophobic and racist appeals, most recently captured in their promise to "stop the inundation by foreign elements" (*Überfremdung*). Nor should one trivialize the dangers to democratic politics represented by Austrian voters' indifference to the FPÖ's racist and xenophobic appeals. Haider is entitled, indeed, should be encouraged, to repudiate his remarks about the Third Reich and his racist asides,[37] though careful listeners will often detect the qualifications he makes to his "apologies." Haider's statements are never "slips" of the tongue; that is simply the way he conducts politics. The relevant question is, then, what does it mean to share power with such a leader, and a party whose campaign in Vienna, for example, was based predominantly, if not exclusively, on appeals to ethnic hostility?

That a high percentage of FPÖ supporters vote for Haider out of protest against entrenched power (for which there is no obvious ethnic motive), however, suggests that Haider's success has been contingent both on the two major parties' unwillingness to inaugurate the policies needed to reassure the insecure and weed out the corruption, which has continued to nourish the current wave of anti-politics, as well as on the inability of the other opposition parties (the Greens and Liberal Forum) to articulate responses to voter disillusionment which could eclipse the authoritarian and ethnically chauvinist scenarios advanced by Jörg Haider and his supporters, and also command the support of protest voters. As a consequence, Haider has dominated Austrian politics since 1986, and has retained the initiative in determining the issues that are debated. As long as the FPÖ remained an opposition party, and Haider continued to disregard conventional norms of political behavior, he would continue to claim the initiative so long as there were scandals to be exposed and there was no other party able to give voice to these kinds of grievances.

The Social Democrats pursued a two-pronged strategy to combat the Haider threat. First of all, the SPÖ used its own variation on the "Nazi" and "foreigner" themes both to demonize Haider and simultaneously to try to outflank him on the right. Franz Vranitzky, Austrian Chancellor from 1986 until 1997, while never openly calling Haider a neo-Nazi, constantly intimated as much. For a while this strategy seemed a promising one. Vranitzky himself was in effect the presentable face of Austria during Kurt Waldheim's presidency, and became the first Austrian chancellor openly to acknowledge the crimes of Austrians during the Holocaust. Haider's own statements on the Third Reich only enhanced the plausibility of Vranitzky's portrayal. At the same time, however, successive Social Democratic interior ministers, beginning with Franz Löschnak in the early 1990s, attempted to defuse Haider's criticism of government policies dealing with the "foreigner problem" by denouncing Haider's xenophobic excesses while imposing increasingly more severe restrictions on immigration.[38] The ÖVP's response was either to promote itself as the guarantor of stability (as part of a grand coalition, whose large parliamentary majority would ensure sufficient support for the difficult reform measures the government was to adopt), or to flirt with the option of forming a coalition with the FPÖ. While the former strategy kept the ÖVP both from running strongly against the SPÖ (it had, after all, approved all government measures), and denied it electoral rewards for the policies it claimed to have pushed through, the latter strategy was hotly disputed within the party itself, for all the usual reasons. The results of this policy oscillation are well known.

Yet just as Haider has dominated Austrian politics, his becoming a political pariah has paralyzed Austrian politics as well. By casting Haider as an extremist, borderline neo-Nazi (the very image that has caused such concern outside Austria), Vranitzky certainly scared some Austrians into voting for the SPÖ, though those voters affected by this appeal appear to have come mainly from previous Green, Liberal

Forum, and ÖVP voters, rather than FPÖ voters. However, the very success of this strategy made it politically nearly impossible to govern with Haider, even assuming it were possible on programmatic grounds.

At the same time, the Social Democrats and People's Party signally neglected to address the larger, *and among Haider's voters far more significant*, issues of corruption and unearned party patronage. In what almost could be seen as a political death wish, the two parties continued to provide Haider with enough ammunition of their complacency on this issue (the crude political horse-trading surrounding the reappointment of the ÖVP's Franz Fischler as the EU Commissioner for Agriculture was only the latest example), and Haider was always only too happy to oblige. All these strategies failed ignominiously: the Social Democrats' 33.15 percent of the vote in the October election was a historic low, the ÖVP slipped into third place (in terms of total votes) for the first time in its history, while with 26.9 percent of the vote the FPÖ registered its most successful election result yet.

After the elections in October 1999, negotiations did take place between the Social Democrats and the People's Party, who between them still commanded the largest parliamentary majority. Yet it is unlikely that the ÖVP was seriously committed to forming a new coalition with the SPÖ. The October election confirmed the trend of all previous elections since 1986: the FPÖ continued to increase its vote at the expense of the two grand coalition parties. But this trend had affected the People's Party more severely than it had the Social Democrats. As the junior partner in the grand coalition, for example, whatever electoral benefits of incumbency that successful government policies might bestow had always redounded more to the SPÖ's favor than to the ÖVP's. Wolfgang Schüssel could thus credibly consider the situation after the October election as a do or die situation for his party (and his leadership). Schüssel's ÖVP had four options: to continue as the junior partner in the grand coalition with the SPÖ; to support an SPÖ-led minority government; to go into opposition; or to form a coalition with the FPÖ. Schüssel must have feared that the Social Democrats, despite their pledge to the contrary, might in the end find a way to form a coalition with the FPÖ, or at least to reach some sort of accommodation. A Social Democratic minority government tolerated by the FPÖ in response for certain concessions, however, would freeze the ÖVP out completely. The most promising option politically for Schüssel was therefore to form a government with the

FPÖ, with himself as chancellor. This solution would break Social Democratic dominance in the government for the first time in thirty years, and would return a People's Party chancellor to office. Schüssel, who has an inordinately high sense of self-esteem, was not unaware of the domestic political risks involved in such a move, though he clearly misjudged the extent of the hostile international reaction. But he seems to have been convinced that, as chancellor, he would be able to achieve important reforms that he claimed had been blocked by the Social Democrats in the grand coalition government, and that he could contain, or even reverse, the FPÖ's continued electoral advance, which would also mean reversing the ÖVP's electoral decline.

Judging by the coalition agreement signed by Schüssel and Haider, the new Austrian government represents a significant shift to the right of the current European norm (though in most respects its policies remain to the left of the Clinton Administration).[39] The ÖVP's role in the Waldheim Affair and the FPÖ's xenophobic election campaigns raise legitimate concerns about this new government's scrupulous observance of minority rights and of its commitment to abide by recognized conventions of tolerance. These dangers should not be overlooked or underestimated. However, the social and economic policies the new coalition has pledged to pursue also represent a radical departure from the previous "Austro-Keynesian" consensus. It is these policies, moreover, rather than the issues of xenophobia or the trivialization of the National Socialism, which will most likely determine the fate of the coalition parties in the next election.

One need not share Schüssel's own sanguine prognosis for the government or for his party to recognize that domestically, the formation of this government *could* have some salutary long-term effects. For one thing, it has, for better or worse, broken the quarantine that had been hung on Haider's FPÖ at the national level. But while the FPÖ is now a governing party, Haider is not in the government. The anomaly of the national party leader not serving in a coalition government of which his party is a member was resolved when Haider formally ceded his position as FPÖ national leader to Vice-Chancellor Susanne Riess-Passer. However, because no one seriously doubts that Haider still calls the shots in the party (he has remained a member of the "coalition committee," which coordinates the work of the two parties in the government), this situation is fraught with risks both for the FPÖ and for the government. The FPÖ's transition from an opposition to a governing party, while difficult in and of itself, is complicated by the fact that Haider is not in the government. Part of the reason for the success of the FPÖ under Haider's leadership has been the freedom it enjoyed as an opposition party. Indeed, most of its voters since 1986 have been protest voters; only a small proportion of them voted for the FPÖ because of its specific policies (many of which were difficult to reconcile with each other in any case). And while Haider will doubtless try to be both a supporter of his party's participation in government, as well as in opposition to that very government, this will not be easy to pull off successfully. Hence the very fact that Haider holds no ministry in the national government is a source of potential conflict between him and the party's ministers. For if these FPÖ ministers (in particular Finance Minister Karl Heinz Grasser and Vice-Chancellor Susanne Riess-Passer) begin to assert their independence from Haider and develop a personal political interest in the success of the government, they might find support within the party, and this would, in turn, limit Haider's overall control of the party. At the same time, if such conflicts between Haider and the FPÖ ministers do arise, it could paralyze the work of the government itself, which would be especially detrimental to Schüssel's plans. Should, however, the government avoid such conflicts because the ÖVP bows to Haider's pressure, then it is not clear who would be rewarded for these governmental successes at the polls. Nonetheless, Schüssel, at least domestically, is playing with some strong cards, and his political gamble might well pay off, ushering in the electoral renaissance of the ÖVP, and either reducing the FPÖ's share of the vote, or forcing it to moderate its racist rhetoric.

Moreover, the ÖVP-FPÖ coalition has also created a new, and quite large, parliamentary opposition comprising the Social Democratic and Green parties, and has, at long last, shaken anti-Haider political forces in Austria out of their passivity. Together with more combative trade unions, which are vehemently opposed to the government's social and economic policies, these forces could exert notable pressure on the government both inside and outside parliament. President Thomas Klestil, who only reluctantly agreed to approve the government,[40] is also in a strong position to exercise influence on the government beyond his constitutional prerogatives per se. Klestil required both Schüssel and Haider to sign a declaration "Responsibility for Austria—A Future in the Heart of Europe." This document expressed the coalition partners' "unshakable commitment to the intellectual and moral values that are the common heritage of the peoples of Europe." In keeping with this heritage, the declaration stated, the government would strive for "an Austria in which xenophobia, anti-Semitism and racism have no place." Indeed, the government pledged itself to oppose all beliefs that show contempt for other human beings. Moreover, Austria acknowledged "its responsibility deriving from the fateful history of the twentieth century and the monstrous crimes of the National Socialist regime." It explicitly noted the "singularity and incomparability of the Holocaust." The best guarantee against the return of this dark chapter of Europe's history, the declaration stated, was the European commitment to peace and the current aims of the European Union. Whatever Klestil's motives, forcing the two to sign the declaration was a potentially shrewd political move, for a perceived violation of one of the provisions could serve as the basis for demanding the dismissal of ministers, a change of government, or even new elections.

The Measures of the Europeans against the Austrian Government

Given the predominantly domestic determinants of the recent elections and the appointment of the current Austrian government, and the equally important domestic factors that will probably decide the political outcome, it is well to examine how the external pressures that have been brought to bear on the current Austrian government might affect this positively or negatively. Acting as the representatives of the individual EU governments, but not as an EU body, the heads of fourteen states decided to end official bilateral contacts with the Austrian government. This means that no state visits by heads of states or governments will take place. While official contacts in official EU bodies will not be affected by this decision, Austrian ambassadors will be received by subaltern foreign ministry officials of these fourteen countries. Finally, Austrians who are nominated for international positions will no longer be supported by the EU and its anti-Haider allies.[41]

In considering the effectiveness of these sanctions, it seems to me that some questions are unavoidable: Are these measures comprehensible? Are they applied consistently? Are they likely to achieve their intended aims? And just what are these aims?

There is something woefully disingenuous about the descriptions of the sanctions by the fourteen EU countries, as well as the varied justifications for their imposition. Though there was no precedent for this form of sanction, nor is it covered by the Amsterdam treaty, the announcement at an official EU gathering that fourteen states were unilaterally imposing sanctions on the Austrian government was nothing other than a sleight of hand clearly intended to convey the impression of EU legitimacy where none exists. The sanctions, though largely symbolic, nonetheless do represent a significant escalation in comparison with the international isolation of Austrian President Kurt Waldheim between 1986 and 1992. Back then, only Israel formally recalled its ambassador, and while many European countries devised various strategies to avoid meeting Kurt Waldheim officially, diplomatic protocol was on the whole observed.

Moreover, the sanctions do not seem terribly consistent. Leaving aside the participation of the Allianze nationale in the Italian government a few years back, consider these facts: in 1999 Jörg Haider was unanimously elected to serve on the EU committee on regions. In other words, the representatives of the very states which have sanctioned Austria for forming a government of which Haider is not a member, voted one year earlier to accept him personally into an official EU body. Moreover, the FPÖ under Haider has served, and is now serving, in several provincial governments in Austria: the provincial governments in Upper Austria, Lower Austria, Burgenland, Vorarlberg, Vienna, and Carinthia all have members of the FPÖ currently in their governments, either because the provincial constitution mandates proportional distribution of government ministries, or because of the party's considerable gains in recent provincial elections. Jörg Haider himself is governor of Carinthia. It is not entirely clear what difference the mere presence of the FPÖ in the government at a national level makes that the presence of Haider as governor of Carinthia does not?

It is not particularly edifying to point out the inconsistency of putatively "moral" stances of states.[42] A far stronger argument can be made, however, that, consistent or not, a policy should at least bear some reasonable chance of achieving its aims. But what are these aims? What exactly is it about the FPÖ that has justified these sanctions? Is it the program of the FPÖ, of individual planks of it, or the demagogic means by which Haider pursues them? If it is the program, does it count for naught that the written coalition agreement, which bears Haider's signature, contains neither a rejection of the eastward expansion of the EU (but a ringing endorsement of European integration), nor a single ethnically discriminatory measure (but states a commitment to integration of immigrants, and makes a firm statement about the Holocaust)?

Since these measures by the non-Austrian members of the EU were announced before any of the leaders could have read the coalition agreement, it is unlikely that the government's program was a consideration. This presumably leaves Haider's, and his party's, consistent use of xenophobic and racist appeals in support of its positions against immigration and the eastern expansion of the Union, and Haider's statements trivializing the Nazi regime. But here one needs to be very clear about what the sanctions hope to achieve: do they wish to exert sufficient pressure until Schüssel bends and ends the coalition with the FPÖ? Or is the aim to convince Austrians to reject these racist politics? Clearly such sanctions would have more chance of achieving the former than the latter, but is the introduction of a kind of informal, supranational European political police regime with no explicit terms of reference, and no accountability, the best way to do this?

It is counter-intuitive to think that Austrians, like citizens of every other European state, would not resent the short-circuiting of their country's democratic procedures. Moreover, where, exactly, does one draw the line on pandering to, or promoting, ethnic prejudice or racism? At what point are such sanctions to be considered? There can be no doubt about the FPÖ's having appealed to racism, but a close look at earlier campaigns of French President Jacques Chirac suggests that it was not wholly free of such pandering. Moreover, FPÖ voters, while not deterred by this politics, do not *necessarily* endorse either Haider's revisionist views on National Socialism or his party's xenophobic politics. Moreover, they, as well as many others, have had good reasons for opposing the SPÖ-ÖVP oligopoly and the corrupt practices it has generated. The Green Party, and the Liberal Forum, have both condemned such practices and offered a political alternative to the FPÖ, while equally explicitly condemning the intolerance preached by the FPÖ. I, personally, would prefer that either or both become the voice of opposition instead of Haider, but, for a number of reasons, some of which I have discussed above, most Austrians to date think otherwise. Finally, the sanctions themselves have impeded the very important political debate in Austria by deflecting it onto the extraneous issue of foreign interference and thus handing the ÖVP-FPÖ government an unearned, but ruthlessly exploited, patriotic bonus.

The virtue of encouraging the efforts of the anti-Haider forces in

Austria, while following a vigilant, but more calibrated and less obviously hypocritical policy of condemnation and isolation of Haider and his party, is that it allows Austrians themselves to observe Haider's inability to fulfill his demagogic promises. It could also force him and his party colleagues to moderate their policies and xenophobic rhetoric. Under the terms of the Amsterdam treaty, the EU has the means to apply swift and effective sanctions to the Austrian government, should it adopt measures that violate European human rights agreements. And, should the Austrian (or the British, Spanish, German or any other) government take similar measures, the appropriate EU bodies should act, and act promptly. Dealing as a European Union with the challenges presented by parties of the FPÖ's ilk in national elections presents a number of very difficult questions, and there are no easy answers. It seems clear, moreover, that these European leaders acted out of genuine political concern, even if not out of particularly honorable motives. The attempt of the European countries to find a face-saving way to end the sanctions by empowering a three-member informal commission to investigate, among other things, the political nature of the FPÖ, will probably deliver a verdict that effectively confers legitimacy on the FPÖ as a party worthy of government, or at least will be promoted as such by the government and the FPÖ. There are thus good reasons to suspect that the European Union's decision will not bring Haider to his knees, and might well even strengthen his hand in Austria. Is this really what they set out to do?

Postscript

This chapter was written in the spring of 2000, as an occasional piece designed to provide some historical and political background to the October 1999 election and formation of the Austrian government in February 2000, and the sanctions imposed on Austria by the other European Union members. Consequently, it was written prior to the submission of the report by the three-member commission appointed by the European Court of Human Rights to investigate the Austrian government and the FPÖ, which led to the lifting of the sanctions against Austria, and prior to the Nice summit meeting of the European Union member countries in December 2000, which officially adopted a procedure to deal with similar political events in a member state of the Union. Apart from typographical and other similar errors, I have not altered the original text, because to have written a new article that was completely current and would evaluate the policies of the government in power not only would have required substantially more research, but would have altered the character of the piece itself. However, it is important to say a word or two about developments since the spring of 2000. In September, the three-member commission comprising Martti Ahtisaari, Jochen Frowein, and Marcelino Oreja, submitted their report on the commitment of the Austrian government to what were called "common European values," in particular relating to the rights of minorities, refugees, and immigrants, and on the nature of the FPÖ.[43] As predicted, this report, while critical of certain aspects of the FPÖ and current government ministers, nonetheless pronounced the Austrian government within the spectrum of mainstream European politics. In light of this finding, the lifting of sanctions against Austria became a foregone conclusion, and duly followed. Thus, in addition to the sanctions having provided the Schüssel government with what I termed its "patriotic bonus," the report of the commission, portrayed as legitimating Schüssel's decision and the defiant stance of the Austrian government itself, was also an implicit criticism of the sanctions regime as well. In addition, since this article was completed, Austrian journalist Gerfried Sperl has published a book dealing with the negotiations between the SPÖ and ÖVP, and between the ÖVP and FPÖ, which led to what he described as the "transfer of power."[44] Sperl conducted dozens of interviews for his book, and provides many more details of the events leading up to Schüssel's decision to break off negotiations with the SPÖ and form a government with the FPÖ. There is, however, nothing in it which requires me to revise my initial, more impressionistic judgment. It is also worth mentioning that it was the ÖVP-FPÖ government, led by Wolfgang Schüssel and supported by Jörg Haider, which finally concluded the negotiations and signed an agreement providing for the restitution of slave laborers who had been employed in firms located on Austrian soil during the Nazi dictatorship. While I still believe that the sanctions of the EU countries themselves were mistaken and ultimately counterproductive, it is nonetheless true that the political pressure under which Schüssel came as a result of his deciding to govern with the FPÖ nonetheless prompted the government to prove its democratic credentials by taking individual measures which to some might seem surprising, but which are laudable in any case. Finally, since the formation of the Schüssel government, the FPÖ has suffered major setbacks in two state elections (in Styria and Burgenland), and current indications at the time of writing suggest that it will do the same in the upcoming Vienna municipal elections. Whether this trend continues, or whether it is just another of the temporary setbacks which have beset the FPÖ since 1986 (since each of these elections had its own local dynamic and issues) remains to be seen. Equally uncertain is whether the FPÖ reacts to this string of setbacks by resuming its radical xenophobic and racist rhetoric, which would threaten the national coalition. But, in the short term, at least, Schüssel's gamble that he could show up the FPÖ by having it serve as the junior partner in his government, appears to have paid off.

Notes

1. The title is a pun on the political colors associated with the respective parties in Austrian political culture: the ÖVP are the "blacks," the FPÖ the "blues," the SPÖ the "reds." The Greens are, of course, the "greens."
2. *Financial Times*, October 4, 1999; *Corriere della Sera*, October 4, 1999.
3. *"Liar's Poker," New York Times*, February 8, 2000.
4. "Haider and the Hypocrites," *The New Republic*, February 21, 2000.
5. George Will, "Europe overreacts on Austria matter," *Washington Post*, February 11, 2000. Friedman also declared that Haider was "a neo-Nazi and a high tech free-marketeer . . . Pat Buchanen *and* Steve Forbes." Wills' judgment about this was, in fact, more perceptive than most.
6. On the effects of the Waldheim debate on Austrian politics more generally, see Richard Mitten, *The Politics of Antisemitic Prejudice. The Waldheim Phenomenon in Austria* (Boulder, CO: Westview Press, 1992), especially Chapter 9.
7. The German word *Überfremdung,* used if not coined under the Nazis, and frequently, if infelicitously, translated as "over-foreignization," connotes images similar to those conveyed by the expression "yellow peril."
8. In the 1988 presidential election, then incumbent Republican Vice-President George Bush ran against former Massachusetts governor Michael Dukakis. As part of his campaign to portray Dukakis as being "soft on crime," the Bush campaign publicized the case of Wille Horten. While on leave during a prison furlough program which Dukakis supported, Horten, an African-American who had been convicted of raping a white women, allegedly committed another crime, for which he was subsequently convicted. Horten's face, shown repeatedly (and menacingly) throughout the spot, was a kind of visual code which triggered unspoken prejudicial beliefs about African-Americans and crime without, however, ever making an explicit appeal to these racist assumptions.
9. *Time*, Vol. 153 no. 17 (May 3, 1999).
10. See, for example, *Le Monde*, February 5, 6, and 7, 2000. To be sure, there have been well-informed and quite subtle explorations of the significance of the elections and the new government which do not exhibit this bias, but they are exceptional. See Anson Rabinbach, "The Specter of Jörg Haider," *Los Angeles Times*,

February 6, 2000, Tony Judt, "Tale from the Vienna Woods," *The New York Review of Books* XLVII, no. 5 (2000, 23 March 2000).

11. See, for example Mark Mazower, "Haider is Not Alone," *Civilization*, no. 4 (2000), *Http://www.civmag.com/articles/-* C0004.wor.html.

12. See Richard Mitten, *The Politics of Antisemitic Prejudice. The Waldheim Phenomenon in Austria* (Boulder, CO: Westview Press, 1992), passim; Richard Mitten, "Jörg Haider, the Anti-Immigrant Petition and Immigration Policy in Austria," *Patterns of Prejudice* 28, no. 2 (1994): 27–47; Richard Mitten, "'Are We Austrians Germans?' Jörg Haider and the Dilemmas of Austrian Identity," *Jewish Quarterly* 43, no. 2 (Summer 1996): 24–28. Richard Mitten, "EU Could Strengthen Haider's Hand in Austria," text found at http://wwics.si.edu/NEWS/mitten.htm.

13. For the historical background to the German national Lager and Liberalism in Austria, see Adam Wandruszka, "Österreichs politische Struktur. Die Entwicklung der Parteien und Politischen Bewegungen," edited by Heinrich Benedikt, in *Geschichte der Republik Österreich* (Munich: R. Oldenburg, 1954), 291–485; Max E. Riedlsperger, *The Lingering Shadow of Nazism: The Austrian Independent Party Movement Since 1945*, East European Monographs (Boulder: East European Quarterly, Distributed by Columbia University Press, 1978); Max E. Riedlsperger, "FPÖ: Liberal or Nazi?" in *Conquering the Past: Austrian Nazism Yesterday and Today*, edited by F. Parkinson (Detroit: Wayne State University Press, 1989), 257–78; Brigitte Bailer and Wolfgang Neugebauer, "Die FPÖ: Vom Liberalismus Zum Rechtsextremismus," in *Rechtsextremismus in Österreich*, edited by Stiftung Dokumentationsarchiv des österreichischen Widerstandes (Vienna: Deuticke, 1993), 327–428; see also Viktor Reimann, *Die Dritte Kraft in Österreich* (Vienna, Munich, Zurich and New York: Verlag Fritz Molden, 1980) and Lothar Höbelt, *Von der vierten Partei zur dritten Kraft. Die Geschichte des VdU* (Graz and Stuttgart: Leopold Stocker Verlag, 1999).

14. For biographical information on Haider's career, see Brigitte Bailer and Wolfgang Neugebauer, "Die FPÖ: Vom Liberalismus Zum Rechtsextremismus," in *Rechtsextremismus in Österreich*, edited by Stiftung Dokumentationsarchiv des österreichischen Widerstandes (Vienna: Deuticke, 1993), 327–39, and more generally, Christa Zöchling, *Haider: Licht und Schatten einer Karriere* (Vienna: Econ Taschenbuch, 2000),7–54.

15. Brigitte Bailer and Wolfgang Neugebauer, "Die FPÖ: Vom Liberalismus Zum Rechtsextremismus," 339–47; Richard Mitten, "Jörg Haider, the Anti-Immigrant Petition and Immigration Policy in Austria," *Patterns of Prejudice* 28, no. 2 (1994): 27–30.

16. See Richard Mitten, *The Politics of Antisemitic Prejudice. The Waldheim Phenomenon in Austria*, 246–59.

17. "Protokoll einer Vernaderung," *Schnell-INFO der FPÖ*, Vol. 5, Issue no. 30/96 (pamphlet published by the Freiheitlichen in Vienna), pp. 10–11; *Kärntner Nachrichten*, February 14, 1985; *Wiener Zeitung*, June 14, 1991.

18. Brigitte Bailer and Wolfgang Neugebauer, "Die FPÖ: Vom Liberalismus Zum Rechtsextremismus," 353–57.

19. Richard Mitten, "Jörg Haider, the Anti-Immigrant Petition and Immigration Policy in Austria," 27–47; Martin Reisigl and Ruth Wodak, "'Aliens' and 'Foreigners': The Political and Media Discourse About the Austria First Petition of Jörg Haider and the Austrian Freedom Party in 1992 and 1993," in *Discourse and Discrimination* (London and New York: Routledge, 2001), 144–204.

20. For a well-informed introduction to the Austrian political structure and its

"corporatist" institutions, see Anton Pelinka, *Austria. Out of the Shadow of the Past* (Boulder, CO: Westview Press, 1998).

21. Fritz Plasser and Peter Ulram, *Radikaler Rechtspopulismus in Österreich. Die FPÖ Unter Jörg Haider*, Final Report. Zentrum für Angewandte Politikforschung, November 1994 (Vienna: Fessel + GFK, 1994); Richard Mitten, "Jörg Haider, the Anti-Immigrant Petition and Immigration Policy in Austria," 27–47.

22. See, for example, Bernd Matouschek, Ruth Wodak, and Franz Janoschek, *Notwendige Maßnamen gegen Fremde? Genese und Formen von rassistischen Diskursen der Differenz* (Vienna: Passagen Verlag, 1995).

23. In making the distinction between xenophobic and racist appeals I am following Gavin Langmuir's argument in his essay "Toward a Definition of Antisemitism." See Gavin I. Langmuir, *Toward a Definition of Antisemitism* (Berkeley, Los Angeles and London: University of California Press, 1990), 311–52.

24. On the phenomenon of prejudice, and the distinctions made here about its mobilization, see Gordon Allport, *The Nature of Prejudice*, reprint, 1954 (Reading, MA.: Addison-Wesley Publishing Company, Inc., 1987); Richard S. Levy, ed., *Antisemitism in the Modern World. An Anthology of Texts*, Sources in Modern History (Lexington, MA and Toronto: D.C. Heath and Company, 1991), 1–11; Ruth Wodak, et al., *"Wir sind Alle Unschuldige Täter!" Diskurshistorische Studien Zum Nachkriegsantisemitismus in Österreich* (Frankfurt: Suhrkamp, 1990); and Richard Mitten, *The Politics of Antisemitic Prejudice. The Waldheim Phenomenon in Austria*, passim.

25. Two surveys were carried out by the Gallup organization in Austria for the American Jewish Committee (AJC) in 1991 and 1993. A third study was conducted by University of Vienna sociologist Hilde Weiss, author of a highly regarded 1987 study of anti-Semitic prejudice in Austria. The results were reported for the sample as a whole, and can be broken down according to sex, age, education, geographical region and political preferences. For reasons of space I will focus on the two AJC studies. With some minor variations, the AJC and Weiss studies reach essentially similar conclusions. See Österreichisches Gallup-Institut, "Antisemitismus in Österreich," June-July-August 1991, Ms. Vienna, 1991; American Jewish Committee, "Current Austrian Attitudes toward Jews and the Holocaust," New York: American Jewish Committee, 1995; Hilde Weiss, *Nationalismus-Studie*, Final rept. (Vienna: Bundesministerium für Wissenschaft, Kunst und Verkehr, 1996); Hilde Weiss, *Stereotyp und Attribution ethnischer Gruppen in Österreich: Komponenten des Vorurteils und soziale Hintergründe.*, Final rept. (Vienna: Bundesministerium für Wissenschaft und Verkehr, 1998); Hilde Weiss, "Alte und neue Minderheiten. Zum Einstellungswandel in Österreich (1984–1998)," *SWS-Rundschau* 40, no. 1 (2000): 25–42.

26. This included the categories "strongly agree" and "mostly agree."

27. Richard Mitten and Ruth Wodak, "Antisemitic Prejudice in Contemporary Austria," *Patterns of Prejudice* 25, no. 2 (Winter 1991): 49–54.

28. Apart from the normal bias inherent in opinion surveys generally, quantitative studies like those commissioned by the AJC or carried out by Weiss face the additional difficulty of ascertaining and measuring from the instruments available (interviews) the precise impact of the official taboo on anti-Semitic prejudice in postwar Austria among respondents. Such studies thus may not reliably show how extensive anti-Jewish prejudice or hostility towards other ethnic groups is, as much as how well those interviewed were aware of the preferred response. Thus, such surveys must be complemented by other, qualitative studies, primarily those

analyzing political discourse, to get a fuller, but by no means definitive, picture. See Ruth Wodak, et al., *"Wir sind Alle Unschuldige Täter!" Diskurshistorische Studien Zum Nachkriegsantisemitismus in Österreich*, 31–58.

29. The following data are taken from Fritz Plasser and Peter Ulram, *Radikaler Rechtspopulismus in Österreich. Die FPÖ Unter Jörg Haider*); Fritz Plasser, Peter A. Ulram, Erich Neuwirth, and Franz Sommer, "Analyse der Nationalratswahl 1995. Muster, Trends, Motive und Wählerströme," In *Politische Macht und Kontrolle*, Informationen zur politischen Bildung, edited by Johann Burger and Elisabeth Morawek (Vienna: Verlag Jugend & Volk, 1996), 109–20. Fritz Plasser, Peter A. Ulram, and Franz Sommer, "Analyse der Nationalratswahl 1995. Muster, Trends, Motive und WählerströMe," in *Analyse der Nationalratswahl 1999. Muster, Trends und Entscheidungsmotive*, in *Politische Macht und Kontrolle*, Informationen zur politischen Bildung, edited by Johann Burger and Elisabeth Morawek (Http://www.gfk.co.at: Fessel-GfK, 1999), 109–20.

30. Fritz Plasser, Peter A. Ulram, and Franz Sommer, "Analyse der Nationalratswahl 1995. Muster, Trends, Motive und Wählerströme," in *Analyse der Nationalratswahl 1999. Muster, Trends und Entscheidungsmotive*, in *Politische Macht und Kontrolle*, Informationen zur politischen Bildung, edited by Johann Burger and Elisabeth Morawek (Http://www.gfk.co.at: Fessel-GfK, 1999), 19.

31. Poll cited in Max Riedelsperger, "Die Freiheitlichen—A View from the U.S.," http://www.multimedia.calpoly.edu/libarts/mriedlsp/Publications/referat.html. Max Riedelsperger is the author of an important study of the FPÖ, and is a prolific writer who has been enjoying a great deal of prominence of late. One can only applaud Riedelsperger's willingness to cut through the hypocritical cant of U.S. politicians when trying to explain the FPÖ to his American readers, and his hard-nosed look at politics frequently yields helpful insights. Unfortunately, Riedelsperger's polemical zeal sometimes leads him to read, or miss, evidence, in a way that distorts, not to say trivializes, Haider's politics. In a brief essay posted on his personal web site, for example, Riedelsperger analyzes the speech Haider gave in Krumpendorf in September 1995. In that speech, Haider praised those present as people "who have character and who remain true to their convictions against strong head winds, and who have remained true to them until today." In his analysis of the Krumpendorf speech, Riedelsperger states, in bold typeface, **"There is no mention in this speech of the Waffen-SS."** He also claims that it was German television's identification of "some of the members of the audience at Krumpendorf as Waffen-SS veterans" which "led to the charge that Haider praised the values of the SS." a charge Riedelsperger, based on his analysis of the text, clearly rejects. While it is certainly true that Haider did not mention the Waffen-SS by name in his speech, what Riedelsperger left unstated is that Haider was addressing a meeting of the Kamaradschaft IV (K-IV for short), which is *the organization of Waffen-SS veterans*. It is named Kamaradschaft-IV because the Waffen-SS considered itself the fourth pillar of the German armed forces. Why, then, would Haider have needed to mention the Waffen-SS by name, when every-one in the audience, and certainly Haider as well, knew very well that his praise of those who had remained "true to their convictions against strong head winds, and who have remained true to them until today" included the members of an organization which comprises principally members of the Waffen-SS? Riedelsperger's view that the Krumpendorf "incident" revealed merely "Haider's historical ignorance and lack of sensitivity" is thus, shall we say, exceedingly generous. Judgments like these reinforce my impression, based on a desultory consultation of the official FPÖ web site, that Riedelsperger has become the

FPÖ's favorite historian for a good reason. See "Jörg Haider and the SS," http://www.multimedia.calpoly.edu/libarts/mriedlsp/Publications/Krumpendorf.html.

32. Richard Mitten, *The Politics of Antisemitic Prejudice. The Waldheim Phenomenon in Austria*; Ruth Wodak, et al., *"Wir sind Alle Unschuldige Täter!" Diskurshistorische Studien Zum Nachkriegsantisemitismus in Österreich.*

33. Bernd Matouschek, Ruth Wodak, and Franz Janoschek, *Notwendige Massnahmen Gegen Fremde? Genese und Formen von Rassistischen Diskursen der Differenz* (Vienna: Passagen Verlag, 1995), passim.

34. *Kurier*, May 27, 1999, 7.

35. "Jeder Buschneger hat in Zukunft die Moeglichkeit, seine Kollegen in Oesterreich zu behandeln" (Haider ueber das neue Aerztegesetz, *Der Standard*, 13.10.1998).

36. "Schwarzafrikaner schauen nicht nur anders aus, (. . .) sondern sie sind auch anders, und zwar sind sie besonders aggressiv" (Helene Partik-Pablé, *Tiroler Tageszeitung,* 20.5. 1999).

37. See, for example, *Washington Post*, November 10, 1999.

38. This strategy was examined in detail in Richard Mitten, "Jörg Haider, the Anti-Immigrant Petition and Immigration Policy in Austria," *Patterns of Prejudice* 28, no. 2 (1994): 27–47.

39. See the coalition agreement and the "Regierungserklärung Bundeskanzler Dr. Wolfgang Schüssel," both MS, Vienna, February 2000. *Neue Zürcher Zeitung*, February 10, 2000.

40. See *Neue Zürcher Zeitung*, February 5, 2000.

41. *Neue Zürcher Zeitung*, February 4, 2000; February 5, 2000.

42. Tony Judt, *"Tale from the Vienna Woods," The New York Review of Books* XLVII, no. 5 (23 March 2000), offers a delightful antidote to the self-righteous utterings of the Europeans on this score.

43. Martti Ahtisaari, Jochen Frowein, and Marcelino Oreja, "Report," Report of the Commission Established by the European Court of Human Rights on Austria (Paris, September 8, 2000).

44. Gerfried Sperl, *Der Machtwechsel. Österreichs politische Krise zu Beginn des 3. Jahrtausend* (Vienna: Molden Verlag, 2000).

10

The FPÖ in the European Context

Anton Pelinka

The Austrian government, appointed and sworn in on Feburary 4, 2000, has provoked a remarkable political turmoil:

- The governments of the (other) fourteen EU member states sanctioned the Austrian government as a consequence of the Freedom Party's (FPÖ's) participation in the government. Bilateral relations between the fourteen and Austria were downgraded to a bureaucratic level. No Austrian representative on the cabinet level was welcome on bilateral missions in the EU capitals. No Austrian ambassador has been allowed to meet cabinet members of the fourteen governments. Other non-EU governments—Canada, Norway, Poland, and the Czech Republic—have followed this pattern.
- The European Commission declared that the Austrian government will be closely observed. If it violates any of the common European values, the Commission willnot hesitate to start the procedure leading to the cancellation of Austria's voting rights in the Council according to Articles 6 and 7 of the Amsterdam Treaty. This could well have been a first step towards Austria's expulsion from the EU.
- The European Parliament passed a resolution condemning the formation of a coalition government that includes the FPÖ. It stated: "The European Parliament . . . believes that the admission of the FPÖ into a coalition government legitimises the extreme right in Europe." (European Parliament resolution, B5–0101, 0103, 0106 and 0107/2000.) The resolution was passed by a majority of 406 votes, with 53 opposed and 60 abstentions.

The front within the EU against the new Austrian government was a kind of "grand coalition": Those who voted in favor of the resolution included not only the (social democratic, socialist, green) left, but also the liberal center and a significant part of the (moderate) right, for example, Spanish Conservatives and French Gaullists. The fourteen governments, represented by the Portuguese Presidency, that had declared their "sanctions" also represented a variety of different party affiliations. Center-left governments like those of Germany, the United Kingdom, Italy, Sweden, Portugal, and Greece acted together with others: The Spanish government is conservative, the French government is characterized by the right-left-"cohabitation," the Irish cannot be called leftist at all, and the Dutch, Belgian, Finnish, Danish, and Luxembourg governments all have rather complex coalition arrangements.

The European uproar has not been completely calmed down by the "lifting" of the bilateral measurements that followed the publication of the report of the three "wise men" in September. The former Finnish president Athisaari, the German international law professor Frowein, and the former Spanish cabinet minister (and EU-commissioner) Oreja were asked by the EU 14 to evaluate the human rights record of the Austrian government and the "nature" of the FPÖ (Kopeinig/Kotanko 2000).

The report's conclusion was the justification for an end to the bilateral boycott by the EU 14. This conclusion reflects the ambivalence of the European attitude towards the Austrian government and especially towards the FPÖ:

> From the material quoted in this part of the report it can be concluded that the present Austrian Government is committed to continue the fight against racism, anti-Semitism, discrimination and xenophobia in Austria.
> The determination of the present Federal Government must, however, be evaluated in the context of what will be described as the ambiguous language being repeatedly used by some high representatives of the FPÖ. (Report 2000, par. 63 f.)

The Real Issue: The FPÖ's Particular Nature

The reason for this unique European response was (and is) the perception of the FPÖ. The EU 14 sees the FPÖ as a party with an openly racist and xenophobic agenda. To build a majority within "cordon sanitaire," the EU 14 wanted to make it clear that such a party should not be tolerated in any decisive role within the Union.

Two questions should be raised: Was the EU's approach legitimate? And: Is the EU's image of the FPÖ correct? As the answer to the second question is the basis for the answer to the first question, the FPÖ's specific character is the real issue.

The FPÖ can be analyzed by looking at two aspects, both of which are of some significance: its historic roots and its present agenda. Historically, the FPÖ must be characterized as a party founded 1956 by former Nazis for former Nazis. The FPÖ's first chairman, Anton Reinthaller, was a former SS-general, and almost all of its rank and file members were former Nazi party members. From its very beginning, the FPÖ represented the tradition of the Pan-German camp in Austria, which became fully integrated into the Austrian NSDAP in the 1930s.

In the 1970s and 1980s, the FPÖ tried to change its image. The party redefined itself as centrist and liberal and formed a coalition with the Social Democrats in 1983. Haider was the most outspoken opponent of these changes. When he became party chairman in 1986, his leadership was perceived as a significant move toward the extreme right. The SPÖ cancelled the coalition agreement, and the FPÖ had to leave the Liberal International (Pelinka 1993). Together with Jean-Marie Le Pen, Haider became the symbol of the New (extreme) Right in Europe.

The price the FPÖ had to pay for this development was its total isolation in Europe. After its expulsion from the Liberal International, the FPÖ did not belong to any European umbrella organization. Within Austria, the FPÖ became the most vocal opponent of Austria's accession to the European Union. The FPÖ repeatedly used an anti-European agenda–in 1994, before a plebiscite legitimated Austria's EU membership; in 1998, before Austria joined the European Monitary Union (the "Euro Zone"); and beginning in 1998, with its principal opposition to the enlargement of the EU through the admission of former communist countries in Central Europe.

The FPÖ's European isolation became obvious when FPÖ-representatives joined the European Parliament in 1995. No party group was interested in welcoming the FPÖ as a member. The FPÖ politicians remained outside of any formalized affiliation while the other Austrian members joined the different factions–the conservative, the social democratic, the green, and the liberal groups. This isolation was a foreshadowing of what was to come in 2000: No one of any significance wanted to have established friendly or even normal relations with the FPÖ. The FPÖ became the most successful outsider of all the EU's parties—successful due to its exploitation of xenophobic and therefore anti-European sentiments, and isolated as a consequence of this very same strategy.

The FPÖ's rise after 1986 has always been seen in the context of the party's right wing past and present. Probably no other Austrian phenomenon of the 1990s has been observed, described, analyzed, and explained as much as the FPÖ (for some examples, see Bailer-Galanda/ Neugebauer 1997; Scharsach 2000; Reinfeldt 2000). There is a broad consensus among those responsible for all this research that the FPÖ is a rather unique example. It must be explained by two main factors, which are not necessarily linked:

- The FPÖ is a "populist" party (see e.g., Betz 1998; Plasser/ Ulram 2000; Reinfeldt 2000). The FPÖ voices the protest of "outsiders" against "insiders," of "have-nots" against "haves," of "modernization losers" against "modernization winners."
- The FPÖ is a "right wing" party (see e.g., Rechtsextremismus in Österreich 1994; Bailer-Galanda 1994; Bailer-Galanda/ Neugebauer 1997). The FPÖ has a tradition of trivializing Nazism as well as mobilizing prejudices against "the others." Xenophobic and (at least indirectly) racist attitudes play a significant role in the FPÖ's outlook.

This was also the understanding of Athisaari's, Frowein's, and Oreja's report:

> The FPÖ has reportedly not taken any action against its members who have used xenophobic statements in public; it has neither condemnded nor suppressed those statements, nor clearly apologized for them. When confronted with these statements the authors will deny that any National Socialist intention or even character really existed.
> There are, unfortunately, several political groupings using similar language in Europe. The FPÖ has, however, become the second strongest party in Austria and has been, since February 2000, a coalition partner in the Austrian Federal Government. We are of the opinion that a government party must be under much heavier scrutiny as far as its language and statements are concerned than opposition parties." (Report 2000, par. 89 f.)

Until 2000, the FPÖ was able to criticize the two other traditional parties–the social democratic SPÖ and the conservative ÖVP–as "old parties," representing an outdated political cartel, due to its outsider position in the post–1945 power arrangement in Austria. The SPÖ and ÖVP established a political culture of "consociationalism," which helped to stabilize a democratic polity by dividing political power between these two parties. The FPÖ was relegated to the role of the outsider. "Social partnership" as a corporatist network was another instrument that excluded the FPÖ from power. During the (first) grand coalition, from 1945 to 1966, the FPÖ was the sole opposition in parliament, but this monopoly did not help the Freedom Party increase the 5 to 7 percent of the votes it got at the national level. This situation did not change during the years of one-party government (1966 to 1983) or even during the SPÖ-FPÖ government. The pre-Haider FPÖ, which finally had its share in the government, was by all appearances stagnant (Pelinka 1993).

The return of the grand coalition after the elections in 1986 was the result of Haider's access to the party leadership, and Haider's further electoral successes were the result of the reestablished coalition. Because the SPÖ had declared it would never ally itself with the Haider FPÖ, and because the ÖVP was divided with respect to a possible alliance with the (new-old) FPÖ, there was no other way to get a parliamentary majority. But unlike the situation during the years of the first grand coalition, opposition to this government florished: The newly established Greens came into parliament as a fourth party, and the FPÖ started a period of rapid growth at the expense of the SPÖ and ÖVP.

The grand coalition as such was not responsible for the FPÖ's new strength; the explanation for Haider's success lies in a combination of social, economic, and political changes. The grand coalition did not create the Haider phenomenon, in fact, the grand coalition was an (ultimately unsuccessful) attempt to prevent Haider's rise to power.

The FPÖ's Structure

Of the two factors, which can explain this development, the "populist" factor must be considered first. Now, almost half a century after the FPÖ was founded, it represents a different, a new generation – one led by politicians born after 1945. The party's electoral success cannot be explained by pointing out a revival of the old type of Nazism. The data electoral research provides gives a clear picture of the FPÖ's electorate, who gave it 27 percent of the votes on October 3, 1999,

Table 10.1
Cleavages in the Austrian Electorate – General Elections 1999 (Plasser/ Ulram 2000:233)

Percentage according to the features	SPÖ	ÖVP	FPÖ	Greens	LIF(Liberals)
Religion					
practicing Catholics	20	59	13	4	1
others	34	22	30	7	3
Labor union membership					
members	49	19	21	6	2
non-members	24	30	30	8	4
Gender					
male	33	26	32	7	3
female	35	27	21	9	4
Education					
basic	37	24	29	3	2
higher	27	30	22	13	7

exit poll, n = 2,200

making it the second largest party after the SPÖ. The FPÖ's followers can be characterized by the following features:

- Youth: The FPÖ is especially successful with younger voters. In 1999, the FPÖ was the strongest party among voters under thirty.
- Gender: The FPÖ has significantly more appeal among men than among women. It has the only male-dominated electorate of all the Austrian parties.
- Class: The FPÖ has become a blue collar party. In 1999, for the first time in Austrian history, more working-class voters cast their ballots for the FPÖ than for the SPÖ.
- Education: The FPÖ has become a party of the lesser well educated. Reflecting the class factor, the FPÖ is successful among people with no higher education.
- Union Membership: The FPÖ has a rather weak presence in organized labor despite its overall popularity with blue-collar voters.
- Religion: The FPÖ is still a rather secular party. The party's followers are mostly non-practicing Catholics or non-Catholics.

The FPÖ electorate changed dramatically after Haider became chairman in 1986. A traditional bourgeois party with a more rural than urban background became a young, male-dominated, and more urbanized blue-collar party. The perception of the FPÖ as a socially conservative "bourgeois" party is no longer accurate. The expectation of the FPÖ-ÖVP coalition as an alliance of the anti-socialist forces is not

Table 10.2
The Dynamics of the FPÖ-Electorate (Plasser/Ulram 2000:231)

Percentage of the FPÖ-voters	1978	1986	1990	1994	1995	1999
men	54	61	60	60	62	62
women	46	39	40	40	38	38
	100	100	100	100	100	100
under 30 years	18	31	27	25	31	27
30–44	28	32	24	27	31	34
45–59	26	15	22	23	20	22
60 and older	28	22	26	26	19	16
	100	100	100	100	100	100
self employed	21	9	8	9	9	10
employed–white collar	24	32	25	24	27	33
employed blue collar	19	22	29	28	35	27
housewives	13	12	9	8	6	8
retired	23	19	27	28	19	18
students, unemployed	1	4	2	4	4	4
	100	100	100	100	100	100

1978: Fessel-GfK, survey of party preferences; 1986–1999, exit polls, n=2,200

compatible with the social composition of the new electorate responsible for the FPÖ's rise.

This alliance is one full of contradictions. Any coalition can be characterized by some contradictions. But the present Austrian coalition includes some very specific contradictions: The ÖVP was the party that started to push for Austria's EU membership in the 1980s. It was the ÖVP that succeeded in convincing the SPÖ of the advantages of membership. The FPÖ had been more pro-European than the two other traditional parties since the 1950s, but it reversed course when the SPÖ-ÖVP coalition applied for EU membership in 1989 and became the most ardent opponent of the EU as an overall concept (Schneider 1990; Pelinka/Schaller/Luif 1994). The FPÖ-ÖVP coalition is thus an alliance of the most active pro-EU party and the most active anti-EU party.

It is a rather characteristic coincidence that Europe became the main problem and even obstacle for this coalition from its very beginning. The EU's policy is directed at an Austrian government that is based on a rather striking inconsistency regarding Europe. Even if it is

Table 10.3
FPÖ-Party Membership and Party Organization (Luther 1997:293)

Party Members (absolute figures)					
1986	1988	1990	1992	1994	1996
36,683	37,958	40,629	41,260	43,764	44,541

Local Party Offices (O) and Organized Groups (G) (absolute figures)					
1984		1992		1996	
O	G	O	G	O	G
676	831	456	1084	215	1217

clear that the sanctions are not justified by the FPÖ's anti-EU record but by its history of xenophobic and racist policies, the European response is also an indirect answer to this contradiction.

Another contradiction inherent in the FPÖ-ÖVP coalition is the alliance of a very traditional party—the People's Party–and one which, despite its roots in Austrian tradition, has become a striking example of "postmodern" politics characterized by sound-bites, video-clips, and entertainment. The FPÖ presents itself as a party that fully accepts the fact that most voters are not especially interested in politics, and it successfully appeals to the majority which shows only occasional interest in politics. The FPÖ does not claim to have a consistent message, a consistent platform. For this audience, a consistent agenda is simply not necessary, and may even be counterproductive. The FPÖ's mixed bag of messages–excluding "them" (especially foreigners) and opposing "them" (the traditional political class)—is the voice of protest of those who feel "in" (as Austrians, as non-foreigners) and "out" (as social underdogs, as excluded from the political class) at the same time. (Reinfeldt 2000: esp.181–190).

The ÖVP, on the other hand, is a very traditionally structured party. Its membership is extremely high and its internal hierarchy is based on extremely well-organized subparties–the "Buende," which follow specific patterns of professional affiliations (farmers, employers, employees). The FPÖ, and especially the FPÖ since 1986, is a party with no traditional organization. It is striking that while the FPÖ's proportion of votes rose from 5 percent to 27 percent, it was not able to attract a significant number of new party members.

This data indicates a significant development: Membership has been on the rise, but to a much lesser degree than the number of popular votes. The FPÖ's "membership density"–the percentage of party members among its voters–declined between 1986 and 1996 from 7.8 to 4.2 percent (Luther 1997:293). The FPÖ was not able to convince its greatly increased electorate to become card-carrying members. Those numbers, unlike the electoral vote, was almost stagnant.

This development is underlined by the changes in the organization itself. During the years of Haider's electoral successes, the FPÖ downsized its party apparatus. The number of local party offices ("Stützpunkte")—usually run by fully paid party employees–declined dramatically. The number of organized local groups ("Ortsgruppen") increased nevertheless.

This indicates that the "new" FPÖ is based on a structure that is rather unusual for Austria: a less traditional organization (expressed by the decline in the number of local party offices), with comparatively little emphasis on membership, but full concentration on voters and elections. In that respect, the FPÖ can be called "postmodern"– especially compared with the ÖVP and the SPÖ, which are still characterized by a traditional emphasis on local organizations and on maximizing membership. The FPÖ has become a political party that concentrates solely on campaigning, neglecting all other activities.

This is all part of a populist agenda directed against the institutions of representative government–especially parties and organized interests, parliament, and the formalized version of democracy represented by parliamentary rule (Reinfeldt 2000: 213—216). This is not a unique phenomenon, and it does not explain the unusual response to the FPÖ's inclusion in the Austrian government. It is an additional factor that must be considered for a better understanding of the FPÖ's specific character. And this additional factor–the X-factor–is the linkage to the party's Nazi roots.

The FPÖ as an Austrian Phenomenon

There is reason to believe that the FPÖ's success and even its special quality would not be possible in any other European democracy, especially not in Germany. The German "re-education" and the re-alignment of the German party system after 1945 had not permitted the existence of a party which demonstrated its ambivalence regarding the NS-regime. Austria already had been under a kind of suspicion after the "Waldheim Affair" provoked critical observers to see Austria double-talking about Nazism: Arguing that Austria was the "first victim" of Hitler's Germany and at the same time appeasing the significant number of (former) members of the NSDAP in Austria. After Waldheim, Haider and his party became the focus of this suspicion.

The FPÖ is an Austrian party. In many respects, it has become the most Austrian of the Austrian parties. During the 1990s, the FPÖ seemed to have overcome the traditional contradiction between "Austrian patriotism" and "Pan-German nationalism." In its early years, the FPÖ opposed the idea of a specific Austrian national identity (Pelinka 1998:15–30). The FPÖ acted as the heir to the Pan-German tradition, which included the years of Nazi rule in Austria. In the party's liberal period, especially between 1978 and 1986, the FPÖ downplayed these roots and pragmatically accepted Austrian patriotism. When Haider became chairman, the party returned to the Pan-German tradition. Haider's well-known remark about the Austrian nation being an "ideological monster" ("ideologische Missgeburt"–Czernin 2000:20) was still in the tradition of Austrian Pan-Germanism, which never accepted the idea that Austria as a country could have a distinct Austrian, non-German character.

But in the 1990s, Haider tried to reconcile his own and his party's Pan-German outlook with Austrian patriotism, which was especially designed to withstand the appeal of Nazism and Nazi-Gemany. Haider's "Contract with Austria," patterned after the ideology of the U.S. Republicans and Newt Gingrich in 1994, was based on a strong "Austria first" emphasis (Reinfeldt 2000:195–212). This patriotic attitude helped the party go beyond the limits of Pan-German traditions, which were not able to attract many Austrians of the younger generation. The FPÖ in the 1990s was the party of German nationalism as well as of Austrian patriotism.

By bridging the gap between an Austrian non-German and an Austrian pan-German orientation, the FPÖ was able to unifiy all the ideological inclusiveness necessary to create a distinct exclusiveness. An analysis of the rhetoric used in the Austrian parliament showed that members of the FPÖ used the most aggressive terms against "them," "foreigners." This was not an exclusively FPÖ practice, but FPÖ representatives clearly lead in the exploitation of xenophobic resentments (Sedlak 2000).

This lingustic aggressiveness was in the tradition of Nazism. When Haider compared the number of foreigners living in Austria with the number of unemployed, he used the same pattern as the Nazis. "Foreigners" had replaced "Jews," but the message was the same: The enemy is responsible for unemployment (Czernin 2000:87). And when Haider used the term "parasites" to explain social problems, he used again a term familiar from the Nazi period (Czernin 2000:122, 124).

It is this parallel to Nazism that is the X-factor–the factor that makes the FPÖ different from general "populism." The FPÖ's populism is specific because it emerges directly from an unbroken Nazi tradition. The largest right-wing party in Europe is not just populist. It does not just use certain xenophobic stereotypes. Its success and its aggressiveness have to be seen in direct connection to the party's beginnings–and to Austria's darker image.

In that respect, the FPÖ phenomenon of 2000 is in direct succession to the Waldheim phenomenon of 1986. When Kurt Waldheim was elected Austrian president in 1986, critical observers realized that a majority of Austrians did not see any reason not to vote for a candidate who was trying to make Austria and the world forget about his years as an intelligence officer in the Wehrmacht. Austria's long tradition of anti-Semitism was suddenly a topic of an international debate (Wodak et al. 1990; Mitten 1992).

Haider had always defended Waldheim against his critics. Haider said that the president of the World Jewish Congress, Edgar Bronfman, was worse than Joseph Goebbels. In 1988, Haider declared that Austria had not to be liberated from its "democratically elected president, . . . (but) . . . from the manipulators of this campaign" (Czernin 2000:19 and 101).

For understandable reasons, Haider's rhetoric is seen as trivializing Nazism. It reminds observers of Austria's tradition of downplaying its involvement in the Nazi past and/or of downplaying the Nazi past itself (Scharsach 1992:97–141; Bailer-Galanda/Neugebauer 1997:50–102). This linkage to Nazism makes the FPÖ's populism specific.

There is an Austrian tendency to see the country as a permanent victim. In 1945, the Austrian government declared itself the "first victim" of Hitler's aggression. This was the term used by the Allies in Moscow in 1943–but the Austrian government usually quoted only the first part of the Moscow Declaration and not the second part, which gave Austria and the Austrians a kind of co-responsibility for Hitler's war. The official Austria wanted to absolve itself of any responsibility for Nazism. This Austrian "amnesia" made it possible after 1945 to integrate former Nazis into the political system (Pelinka 1998:183–194). And the very same amnesia made it possible for Austria to invent and then sell a "usable past" (Bischof 1999:52–67).

Westernization–Revisited ?

The EU's response to the new government in February 2000 may unleash a new wave of victimization in Austria and as a consequence create a distance between the EU and Austria. Almost immediately after 1945, Austria and the Austrian government began to build a special relationship with the Western powers, especially with the United States and Western Europe, which was a step toward an integrated Europe. In 1947, the Austrian government decided to accept the American invitation to participate in the Marshall Plan (Bischof 1999). This was the beginning of a long-term strategy: Despite having one-third of its territory occupied by Soviet forces, Austria followed the path of Western orientation. And despite declaring its neutrality in 1955–part of a bargain for the withdrawal the of occupying powers–Austria exploited every possible link to the West with the exception of NATO membership.

This Western orientation was the basis of Austria's decision to join the EU: As soon as the East-West conflict ended, Austria applied for EU membership and became a member in 1995. This was the logical consequence of decades of specific orientation. And even the principle of "permanent neutrality" had lost most of its significance (Pelinka 1998:157–172). In 1999, Austria seemed to have reached the final destination on its Western orientation path–full integration into Western Europe.

Since then, things have changed dramatically. Austria's Western orientation is now in a deep crisis due to the FPÖ's governing position. Western governments do not see the FPÖ-ÖVP coalition as business as usual. For the established Western democracies, a party like the FPÖ in a European government sets off alarm bells. The EU 14 started its "cordon sanitaire" policy as a warning signal to both present and future member states. And even by lifting the boycott, the EU 14 declared that they will observe the FPÖ in a particular way–a rather unique policy within the European Union.

Is this intervention in Austria's internal affairs? The answer is no, neither in theory nor in practice. The EU is at the same time a federa-

tion and a confederation. Its federal character has been strengthened
by the treaties of Maastricht and Amsterdam. Membership in this federation is like membership in a club, and the other club members insist
on their right to stop speaking to one member who does not behave
properly. The EU does not dictate who should govern in Austria. The
EU (speaking through the fourteen other members) simply doesn't
want to be friendly with a party that violates the basic values for
which the EU stands.

Is this a double standard? Why didn't the EU react in a similar way
when the Alleanza Nazionale, the "postfascist" Italian party, was part
of the coalition government under Silvio Berlusconi in 1994? The
explanation is that in 1994, when the Maastricht treaty was being
ratified and before the Intergovernmental Conference which led to the
Amsterdam treaty had even started, there was less emphasis on the
EU's federal character. There is also reason for Europe to see the
trivialization of German fascism (Nazism) in a more critical light than
the trivialization of Italian fascism: Nazism, not Italian fascism, was
responsible for the Holocaust.

Neither of these arguments–"intervention into internal affairs" and
"double standard"–are in line with the nature of the policy the EU 14
introduced as a response to the FPÖ-ÖVP coalition. This response was
political, not judicial, and it must be evaluated from a political, not
from a legal perspective.

The European Union has entered new territory. It has begun to use
specific values as a standard for democratic governments within the
Union. This marks a beginning, not an end. For that reason, it is
understandable that there is criticism, calling the EU's response an
overreaction. But this criticism could imply the beginning of an alienation between Austria and the EU. There is the possibility of a
"Serbianization" of Austria: In their anger, a majority of Austrians
could rally around the government and accept the FPÖ as a party
wronged by Europe.

Of course, Austria is not Serbia and Chancellor Schuessel is not
(former) President Milosevic. Austria has not stopped to be a liberal
democracy. But the attitude of "victimization" creates a certain parallel atmosphere: The Austrian government and a significant part of
Austrian public opinion view the country (not the government) as
victim of a kind of conspiracy, directed by some sinister (French and/
or leftist) center.

Such a reaction is possible because of a lack of sensitivity to right-wing extremism in a country which, together with Germany, has a historical responsibility for Nazism. There has been significant tolerance in Austria even for high-ranking former Nazis who reentered Austrian politics after 1945 (Scharsach 2000: esp. 22–66, 105–127, 188–226). There has been significant tolerance in Austria for historical revisionism–honoring ardent Nazis and neglecting their victims (Rechtsextremismus in Östereich 1994: esp. 309–356). And there has been significant tolerance for the intolerance of right-wing violence (Rechtsextremismus in Österreich 1994:esp. 97–269).

This negligence has served as the background for Haider's populism. The FPÖ's success is the product both of Austria's leniency towards the Nazi past and Austria's modernization crisis, which brought about a dramatic de-alignment of political loyalties.

Strategic Perspectives: The "People" and the "Elites"

What went wrong, and what can be done about this kind of right-wing populism, the mobilization of xenophobic resentments, the acceptance of aggressive exclusiveness, the perpetuation of Nazi elements? The FPÖ-ÖVP coalition tried to convince Europe of its mainstream character by issuing "Responsibility for Austria–A Future in the Heart of Europe" (Preamble 2000).

This document was the preamble that, at the insistence of Federal President Thomas Klestil, the two coalition partners officially signed and made part of their coalition agreement. In this declaration, the government "condemns and actively combats any form of discrimination, intolerance and demagoguery in all areas. . . . The Federal Government works for an Austria in which xenophobia, anti-Semitism and racism have no place. . . . The Federal Government supports the Charter of European Political Parties for a Non-Racist Society and commits itself to work for the exemplary realisation of its fundamental principles in Austria" (Preamble 2000).

The FPÖ and ÖVP signed a declaration, which referred to a "Charter" signed by many European and some Austrian parties (SPÖ, Greens, LIF)–but not by the FPÖ or the ÖVP. To make this credibility gap even wider, two of the candidates the FPÖ and ÖVP nominated for cabinet positions were not appointed by the federal president: Klestil would not accept persons who had clearly violated the principles of this charter. The chairman of the FPÖ's Viennese regional branch,

Hilmar Kabas, who was responsible for a vitriolic electoral campaign in Vienna full of open xenophobia and racism, had been nominated for the position of defense minister. And Thomas Prinzhorn, one of the leading FPÖ candidates for the 1999 elections, known for his blatantly xenophobic remarks during that campaign, was to become the minister of finance.

The "Charter of European Political Parties for a Non-Racist Society" prohibits parties from stirring up prejudices related to race, ethnicity, national identity, and religious creed (Charter 1998). This was precisely what Kabas and Prinzhorn had done. Despite having signed an agreement to respect the principles of the charter, the FPÖ and the ÖVP ignored their promises by nominating Kabas and Prinzhorn.

This contradiction between the acceptance of an official obligation and the violation of the very same obligation at the very same time demonstrates the failure of Austrian political elites. To make the federal president and the international community believe that the new coalition cabinet would respect the values formulated in the charter, the leaders of the FPÖ (Joerg Haider) and the ÖVP (Wolfgang Schuessel) signed a document with no intention of respecting its values. By nominating Kabas and Prinzhorn, the FPÖ and the ÖVP ridiculed the values they had just promised to cherish.

The message they sent to the Austrian public was clear: The values of the European Union are not to be taken seriously. We can fool Europe by paying lip service to these values, but then we'll continue as before. A couple of signatures won't change anything. The new government had tried to fool Europe. The Union's response must be seen from the viewpoint of this experience.

Austrian polity has to learn the lesson that Europe cannot be fooled all the time. In order to be accepted by Europe, Austrian society has to move in the direction it should have taken decades ago:

- To deal with Austria's Nazi experience and with Austrian co-responsibility for the Holocaust, taboos must be established: Playing with racist, anti-semitic, xenophobic resentments is not to be tolerated in a democratic society. Anyone who appeals to these instincts must be thrown out of the circle of credible politicians.
- To overcome the tendency toward ethnic or racist exclusion, the political decision makers should make a deal that this tendency may not be used for political purposes. A strong elitist consensus must prevent any ethnic or racist demagoguery.

- To change the traditions of aggressive exclusion inherent in the Austrian society, a long-term program of political education and enlightenment should be implemented. Much has been done already, but it has not been enough.

The end of the bilateral boycott has not ended completely Austria's isolation within the EU. Austrian democracy will overcome the isolation that was created by the FPÖ and its access to the government when the electorate–"the people"–learns to accept democracy not only as party competition but also as a set of undisputed values. The measures by the EU 14 could have a positive impact: Once the isolation starts to hurt, Austria could start to learn.

References

Bailer-Galanda, Brigitte Bailer-Galanda. 1995: *Haider wörtlich. Führer in die Dritte Republik*. Vienna: Löcker.

Bailer-Galanda, Brigitte, and Wolfgang Neugebauer. 1997. *Haider und die "Freiheitlichen" in Österreich*. Berlin: Elefanten Press.

Betz, Hans-Georg. 1998. *New Politics of the Right*. London: Macmillan.

Bischof, Günter. 1999. *Austria in the First Cold War, 1945 – 1955. The Leverage of the Weak*. London and New York: Macmillan and St. Martin's Press.

Charter of European Political Parties for a Non-Racist Society. 1998. Document. Utrecht, February 28.

Czernin Hubertus, (ed.). 2000. *Wofür ich mich meinetwegen entschuldige. Haider, beim Wort genommen*. Vienna: Cerznin.

Kopeinig, Margaretha, and Christoph Kotanko. 2000. *Eine europäische Affäre. Der Weisen-Bericht und die Sanktionen gegen Österreich*. Vienna: Czernin.

Luther, Kurt Richard. 1997. "Die Freiheitlichen," in Herbert Dachs et al. (eds.), *Handbuch des Politischen Systems Österreichs*, 3ª ed. Vienna: Manz.

Mitten, Richard. 1992. *The Politics of Anti-Semitic Prejudice. The Waldheim Phenomenon in Austria*. Boulder, CO: Westview Press.

Pelinka, Anton. 1993. *Kleine Koalition. SPÖ–FPÖ. 1983–1986*. Vienna: Böhlau.

_____. 1998. *Austria. Out of the Shadow of the Past*. Boulder, CO: Westview Press.

Pelinka, Anton, Christian Schaller, and Paul Luif. 1994. *Ausweg EG? Innenpolitische Motive einer außenpolitischen Umorientierung*. Vienna: Böhlau.

Plasser, Fritz, and Peter A.Ulram. 2000. "Rechtspopulistische Resonanzen. Die Wählerschaft der FPÖ," in Fritz Plasser, Peter A.Ulram, and Franz Sommer (eds.). *Das österreichische Wahlverhalten*. Vienna: Signum.

Preamble. 2000. Declaration "Responsibility for Austria–A Future in the Heart of Europe," in *International Herald Tribune*, 5, 8 February.

Rechtsextremismus in Österreich 1994: Handbuch des österreichischen Rechtsextremismus. (ed. Stiftung Dokumentationsarchiv des österreichischen Widerstandes). Vienna: Deuticke.

Reinfeldt, Sebastian. 2000. *Nicht-wir und Die-da. Studien zum rechten Populismus*. Vienna: Braumüller.

Report of Matti Ahtisaari, Jochen Frowein, and Marcelino Oreja on Austria. 2000. Published September 8.

Scharsach, Hans-Henning. 1992. *Haiders Kampf.* Vienna: Orac.

_____. 1995. *Haiders Clan. Wie Gewalt entsteht.* Vienna: Orac.

_____ (ed.). 2000. *Haider. Österreich und die rechte Versuchung.* Reinbek: Rowohlt.

Schneider, Heinrich. 1990. *Alleingang nach Brüssel. Österreichs EG-Politik.* Bonn: Europa Union.

Sedlak, Maria. 2000. "You really do make an Unrespectable Foreigner Policy . . . Discourse on Ethnic Issues in the Austrian Parliament," in Ruth Wodak and Teun A.van Dijk (eds.), *Racism at the Top. Parliamentary Discourses on Ethnic Issues in Six European States.* Klenfurt/Celovec: Drava.

Wodak, Ruth et al. 1990. *"Wir sind alle unschuldige Täter." Diskurshistorische Studien zum Nachkriegsantisemitismus.* Franfurt: Suhrkamp.

11

Constructing the Boundaries of the Volk: Nation-Building and National Populism in Austrian Politics

Rainer Bauböck

How was it possible for a political party like the FPÖ to gain 27 percent of the vote in the general elections and to enter a government coalition in one of the most stable and wealthy democracies of Europe? Most serious analyses mention four causes. First, there is a specific Austrian syndrome of repressing memories of the National Socialism era that is markedly different from German style *Vergangenheitsbewältigung*. This is said to explain the broader political leeway for a party whose ideological roots lie in the German nationalist camp and whose functionaries are notorious for trivializing the NS-Regime. Second, Austria's position in the international system has changed since the end of the Cold War. In 1955, when Austria's sovereignty was fully restored, the country adopted a position of permanent neutrality. Bruno Kreisky, social democratic chancellor from 1970 to 1983, skillfully used this position to push Austria into the limelight of world politics by offering her good services for the resolution of international conflicts. Neutrality became thus an important ingredient of Austria's national identity.[1] After the fall of the Iron Curtain and the intensification of economic and political integration in the European Union, there was a need to reorient shattered illusions of grandeur that had been fostered by Kreisky's policy. When Austria's

Green Party changed its position to advocate integration in the EU framework, the FPÖ gained a monopoly over the anti-European protest vote. Third, hyperstability in Austrian politics was largely due to social partnership, i.e., institutionalized cooperation by organizations representing employers, workers, and farmers, and to consociational government with two long periods of grand coalition between the Social Democratic (SPÖ) and the Conservative Party (ÖVP) from 1945 to 1966 and 1986 to 1999. Over the last decades this system came into conflict with neoliberal economic reforms that led to the formation of new groups at the lower as well as the upper end of the income scale who no longer felt represented by the traditional parties and interest organizations. At the same time the continuous electoral growth of the FPÖ welded together the ruling coalition, thus impeding a normal democratic change of government that could have unleashed a stronger reform impetus. In this vicious circle the strength of the FPÖ was both an effect and a cause of paralysis in the Austrian political system. Fourth, the early 1990s had witnessed a strong immigration of foreign workers, family members of settled immigrants and war refugees from Croatia and Bosnia. The government responded not only by tightening laws on asylum and immigration but campaigned also actively on this issue among their core electorates to show that they took seriously their "legitimate worries." This gave added credibility to the virulent xenophobic propaganda of the FPÖ, which gained the thematic leadership in this field and appeared to pull the ruling parties towards its own positions.

Each of these four separate reasons is entirely plausible, but it is not obvious how they fit together. Instead of lengthening the list of ad hoc explanations I want to search for the chain that links this series of apparently contingent circumstances. This connection can be summed up in three hypotheses: (1) All four elements illustrate democratic deficits of Austrian nation-building since 1945. (2) Today the FPÖ is the driving force in an austro-nationalist discourse that mobilizes collective identity through drawing boundaries. (3) The terrain for this discourse was originally prepared by the traditional parties SPÖ and ÖVP but gradually abandoned by them.

Continuity and Contingency

Before explaining these ideas I would like to clear the path of some misunderstandings that might be caused by alleging a connection between the constructions of an Austrian national identity and the rise of right-wing populism. First, I do not want to claim that there is an Austrian national character that makes this people especially susceptible to succumb to the populist temptation. Such an explanation would only replicate a basic postulate of nationalist ideology: the idea that nations are communities of character and fate that determine the political culture of a country as well as the basic political attitudes of its citizens.[2] In contrast with this view, I want to emphasize that the external boundaries and identity markers of an Austrian nation after 1945 emerged from historically contingent circumstances and are still being reshaped today through an ongoing elite discourse.

Second, analyzing nation-building and nationalism draws attention to the historical particularities of the country that is being researched. However, describing the *special* reasons for the success of what I will call Austrian national populism does not imply a claim that this is a *singular* phenomenon. Parties of a similar ideological makeup as the FPÖ have flourished in other political climates as well. There is obviously a European and possibly also a more specific Alpine dimension of right-wing populism. But in each case a full explanation has to refer to the respective country's recent history. Outside that context we cannot understand the political agenda of such movements and the potential danger they represent for democracy. National populism is thus neither a character trait of a certain society nor is it an unavoidable reaction to economic globalization and supranational political integration.[3] It responds to a general perception of loss of sovereignty and political steering capacity with the mobilization of specific historical traumata and nationalist traditions that are available in all Western democracies.

Third, a special Austrian *dispositif* for national populism still cannot explain its phenomenal electoral growth or its participation in government as one of two parties of equal size, which is truly unique in European postwar history. The conjectures I offer describe a potential more than the conditions for its activation. In the early 1980s, when the share of the FPÖ's vote was about 6 percent and decreasing, this potential was not much smaller than it is today. What boosted the electoral success was the aggressive and charismatic leadership of Jörg Haider, which coincided with a structural decline in traditional party loyalties, opening up a new market in votes. Even more obviously, the FPÖ's entry into government on February 4, 2000, was not in any way predetermined, but resulted from a strategic move by another player. The ÖVP's chairperson Wolfgang Schüssel maintained that there was no other option left after the failure of his protracted government negotiations with the SPÖ. However, many observers doubted that these had been conducted in good faith. What is obviously false is the perception from abroad that in the general elections of October 3, 1999, a majority of Austrian citizens had voted for the new government. This vote had in no way changed the previous arithmetic possibilities of combining parties to form a majority in the legislature. Moreover, opinion polls at this time showed that among the available coalition options only a small minority supported the one that was ultimately realized.[4]

However, the balance of political forces and strategic moves of agents cannot explain the glaring discrepancy between the domestic and the European assessment of the new government. In the eyes of the other EU partner states this was a blatant breach of liberal democratic standards, whereas even many critical observers in Austria saw it as a legitimate democratic change. The harsh reaction in "European domestic politics" is not so difficult to understand. There are a number of good reasons for this: special sensitivity towards any trivialization of the Nazi regime and the fear that Austria might set an example for right extremist parties both in EU member states and among the candidate countries for enlargement. What really needs explaining is the widespread assumption in Austria that government responsibility for a party like the FPÖ is unproblematic from a democratic perspective. In the other fourteen EU member states even politicians that criticize the bilateral sanctions taken against the Austrian government as excessive or counterproductive generally do not consider the FPÖ a normal right-wing party that could under similar circumstances participate in government in their own states.

Every crisis is also an opportunity for change. This applies to the crisis in the relation between Austria and the other EU member states, too. The chance is a new European-wide differentiation between democratic and national-populist parties. However, such a necessary borderline cannot be drawn by the law. In liberal democracies, legal prohibitions of political organizations or restrictions of free speech are only legitimate in extreme cases where the banned activity is explicitly or implicitly linked with an incitement to violence against others. The German and Austrian laws against reviving Nazi organizations or propagating the "Auschwitz lie" must, moreover, be understood in the context of the particular histories of these countries. Such laws, however one evaluates them, may apply to occasional public statements by individual right-wing populist politicians,[5] but the penal code is not a good weapon to fight a party like the FPÖ. The boundary that must be drawn is a political, not a legal one. It is created by a dual self-commitment of democratic parties not to regard national populists as potential coalition partners and to refrain in their own politics from any appeal to racist, xenophobic or anti-Semitic attitudes.[6] Even those parties that today draw a *cordon sanitaire* around right extremists in their own countries have quite often violated the second commitment and may therefore be rightly accused of hypocrisy. One must also recognize that it was a novelty in European politics to turn the participation of such parties into a matter of common concern for all EU member states. Yet norms such as these are often clearly stated only after they have been massively violated. In this sense the Austrian crisis could have become productive for a democratic consensus that still has yet to be developed.

On September 9, 2000, the diplomatic measures of the EU governments against the Austrian government were lifted and on December 9 of the same year the EU summit in Nice adopted new procedures for deciding sanctions against member states, "in case of a clear risk of violation of fundamental principles" of the Union, which include liberty, democracy, respect for human rights and fundamental freedoms, and the rule of law. While it may be useful to establish a mechanism of this sort, this is a very limited response to the problem at stake. Such a procedure can only refer to the current activities of a government that has already taken office, but not to the purely political questions that emerged in the Austrian case and may arise again in the future formation of new governments in other member states. From the domestic perspective the question is whether a legal party that is legitimately represented in parliament should, nonetheless, be excluded from executive power through a consensus of the other parties in parliament; from a European perspective the question is whether a government that includes such a party should be fully respected as an equal partner in the institutions of supranational European governance. Neither of these questions has been answered and in this sense the Austrian crisis has not been resolved.

As far as Austrian domestic politics is concerned, the broad political front against the "EU sanctions" recalled Karl Marx's well-known quip that on the stage of world history all events and persons appear twice: "first as a tragedy and the second time as a farce."[7] Suppressing the cause of the crisis by presenting oneself as the victim, mobilizing collective identity through a closing of ranks against supervision by foreign powers (while at the same time professing loyalty towards them), all these patterns from the first postwar decade resurfaced in 2000 without many people noticing the historical parallels. This seems another good reason to search for the lines of continuity between the ideological constructions of national populism and the deeper structural characteristics of Austrian nation-building.

The Boundary between the Present and the Past

Austria is a model-case for illustrating Ernest Gellner's and Eric Hobsbawms' claim that nations can be invented.[8] In the Habsburg monarchy "Austrian" did not signify a nationality but referred instead to the dynasty as the bond that united the multinational Empire. The First Republic of the interwar period was formed in the remaining contiguous German-speaking territories. Its political elites overwhelmingly regarded it as a preliminary state whose borders had been determined by the allied forces and whose people belonged to the German nation. It was only towards the end of the Nazi Reich when Social Democratic, Christian Conservative, and Communist leaders agreed to cooperate to form an independent state. This elite consensus was the real basis for the project of building an Austrian nation. From the very beginning the new national consciousness had been marked by a strong ambivalence: On the one hand, there was an attempt to foster a state-centered Austrian *patriotism* in contrast with German *nationalism*. On the other hand, the postwar political elites missed the opportunity to ground a republican identity in a new constitution, whose core would be the liberties and rights of citizens. Instead, the constitution of 1929 was quickly reestablished based on the legal fiction that the legal personality of the state had been merely temporarily suspended by a foreign occupying regime. Constitutional continuity had thus the fatal implication of supporting the national myth of Austria as Hitler's first victim.[9] Moreover, this constitution lacked a unified catalogue of basic rights.[10] Generations of parliamentarians have since tried in vain to mend this hole. The desire to not to upset the elite consensus and to regain full independence as soon as possible made it difficult to engage in a protracted constitutional debate about the political content of Austrian republicanism.[11]

A similar ambiguity exists with regard to the cultural content of the newly won nationhood. The founding fathers of the Second Republic missed the opportunity to conceive of Austrian nationhood as a pluralistic identity that would turn the multiplicity of languages and ethnic origins of the late Habsburg monarchy into a positive aspect of the Austrian self-image. Instead, cultural unity became once again associated with the German language and assimilation into a linguistic community went hand in hand with suppressing collective memories of the diversity of ethnic origins. The Austrian negotiators of the State Treaty of 1955 agreed only reluctantly to recognize the country's regional linguistic minorities in the provinces of Carinthia, Styria, and Burgenland and the Treaty's provisions have still not been fully implemented in domestic legislation today.

The project of Austrian nationhood suffered thus from a dual deficit: its republican identity was derived from negating the preceding authoritarian and totalitarian regimes but lacked the positive reference point of a new constitution; and its cultural identity was determined as German-speaking while simultaneously negating a unifying German nationalism. Unintentionally, this created a real contrast with the path taken by the German Federal Republic. The FRG's postwar identity is also ambiguous between republican and ethnic elements, but in contrast to Austria's dual deficit on both dimensions it appears as overdetermined with a strand of constitutional patriotism running alongside an ethnic conception of nationhood and both finding their expression in the German Basic Law of 1949.

The FPÖ's national populist project is not about reinventing an Austrian nation, but rearticulates instead the negations from which this nationhood has emerged. The republican deficit opens a political space for the idea of a plebiscitary democracy with a strong political leadership; the cultural deficit permits conjuring up an ethnic "Austrianness" whose content is mainly determined through the exclusion of foreign immigrants. The FPÖ's roots in the political camp of German nationalism prevented the party from participating in the growing consensus about the existence of an Austrian nation for a long time. In its programs it explicitly condemned this idea and distinguished between Austrian statehood, which it accepted as a historical fact, and German nationhood, which was still seen to include the Austrian people. As late as 1988 Jörg Haider confirmed this by characterizing the Austrian nation as an "ideological miscarriage."[12] As the population increasingly supported the idea of nationhood,[13] this strong link with German nationalism turned into a political liability. Without programmatically breaking with its traditions the FPÖ has since 1995 revamped its political rhetoric and avoids now overly Teutonic tunes.[14] In a complete reversal of the postwar political constellation it parades today as the defender of Austrian national and patriotic interests against the Social Democrats whom it accuses of high treason for their alleged support of sanctions against the new government.

Such a turnabout can only succeed if the origin of Austrian nationhood is dissociated from its entrapments with National Socialism. The line that cuts off this past is the first of the four boundaries that define the national populist project. The FPÖ does not have to draw itself this final stroke; it can easily relate to a widespread public attitude during the postwar era. One should not imagine this lack of *Vergangenheitsbewältigung* as simply a collective amnesia. The problem is less an incapacity to remember than an unwillingness to do so, an intense desire that, as a nation, Austria should be able to close this chapter for good. This was first articulated through presenting the nation itself as a victim of NS aggression and later through the attempt to demonstrate that Austria had already sufficiently fulfilled its duties of remembrance and compensation. The Waldheim years marked an important change in this attitude towards the Nazi years. But even the serious endeavors of historical documentation, memorial events, negotiations about slave labor, debates about stolen art and restitution of aryanized property do not mark a decisive break with this longing for an "end of history," for an Austrian national consciousness that would no longer be tainted by this past. Occasional utterances by FPÖ politicians that can be understood as trivializing National Socialism are counterproductive for these efforts because they bring no additional votes but guarantee a continuation of a debate that the party would rather avoid. Politically, the FPÖ is not interested in rehabilitating the NS regime, but in detaching it from Austrian history. This is the condition for the FPÖ to gain credibility as an austro-nationalist party in spite of its ideological and historical roots. Such an attempt to disconnect the fascist and Nazi experience from the country's history would have no chance in Italy or Germany. In Austria, however, it can appear as an organic continuation of a tradition that had been previously associated with the political center. Today the FPÖ occupies in this area of "the politics of history" almost the same positions that the SPÖ and the ÖVP had previously occupied but had abandoned under an increasing pressure of international criticism. If it refrains from propagating German nationalism, the FPÖ can thus present itself as the true defender of the Austrian nation against accusations that its past is polluted by brown stains.

Of course every nation is an "imagined community"[15] that links the generations of "the living, the dead, and those who are to be born."[16] Nationalist mythologies differ in whether they project their origins back into an indeterminate and distant past (as they do when they claim that their people descended from the Romans or Germanic and Gallic tribes) or whether they refer to an foundational event when the polity was self-consciously created (such as the French or American revolutions). In the latter case there is also a final stroke that separates the *ancien regime* from the birth of the nation, but of an entirely different nature. For Austria these two commonly intertwined interpretations are diametrically opposed to each other. On the one side, National Socialism is regarded as a mere interruption of the national history, while, on the other side, the nation is seen to have emerged from resistance against Nazism. The first of these two views allows for constructing a long continuity of nationhood based on shared ethnic descent; for the second, National Socialism cannot be bracketed but will forever remain constitutive for the self-identity of the political community that resulted from its collapse.[17] Both readings of history have had their defenders in the Second Republic, but the former was certainly the hegemonic view. Had the second view prevailed it would have hardly been possible for a party like the FPÖ to gain a place at the center of political power.

The Boundary between Us and Abroad

Every national identity needs an external boundary that separates it from other nations. This boundary is always imagined as a cultural difference. There is no purely civic nation in this sense because principles of civic republicanism are universal in their contents and cannot identify the particular national territory and community to which one belongs or ought to be loyal.[18] Yet the imagined cultural boundary is also a constructed one. It dichotomizes differences that otherwise could be perceived as quite fluid. Rather than cultural distance predetermining the location of the boundary, it is the historically contingent boundary that shapes the perception of cultural distance.

Austria's educational and cultural policies in the postwar era illustrate this phenomenon quite well. There was a strong effort to emphasize the peculiarities of an Austrian variety of standard German, for example, by issuing an Austrian dictionary for elementary schools. In the early 1990s official recognition of Austrian terms for various food items became an important issue during the negotiations over joining the European Union. German is a pluricentric language just as English. This makes it possible to instrumentalize regional variations for asserting a national difference. In purely linguistic terms, the distance between Munich and Hamburg is certainly greater than that between the Bavarian capital and Vienna. However, once national boundaries have been consolidated, cultural standardization through public education and mass media within these territories contributes to the emergence of standard varieties. Today, it is easy to recognize a German, Swiss, and Austrian variety of the German language. These differences are constructed from existing linguistic material rather than purely invented. But in the end it is the political project of national self-determination within contingently given territorial borders that sorts the finely graded cultural practices and identities into large and homogenous national blocks.

External sovereignty within a given territory does not merely imply the need for highlighting a boundary with neighboring nations but also for determining a geopolitical position within the international system of states. What may appear as a purely rational state interest in a certain foreign policy orientation is always translated into national self-perceptions that support a particular conception of collective identity. Just as the past must always appear glorious in nationalist ideology so sovereignty must be absolute and recognized to be so by all other states. The ten years between the end of the war and the Austrian State Treaty of 1955 are traumatic in this regard because they were experienced as an incapacitation imposed by the four occupying powers. The EU diplomatic sanctions conjured up once more the small country's fear of the great powers' desire to rule it from abroad. In the forty-five years before Austrian foreign policy had succeeded in overcoming this primal fear through two strategic projects of integration:

active neutrality during the Cold War and West European integration after its end. Neutrality, which was originally thrust upon the country as a condition for full sovereignty rather than freely chosen[19] turned into a historical asset. Military neutrality shielded the country from Soviet pressure while permitting a political and economic orientation towards the West. During the Kreisky years Austria developed an international profile as a mediator and meeting place in various international conflicts. This fostered a self-congratulatory attitude and occasional illusions of grandeur. After the fall of the Iron Curtain the overestimation of Austria's role in world politics gave way rapidly to fears of missing the West European train. The campaign for membership in the European Union in 1994 was a last joint effort of the two government parties to redefine Austria's place in the international system. In the referendum of June 12, 1994, a two-thirds majority said yes, but this great political success was due to an ambivalent mixture of motives based on resignation ("Given the level of economic interdependence we have no other choice") and self-esteem ("We are recognized in Europe and can participate in decisions"). The reaction of Austria's EU partners to the formation of the new government has so far not affected the first attitude, but it is a narcissistic insult to national pride and self-esteem.

Such resentment is a breeding ground for the national populist rejection of the European project. Over recent years the FPÖ has primarily mobilized fears about the effects of Eastern enlargement. Now a deepening of political integration is painted in similar dark colors. Has it not already paved the way for the other EU governments' attempts to interfere in Austrian domestic politics? By articulating this dual boundary within Europe against East and West the FPÖ restates Austria's position during the Cold War. In this regard, too, the two mainstream parties had prepared the political terrain that they have to abandon to national populism today. Integration into the EU has not shifted the center of the national discourse in a way that would leave the FPÖ in an outsider's position. Instead of responding to the factual transfers of sovereignty to a supranational level with a corresponding effort to democratize EU institutions and to strengthen supranational citizenship, both the SPÖ and the ÖVP engaged in a symbolic struggle to reassert the lost national competencies, fostering thus the illusion that the EU could still be governed from its fifteen capitals. Moreover, they fought this struggle not so much on a European level but domestically and against each other. Such an attitude of political elites who do not dare to sell supranational integration to their constituencies is certainly not a unique Austrian problem but contributes to a general European malaise. However, given Austria's political traditions and the current crisis in relations with the other member states this deficit in Europeanization could lead to a more dangerous backlash.

The Boundary between Us and Them

In its critical initial stages nation-building requires vertical integration between political elites and the mass of the population as well as horizontal integration among these elites themselves that bridges their ideological differences. Both were achieved to a high degree during the postwar years. While the "founding fathers" established continuity with the First Republic at the level of statehood and the constitution, they also created an entirely different political system that overcame the disastrous cleavage between the ideological camps. This confrontation had paved the way for the elimination of parliamentary democracy by Austrofascism in March 1933 and for civil war in February 1934 that crushed Social Democratic resistance. Austria was reconstructed politically as a consociational democracy with institutionalized power sharing between the Christian Conservative and Social Democratic Parties and rebuilt economically with a strong state-owned industrial sector and neocorporatist regulation of the wider market economy. Even during the periods of single party government (by the ÖVP from 1966 to 1970 and by the SPÖ from 1970 to1983), the system of social partnership guaranteed stability through negotiating economic conflicts behind closed doors and giving each institution a say over government policies that affect its interests. However, in contrast with the first period of grand coalition, the second one became increasingly an unwilling partnership with a declining reform potential. This was not at all due to ideological polarization. On the contrary, the deep rifts that consociational democracy had helped to bridge had been filled long ago. Both parties moved towards the center in an attempt to attract the new volatile votes. This grinding away of ideological contrasts is a well-known phenomenon in Western democracies and would have presented few problems had there been changing governing majorities. When the FPÖ attacked the government coalition as a "united party" in power, it was not the ideological rapprochement itself that lent some credibility to this notion. Paradoxically, the more unwilling the two parties became to continue their cooperation, the easier it became for the FPÖ to target them as a homogenous power block. The existing form of government had lost its previous intrinsic justification and was now only kept together by the rise of the political opponent FPÖ. Even more importantly, institutionalized cooperation between interest organizations and government parties was maintained despite an erosion of their social bases. With a rapid decline in membership rates and everyday activities of political organizations and unions the whole system became increasingly top-heavy. What was really an unleashing of civil society from paternalistic tutelage and the strings that tied its associations to political camps could thus be portrayed inversely as the increasing detachment of smug and corrupt politicians from the "man in the street."

The new rifts between the two mainstream parties as well as between their apparatuses and their social bases opened a breach for the national populist offensive. This movement combines the rhetorics of nationalism and of populism. While nationalism separates the political community from others of the same kind, populism articulates an internal difference between the people and a ruling caste. The latter contains thus an apparently progressive or left element. In Sebastian Reinfeldt's recent analysis, its rhetoric constructs not only a contradiction between "us" and the others who are "not-we," but also a contrast between "us" and "them," i.e., the SP and VP politicians.[20] Other than the two boundaries described so far this third one has, of course, not been previously drawn by the traditional parties themselves, who are the targets at the other side of the line. Yet even in constructing the contrast between the people below and the elite above the FPÖ can make use of attitudes and expectations that have been shaped during the long era of social partnership consensus.

This boundary obviously does not refer to a difference in social status or class. The political leaders of national populist parties are themselves members of the political class whom they condemn, and often they also own great fortunes.[21] Ostentatious wealth and conspicuous consumption belong to the image of the successful political pop-star and of the self-made man who pushed his way to the top against all odds in a system that punishes the diligent and ambitious ones. Only by provoking his own exclusion from established politics and presenting himself as the victim can the populist leader prove that he does not belong to "them."

The populist project is thus not directed against social inequalities but against representative democracy.[22] The alternative of plebiscitary democracy that populism propagates would in no way remove the contrast between below and above. Charismatic and authoritarian rule is often legitimated through plebiscites. After all, the people cannot determine itself the questions that it will be asked. Someone else must formulate them and choose the time for the vote. Rather than strengthening democratic accountability of political leadership, populism attacks instead the constraints imposed on it by the rule of law. It rejects procedural legitimacy and the mediating role of representative institutions. Such affinity between plebiscitary democracy and authoritarian rule is reinforced where the people is imagined as homogenous and where the polity is organized as a unitary state. In Switzerland, by contrast, a rather extreme form of federal division of powers allows to make a strong plebiscitary element well compatible with representative democracy. Such immunizing effects of heterogeneity are much weaker in a country like Austria where an institutionally weak federalism[23] combines with a unitary conception of the people as a cultural and political community.

In its programmatic defense of plebiscitary democracy national populism breaks with the traditions of the postwar political system and aspires to create a "Third Republic." There is, however, a strong continuity at another level concerning the relation between "ordinary people" and those who represent them. In Austria's mainstream political culture this relation has been neither understood as a *representation* of rational interests, which aggregates them and makes them negotiable, nor as *mobilization*, through which political leaders incite the people to mass action. The dominant view is instead a *delegation* of interests into the hands of political leaders. Populism and neocorporatism share this common mechanism for the mobilization of diffuse support[24] by the political leader. The link between him and those whom he represents is one of identity: "He is one of us and this is why we can trust him to best represent our interests, which he understands better than we ourselves do." For traditional neocorporatism, this relation of identity was still positively embedded in ideological camps and social life-worlds differentiated along class lines; for contemporary national populism it is defined purely negatively through the contrast with a ruling elite.[25] What both have in common is the moment of delegation, the quest for unspecified trust that makes the political leader unaccountable and reduces those represented to the role of spectators. Such an attitude of passive trust has been shaped by decades of social partnership and grand coalition politics. Ideological conflicts were publicly articulated in parliamentary and electoral skirmishes but increasingly disconnected from the ongoing negotiation of compromise solutions behind closed doors. Although there is no evidence that neocorporatist arrangements have reduced social inequality, they seemed to guarantee a continuous improvement of living standards for all groups in society. Today this expectation has evaporated. Many voters no longer delegate their hopes but their frustrations with the traditional parties' incapacity to live up to these past promises. The FPÖ is thus not a party of social protest but a party of voters who delegate their protest. It has hardly any roots in the self-organized political movements of Austrian civil society and has itself become the target of the most sustained mobilization of protest in recent history.[26] It is, therefore, hardly paradoxical that the party is unable to benefit even from those forms of plebiscitary participation that it advocates in its program. Among the most serious political setbacks it has suffered were its referendum initiatives against immigrants ("Austria first" referendum in January and February 1993) and against a common European currency in November and December 1997, as well as its defeat in the June 1994 plebiscite on joining the European Union.

The FPÖ's appeal to the people is a purely symbolic act, the movement remains an electoral movement. This facilitates the integration of the party into the established political system. It also separates the national populists from the activist fringe of right-wing extremism. The FPÖ's political tool is verbal, not physical violence. In this sense it is also not a fascist party. What distinguishes it from fascism is not only its incoherent ideology but even more so its form of organization and its political project. Fascist parties attempt to organize mass movements and paramilitary associations for smashing democracy. In today's Europe there are, on the one hand, activist groups with fascist ideologies that are prepared to use physical violence but are isolated from the wider society and, on the other hand, broad national populist parties that fight for exercising political power in the existing constitutional framework. The fusion of both can only occur in another crisis of major proportions. The contemporary danger that emanates from the latter is the destruction not of parliamentary democracy but of a political culture that sustains the precarious integration of heterogeneous societies as democratic polities. By lowering cognitive and verbal inhibition thresholds, national populism undermines the ongoing management of conflicts that are inherent in pluralistic societies. In the long run this may create greater hazards for maintaining democratic rule in times of crisis than the occasional acts of violence by almost universally despised right-wing radicals.

The Boundary between Us and the Others

The fourth boundary national populism needs for its construction of the Volk is an external and, at the same time, an internal one. It separates the native population from immigrants, or, more precisely, it divides the resident population into co-nationals and strangers who may have been born in the country but do not belong to the national community. This distinction is the hard core of the political project. The other three boundaries are more or less variable. The FPÖ has transformed from an explicitly German nationalist party into an austro-nationalist one; in the early 1990s it took a 180 degree turn from advocating Austria's EU membership to opposing it; in 2000 it helped the VP, whom it had denounced as a party of "the system," to regain the chancellery. Its anti-immigrant stance is the only policy on which it has remained constant and consistent. And in no other area are the lines that connect its program to the policies of the old coalition parties so obvious.

Austria is an immigration society that does not regard itself as an immigrant nation. It has a higher percentage of immigrants than the U.S. (although a lower one than countries like Canada, Australia or Israel). Nine percent of the Austrian population are foreign citizens, another 4–5 percent are foreign born but naturalized. Yet this fact has not shaped a new national self-image. All great immigrations of the twentieth century have been treated as "special cases," and this permitted the maintenance of the mental boundary that defines the nation.[27]

Of course, Austria's history is different from that of traditional overseas countries of immigration, which were originally white settler societies. Yet immigration goes back quite a long way. Especially the inhabitants of the Vienna Metro area have been shaped by migration in the two decades before and after 1900. The First Republic tried to unscramble the ethnic mix generated by the late Habsburg Empire by excluding groups that were "foreign by language and race" from access to Austrian nationality.[28] Those of immigrant descent who had survived the Third Reich and the Second World War in Austria did not want to be reminded of ethnic origins that had been a predicament rather than a source of pride. The Austrian population increasingly imagined itself as a homogenous ethnic community and this perception shaped public attitudes towards newcomers. In the immediate postwar period there were two major groups. The Austrian government rejected any responsibility for DPs (displaced persons), who generally did not speak German and were composed of prisoners of war, former slave laborers and Jewish survivors of the Shoa. The other group were ethnic German expellees who came mainly from Czechoslovakia. During the initial years of food and accommodation shortages they were no more welcome. However, when economic reconstruction took off in the early 1950s they were collectively naturalized and fully integrated into Austrian society.[29]

Neither the "guest workers" of the 1970s, nor refugees from the crises in Hungary 1956, Czechoslovakia 1968–69, and Poland 1981–82 were regarded as immigrants. The former had been recruited as temporary labor, for the latter Austria offered its good services as a country of transit on their way to the U.S. or Western Europe. Persistent demand by employers eventually stimulated family reunification and permanent settlement of migrant workers as well as the integration of a considerable number of refugees. The legal framework for residence, employment, and admission to citizenship remained, however, wedded to the "guest worker model." Immigrants were thus distinguished from Austrians not only culturally but also by their precarious legal status that contributed to low job mobility, bad housing conditions and segregation from the native population. Moreover, Austria has today one the purest regimes of *ius sanguinis* transmission of citizenship by descent.[30] Those born of foreign parents grow up as foreign citizens. Individual naturalization is, of course, possible but it requires renunciation of a presently held nationality, is refused after a record of minor misdemeanors, and remains discretionary even after ten years of legal residence.[31] The total effect of the laws on foreign nationals is to reinforce and legitimate social discrimination.

In the 1970s and 1980s immigration policy was primarily handled in the closed forums of social partnership. Employer federations and trade unions negotiated guest-worker contingents and policy guidelines. Responsibility for implementation lay with the Ministry of Social Affairs.[32] In the 1990s the initiative for policy reform shifted to the Ministry of Interior. From now on, internal and external security aspects dominated the political discourse and immigration turned into a major theme during electoral campaigns. The admission of about 90,000 Bosnian war refugees contrasts with a marked deterioration of the legal status of long-term resident foreigners in the context of a new law that was originally meant to regulate new entries only. "Integration before new admissions" became the catchphrase for the new policy, but its real effect was the postponement of an integration agenda in the name of first stemming the inflows. Only in 1997 a substantial improvement in the security of legal residence was achieved, but access to the labor market for family members and to citizenship remain severely limited compared to most other EU member states.[33] Nevertheless, immigrants have become an integral part of Austrian economy, society, and culture. Segmented and uneven integration in these areas contrasts with the invisibility of immigrants as members of the political community. This shows in a pervasive deficit of political representation. There is not a single member of parliament from the post–1960s immigration. Non-EU citizens are even ineligible for workers councils, which are elected in all medium and large enterprises, and they generally are barred from jobs in the civil service, which is a very large employer in Austria.

This background makes it easy for the FPÖ to portray its anti-immigrant platform as a mere continuation of the government parties' policies. The SPÖ's and ÖVP's counter-strategies fall short of their target because they do not touch the core of the national populist project. They engage instead in two separate discourses, a humanitarian and a socioeconomic one. In the first discourse the two mainstream parties have condemned xenophobic utterances by FPÖ leaders, but their policies on the admission of refugees is not clearly different from the FPÖ's stance. All three parties assert the legitimate claims of "genuine refugees." At the same time they maintain that the vast majority of asylum applicants are abusing the system and that war refugees should be admitted only on a temporary basis without gaining recognition under the Geneva Refugee Convention. The second discourse is about the economic effects of migrant workers. Here, the ÖVP emphasizes the economic benefits from employing foreign labor whereas the SPÖ argues that economic and social integration require a strict control over new admissions. The FPÖ sides with the ÖVP on the need for more seasonal migrants and with the SPÖ in demanding long transition periods for labor mobility when the EU expands towards the East. Neither the humanistic discourse against xenophobia nor the debate about displacement effects in the labor market draw a clear line between democratic and populist perspectives because both do not address the decisive question: the need for a new collective self-understanding that regards migrants no longer merely as refugees in need of assistance or as a temporary work force but also as future citizens.

Conclusions

A telling silence about the NS past, resistance against European political integration, defending the "little man" against the powerful ones, campaigning against "over-alienation," these are the most important characteristics of Austrian national populism. I have offered two reasons that may help to account for the extraordinary success of this ideological mix. First, it is not perceived as a radical alternative to established political traditions, but appears instead as a continuation that merely turns them against their original carriers. The FPÖ can thus benefit from the legitimacy its political opponents have provided for its major programmatic planks. Second, the apparently heterogeneous elements of its political rhetoric form really a coherent pattern. This is the image of a political community that can only identify itself negatively through denying its own history, questioning its institutions of representative democracy and separating itself from the larger European community as well as from the immigrant population in its midst. A great majority of Austrian voters reject such a self-image based on resentment rather than on a vision of the public good. Yet the minority that finds this image attractive is comparatively large. This should be sufficient reason to reflect on how the postwar model of an Austrian nation could be adapted to a context of transnational migration and supranational democracy.

Notes

1. See Haller (1986: 89, 503).
2. In the late years of the Habsburg monarchy, Otto Bauer, the most important theorist of the Austromarxist school of Social Democracy, defended such an essentialist conception when he defined the nation as "the totality of persons connected through a community of fate into a community of character" (Bauer 1907: 118, my translation).
3. Benjamin Barber defends the latter conjecture in his bestseller *Jihad versus MacWorld* (Barber 1995).
4. An opinion poll of 9–11 December, i.e., before negotiations started about forming the new government, showed 37 percent of voters unconditionally in favor of a SP-VP coalition, 24 percent for deciding the party composition of the new government after the end of negotiations, 20 percent in favor of the VP going into opposition and only 11 percent in support of a coalition between the VP and the FP (*Der Standard*, 22 December 1999).
5. According to some legal scholars, Jörg Haider's praise for the Waffen-SS in a speech in front of war veterans on September 30, 1995 might qualify as a violation under the Austrian law. See Scharsach (2000: 192).
6. These are principles of a 1998 "Charter of European Political Parties for a Non-Racist Society." As of May 11, 2000, this text had been signed by 84 conservative, liberal, social democratic and green parties. The Austrian signatories are the SPÖ, the Green Party and the Liberal Forum.
7. Karl Marx (1970: 115).
8. See Gellner (1983); Hobsbawm (1990).
9. In November 2000 Chancellor Schüssel said in an interview with the Jerusalem Post: "The Nazis occupied Austria by force. The Austrians were the first victim." This remark characteristically blurs the difference between the Austrian state and the Austrian population. While the Nazi regime annihilated Austria as a *state*, it attempted to annihilate Jews and Roma as *peoples*. Calling "the Austrians" victims of Hitler's aggression is not only an attempt to downplay the large support for Nazism before the Anschluss but suggests also a dubious comparison with the victims of genocide.
10. Today the most important domestic legal sources for basic individual rights is still the Basic Law of the State of 1867. To this have been added international legal conventions that have been transferred into domestic law, such as the European Convention on Human Rights of 1950.
11. In his memoirs, Adolf Schärf, Austrian federal president from 1957 to 1965, gives three reasons for reinstalling the prewar constitution: first, the immediate abolition of constitutional legislation created by the Austrofascist and Nazi Regimes after 1933 and 1938; second, forestalling political disputes between Social Democrats and Conservatives about a new federal division of powers; third, giving the Allied Powers, and most importantly the Soviet Union, no opportunity to impose their will during protracted constitutional negotiations.
12. See Bruckmüller (1996: 40).
13. Support for the statement "Austrians are a nation" grew from only 47 percent in 1964 to 85 percent in 1995. The idea that Austria was only gradually becoming a nation was shared by 23 percent in 1964 but only 9 percent in 1995, while the denial that Austria is a nation fell from 15 percent to a mere 4 percent over the same period (Haller 1996: 67; see also Bruckmüller 1996: 61–7).

14. See Reinfeldt (2000: 99).
15. Anderson (1983).
16. Burke (1987: 118).
17. This is not only due to a lack of political will by the political elites of the postwar period, but also to the weakness of domestic resistance against the Nazi regime. Nevertheless, even its military defeat by external forces, which the majority of the population had experienced as a breakdown, could in retrospect have been interpreted as a liberation. The discourses about Austrian national identity were, however, rather focused on pride in the achievements of rebuilding the economy and of wrestling independence from the occupying powers than in the liberation of 1945 (Bruckmüller 1996: 348–55; 384).
18. See Yack (1996); Levy (2000: 84–91).
19. The provisions on permanent neutrality are not part of the State Treaty of 1955. They were instead adopted by the Austrian parliament on 26 October 1955 after the Treaty had already been adopted and one day after the end of the deadline for the withdrawal of foreign troops. This date is today celebrated as Austria's national holiday. Formally, neutrality is thus based on a free decision by the Austrian legislature. However, neutrality and independence were quite obviously linked *politically*. Back from his mission to Moscow that brought the breakthrough, federal chancellor Julius Raab reported that the declaration of neutrality was the *conditio sine qua non* for the Treaty as a whole (Stourzh 1998: 491).
20. Reinfeldt (2000: 132–7).
21. Haider has inherited a large estate in the province of Carinthia, of which he is governor. In 1999 he chose Thomas Prinzhorn, one of Austria's wealthiest industrialists, as the frontrunner in the 1999 general elections. Haider's Swiss counterpart Christoph Blocher combines the social and political profiles of these two men.
22. Jörg Haider has announced this goal very explicitly, not only in his speeches but also in a programmatic text of 1993 where he claims "representative democracy is outdated" (quoted from Reinfeldt 2000: 198).
23. In contrast with Switzerland, Canada or Belgium, Austrian federalism is monocultural – no provincial borders coincide with boundaries between linguistic groups or nationalities; in contrast with the U.S. or Germany, Austrian federalism is weak – the federal chamber in parliament is neither directly elected by the citizens nor has it any power to initiate legislation. It may only temporarily delay legislation proposed by the national assembly.
24. See Easton (1953).
25. An FPÖ election poster from the mid–1990s illustrates this negative identity relation very well. It shows Jörg Haider's face with the following text: "They are against him, because he is for you" (see Reinfeldt 2000: 196).
26. As other countries in continental Europe, Austria had its student, feminist and peace movements. What is exceptional is the strength of environmentalist movements, which succeeded in 1978 in forcing the closure of the country's only nuclear power plant and in 1984/85 in stopping a dam project on the river Danube. On January 23, 1993, the biggest mass demonstration of the Second Republic mobilized about 300,000 in Vienna in protest against an anti-immigrant referendum initiated by the FPÖ. Similar numbers demonstrated against the FPÖ's participation in government on February 19, 2000.
27. For an overview see Bauböck (1999).
28. See Grandner (1995).
29. See Stieber (1995).

30. See Bauböck and Cinar (2001).
31. A full legal entitlement to naturalization requires thirty years of residence. After fifteen years the applicant has a right to naturalization if she or he can prove "personal and professional integration" in the Austrian society. The new German nationality law that came into force on January 1, 2000, is much more generous than the Austrian one. Among Europe's major immigration countries, only Switzerland and Luxemburg have similarly tough laws as Austria with Switzerland, however, permitting one to keep a foreign citizenship in naturalizations.
32. See Wimmer (1986).
33. For a systematic comparison of legal obstacles of integration in Austria and seven other European countries of immigration, see the contributions in Davy (2001) and Waldrauch (2001).

References

Anderson, Benedict. (1983). *Imagined Communities. Reflections on the origins and spread of nationalism.* London:Verso Editions and New Left Books.

Barber, Benjamin. (1995.) *Jihad vs. McWorld. How Globalism and Tribalism are Reshaping the World.* New York: Ballatine Books.

Bauböck, Rainer. (1999). "Immigration Control without Integration Policy. An Austrian Dilemma," in Grete Brochmann and Tomas Hammar (eds.), *The Mechanisms of Immigration Control, A Comparative Analysis of European Regulation Policies in the Late 20th Century.* London and Oslo: Berg.

Bauböck, Rainer, and Çinar, Dilek .(2001). "Austrian Nationality Law," (co-authored with) in Randall Hansen, and Patrick Weil (eds.), *Towards a European Nationality: Citizenship, Immigration and Nationality Law in the European Union.* London: Macmillan, forthcoming.

Bauer, Otto. (1907). *Die Nationalitätenfrage und die Sozialdemokratie.* Wien: Ignaz Brand.

Bruckmüller, Ernst. (1996.) *Nation Österreich. Kulturelles Bewußtsein und gesellschaftlich-politische Prozesse,* 2nd edition. Wien: Böhlau-Verlag.

Burke, Edmund. (1987). "Reflections on the Revolution in France," in Jeremy Waldron (ed.), *Nonsense upon Stilts. Bentham, Burke and Marx on the Rights of Man.* London: Methuen.

Davy, Ulrike (ed.). (2001). *Die Integration von Einwanderern. Band 1: Rechtliche Regelungen im europäischen Vergleich.* Wohlfahrtspolitik und Sozialforschung, Band 9.1, herausgegeben vom Europäischen Zentrum Wien. Frankfurt, New York: Campus Verlag, forthcoming.

Easton, David. (1953). *The Political System: An Inquiry into the State of Political Science.* New York: Alfred A. Knopf.

Gellner, Ernest. (1983). *Nations and Nationalism.* Oxford: Basil Blackwell.

Grandner, Margarete. (1995). "Staatsbürger und Ausländer. Zum Umgang Österreichs mit den jüdischen Flüchtlingen nach 1918," in Gernot Heiss and Oliver Rathkolb (eds.). *Asylland wider Willen. Flüchtlinge im europäischen Kontext seit 1914.* Wien: Jugend und Volk.

Haller, Max. (1996). *Identität und Nationalstolz der Österreicher. Gesellschaftliche Ursachen und Funktionen. Herausbildung und Transformation seit 1945. Internationaler Vergleich.* Wien: Böhlau Verlag.

Hobsbawm, Eric. (1990). *Nations and Nationalism since 1780. Programme, Myth, Reality.* Cambridge: Cambridge University Press.

Levy, Jacob T. (2000). *The Multiculturalism of Fear.* Oxford: Oxford University Press.

Marx, Karl. (1973). "Der Achtzehnte Brumaire des Louis Bonaparte," in *Marx-Engels Werke* Bd. 8. Berlin: Dietz Verlag.

Reinfeldt, Sebastian. (2000). *Nicht-wir und Die-da. Studien zum rechte Populismus.* Wien: Braumüller.

Renan, Ernest. *(1882). "Qu'est-ce qu'une nation?"* in Oeuvres Complètes de Ernest Renan, *Tome 1. Paris: Calman-Lévy, 1947: 887–906.*

Schärf, Adolf. (1955). *Österreichs Erneuerung. 1945–1955. Das erste Jahrzehnt der Zweiten Republik.* Wien: Verlag der Wiener Volksbuchhandlung.

Scharsach, Hans-Henning. (2000). "Bekenntnis zur sozialen Volksgemeinschaft. Braune Markierungen auf dem Weg in die 'Dritte Republik,'" in Hans-Henning Scharsach (Hg.), *Haider. Österreich und die rechte Versuchung.* Hamburg: Rowohlt Taschenbuch Verlag.

Stieber, Gabriele. (1995). "Volksdeutsche und Displaced Persons," in Gernot Heiss and Oliver Rathkolb (eds.), *Asylland wider Willen. Flüchtlinge im europäischen Kontext seit 1914.* Wien: Jugend und Volk.

Stourzh, Gerald. (1998). *Um Einheit und Freiheit. Staatsvertrag, Neutralität und das Ende der Ost-West-Besetzung Österreichs 1945–1955.* Wien: Böhlau.

Waldrauch, Harald (ed.). (2001). *Die Integration von Einwanderern. Band 2: Ein Index rechtlicher Diskriminierung.* Wohlfahrtspolitik und Sozialforschung, Band 9.2, herausgegeben vom Europäischen Zentrum Wien. Frankfurt, New York: Campus Verlag, forthcoming.

Wimmer, Hannes. (1986). "Zur Ausländerbeschäftigungspolitik in Österreich," in Hannes Wimmer (ed.), *Ausländische Arbeitskräfte in Österreich.* Frankfurt am Main: Campus Verlag.

Yack, Bernard. (1996). "The Myth of the Civic Nation." *Critical Review* 10, no. 2, spring: 193–211.

Contributors

Rainer Bauböck is associate professor of political science at the Austrian Academy of Sciences, Vienna.

John Bunzl, is professor of political science at the Austrian Institute of International Affairs, Vienna.

Reinhold Gärtner is professor of political science at the University of Innsbruck.

Andre Gingrich is professor of social anthropology at the University of Vienna.

Michal Krzyzanowski is a Ph.D. candidate in the School of English, Adam Mickiewicz University, Poznan.

Walter Manoschek is assistant professor of political science at the University of Vienna and editor-in-chief of the *Öesterreichische Zeitschrift füer Politikwissenschaft.*

Andrei S. Markovits is professor of politics in the Department of Germanic Languages and Literatures at the University of Michigan, Ann Arbor.

Richard Mitten is associate professor of history at Trinity College, Hartford, Connecticut.

Anton Pelinka is professor of political science at the University of Innsbruck.

Jessika ter Wal is a Ph.D., research fellow at Utrecht University, the Netherlands, European Research Centre on Migration and Ethnic Relations.

Ruth Wodak is professor of linguistics at the University of Vienna and director of the Research Center "Discourse, Politics, Identity" at the Austrian Academy of Sciences.

Index